THE NATURAL DIVIDEND

THE NATURAL DIVIDEND

Just Management of Our Common Resources

JONATHON W. MOSES AND
ANNE MARGRETHE BRIGHAM

agenda
publishing

To Aurora and Thandeka

First published in 2023 by Agenda Publishing

Agenda Publishing Limited
PO Box 185
Newcastle upon Tyne
NE20 2DH
www.agendapub.com

ISBN 978-1-78821-439-1 (hardcover)
ISBN 978-1-78821-440-7 (paperback)

British Library Cataloguing-in-Publication Data
A catalogue record for this book is available from the British Library

Typeset by Newgen Publishing UK
Printed and bound in the UK by CPI Group (UK) Ltd, Croydon, CR0 4YY

The law locks up the man or woman
Who steals the goose from off the common,
But leaves the greater villain loose
Who steals the common from off the goose.
The law demands that we atone
When we take things we do not own,
But leaves the lords and ladies fine
Who take things that are yours and mine.
The poor and wretched don't escape
If they conspire the law to break;
This must be so, but they endure
Those who conspire to make the law.
The law locks up the man or woman
Who steal the goose from off the common;
And geese will still a common lack
Till they go and steal it back.

Old English folk song

CONTENTS

ACKNOWLEDGEMENTS

In 2019 the Norwegian journalist Jon Hustad referred to Norway as "grunnrentelandet",[1] or (less eloquently) *the nation of resource rents*. This is because Norway has a history of managing its natural resources for the good of its people. The history of this *grunnrenteland* began at the turn of the last century, when a young country – newly independent from Sweden – decided to stop foreigners from absconding with the surplus value produced by its (Norwegian) waterfalls. Later, this approach became central to the way that Norway managed its vast petroleum resources, to the benefit of its people.

As long-time residents of Norway, we are intimately familiar with this history of the *grunnrenteland*, and we wish to share the lessons of this management regime both with younger Norwegians and with a more global readership. As the reader will soon learn, many of the tools used by Norwegian officials to manage their natural resources can be found elsewhere: similar management tools are employed by other countries, and in the management of other types of resources. Indeed, this is not a book about Norway; it is simply inspired by the Norwegian experience. There is nothing particularly unique about the Norwegian approach to managing natural resources, but it offers a glimpse of what is possible to achieve (as well as clear lessons about the dangers of waiting). In the Norwegian case, we see how it is possible to introduce a new and more just management regime for natural resources, but that it is difficult to do so after strong vested interests have been allowed to take root.

We think it is particularly important that a new generation of policy-makers and civil servants become aware of alternative management models, as the history of resource management, or the lessons from comparative policy-making, are often sacrificed on the mantle of economic efficiency. It is for this reason that we have pitched our argument in the direction of academics, policy-makers and civil servants, more than activists or the general public.

This work is inspired by both words and deeds. The first can be found in two remarkable, if underappreciated, works: Thomas Paine's *Agrarian Justice*

---

1. Hustad (2019).

and Henry George's *Progress and Poverty*. These two publications are as important and gripping today as when they first were published (1797 and 1879, respectively). They come highly recommended. But we are also inspired by the way in which Norway has come to manage its petroleum resources. Although many people have contributed to this special management approach, the deeds of one person, in particular, have made a strong impression upon us: Farouk Al-Kasim.[2] Al-Kasim's work was central to what became the "Norwegian model" for petroleum resource management. The success of this model should encourage more countries to secure the Natural Dividend that belongs to us all.

Thus inspired, the impetus for this project can be found in a 2018 funding application to the Norwegian Research Council's "Bionær" programme. This application, entitled "Funding future welfare: bioeconomy as the 'new oil' and the sharing of benefits from natural resources" (BioShare), was spearheaded by Frode Flemsæter and Katrina Rønningen at Ruralis. It resulted in a four-year, broad-based research project that aimed to "develop the knowledge and analytical understanding necessary to assess, organise and manage the sharing of benefits from the utilization of bioresources, and provide policy recommendations accordingly to reinforce the basis for the future welfare state" (quoted from the original application).

This research project provided us with a welcomed opportunity to work together, and our collaboration began with two article publications. The first was entitled "Den nye oljen" ("The new oil"),[3] published in the Norwegian political science journal *Norsk statsvitenskapelig tidskrift* (*NST*: Brigham & Moses, 2021). In this article, we consider whether Norway will be able to maintain its standard of living as the country transitions to a post-oil economy. In doing so, we reveal how Norwegian policy-makers have largely abandoned the *grunnrenteland* model in their approach to managing new natural resources. We were surprised that such a successful model was not being repurposed (as was done earlier with oil), and we began to search for other examples of successful, but ignored, approaches to managing our natural resources in a just fashion.

Later in that same year we published a related article in *Marine Policy*, entitled "Whose benefit? A comparative perspective for the ISA" (Moses & Brigham 2021), which takes a critical look at the way the international community approaches the management of our deep-sea mineral resources. As in so many national contexts, the international community seems to be unaware of the need to secure the Natural Dividend generated by our common natural resources, and we sketched a brief outline of what the International Seabed Authority (ISA)

---

2. See, for example, Al-Kasim (2006).
3. An online English translation of this article by Lars Douceet can be found at https://slimemold timemold.com/2022/05/17/norway-the-once-and-future-georgist-kingdom.

might do to secure some of that Natural Dividend. In researching this article we came to realize how unprepared the global community is to deal with the expected future rush on natural resources found in the global commons.

As our argument is novel, and may prove controversial in some circles, we have striven to provide sufficient documentation, references and cross-referencing. We recognize that this can interrupt the reader's momentum, but we felt it was necessary on two grounds: to show that our work is not idle speculation (but builds on an established and respectable literature and policy experiences); and to help curious readers track the argument closely, and retrace the foundations upon which our argument rests. We recommend that the first-time reader ignore the frequent references, footnotes and cross-referencing, and simply plough through the book, from one end to the other. Those readers who want to dive deeper into the subject material might return, reread and follow up on all or some of the references and cross-references.

Over the course of researching and writing this book, we have received the help and support of many different people. We are thankful to colleagues and friends for their support and assistance. First among these is Alison Howson, our editor at Agenda. Alison planted the seed for this book project and helped nourish its early development. She saw the potential early on and encouraged us to pursue it by securing a number of excellent, anonymous and critical reviewers from distant intellectual and political corners. In doing so, she introduced us to a much broader swathe of the literature. In short, this project would never have seen the light of day had it not been for Alison's strong support and encouragement.

We are lucky to be surrounded by a community of like-minded scholars, at both the Norwegian University of Science and Technology (NTNU) and Ruralis (the Institute for Rural and Regional Research), who are also interested in resource rents. This has led to many informal exchanges in Trondheim, where the main office of Ruralis is located, either in more general conference settings or in our focused reading group. At Ruralis, we would like to thank members of the Ground Rent reading group and the broader BIOSHARE research community, especially Eirik Magnus Fuglestad and Katrina Rønningen. At NTNU, we have benefited greatly from the critical comments of several colleagues working in nearby fields.

As this book grew out of two earlier publications, we are indebted to the many commenters and reviewers who have combed through these article manuscripts. We are grateful to the anonymous reviewers at both *NST* and *Marine Policy*, but also to several friends and colleagues who have helped along the way. Several people have read and commented on article and chapter drafts that were first used to sketch out the ideas in this book: Reidar Almås, Michael Alvarez, Rahul Basu, Eirik Magnus Fuglestad, Paul Harnett, Espen Moe, Rune Skarstein, Anders Skonhoft, Jostein Vik, Anna Zalik and Heidrum Åm. We are also indebted to

Lars Douceet for translating our *NST* article into English, making it accessible to a wider audience.

Finally, we are most indebted to a number of friends and colleagues who have read and commented on the entire manuscript. In addition to the two anonymous reviewers, we would like to thank Michael Alvarez, Rahul Basu, Eirik Magnus Fuglestad and Bjørn Letnes for their useful remarks and criticisms.

It should go without saying, but we mean to make it explicit: despite the generous help and support of all these people, we take full responsibility for any errors that might somehow persist. What remains is our argument alone, although we have benefited greatly from friends and colleagues who have both agreed and disagreed with us along the way.

Trondheim
Norway

ABBREVIATIONS

ABSCH	Access and Benefit-Sharing Clearing-House
AfDB	African Development Bank
ATS	Antarctic Treaty System
BBN	big bang nucleosynthesis
BOT	build–operate–transfer
CBD	Convention on Biological Diversity
CHM	common heritage of mankind
CIA	Central Intelligence Agency (US)
CIT	corporate income tax
COPUOS	Committee on the Peaceful Uses of Outer Space
CPR	common-pool resource
CSP	concentrated solar power
DR	differential rent
EEA	European Economic Area
EEZ	exclusive economic zone
FAO	Food and Agriculture Organization
FIP	feed-in premium
FIT	feed-in tariff
G-77	Group of 77
GPFG	Government Pension Fund Global
HDI	Human Development Index
HSRGWG	Hague Space Resources Governance Working Group
IEA	International Energy Agency
IRENA	International Renewable Energy Agency
ISA	International Seabed Authority
ISDS	investor–state dispute settlement
JV	joint venture
LCP	local content policy
LVT	land value tax
MAB	maximum allowable biomass

MENA	Middle East and North Africa
MSL	Materials System Laboratory
NCS	Norwegian continental shelf
NIMBY	not in my back yard
NOU	Norges offentlige utredninger (Norwegian official report)
NRC	national resource company
NRM	natural resource management
OBM	obsolescing bargaining mechanism
OECD	Organisation for Economic Co-operation and Development
OPEC	Organization of Petroleum Exporting Countries
OPEX	operating expenses
PPA	power purchase agreement
PSC	production-sharing contract
PV	photovoltaic
RBOB	reformulated blendstock for oxygenate blending
RE	renewable energy
REE	renewable energy entrepreneur
REPIM	Research on Economic Policy Implementation and Management
RFMO	regional fisheries management organization
RPO	renewable purchase obligation
RPS	renewable portfolio standard
RRT	resource rent tax
SC	service contract
SDG	Sustainable Development Goal
SEPA	Scottish Environmental Protection Agency
TRIP	trade-related intellectual property
ULSD	ultra-low-sulphur diesel
UNCLOS	United Nations Convention on the Law of the Sea
UNDP	United Nations Development Programme
UNGA	United Nations General Assembly
UNOOSA	UN Office for Outer Space Affairs
USBLM	US Bureau of Land Management
WTI	West Texas Intermediate
WTO	World Trade Organization

1

INTRODUCTION

We are being thrust, full force, into a new world. In response to constant demands for growth, a dwindling supply of natural resources, environmental perils and the threat of climate change, we need to embrace a post-carbon world – or risk serious damage to our planet. Our generation has begun a frantic race to find alternatives for the scarce resources that previous generations have relied upon. In our pursuit of these alternatives, however, we must avoid the pitfalls of the past. This is the motivation for the book in your hands.

The scientific evidence and consensus is clear: we need to quit oil, gas and coal, and do so quickly. We cannot continue as before, and the war in Ukraine has not blunted that consensus. Already in 2015 it was known that we needed to leave "a third of oil reserves, half of gas reserves and over 80 per cent of the current coal reserves" in the ground if we hoped to meet the 2°C Paris climate goals (McGlade & Ekins 2015: 187). To replace these important sources of energy, the world is rushing to discover and develop new resources on two very different fronts.

The first front is aimed at renewables. The demand for new renewable energy resources – such as wind, solar, bio-, geothermal and hydro – is proving insatiable, and global investment in this sector has been extraordinary. BloombergNEF estimates that global investments in this energy transition totalled $755 billion in 2021 – a phenomenal increase from the $32 billion invested in 2004 (BloombergNEF 2022). Much of this investment activity has been spurred by the sundry incentives provided by political authorities that are eager to expand access to nature's renewable resources.

The second front seeks non-renewables. Although there are many advantages in transitioning from carbon-based energy (coal, oil, gas) to more renewable sources of energy (fuelled by, e.g., the sun and the wind), we cannot escape our dependence on non-renewable resources. This transition will require millions of tonnes[1] of new raw materials to be mined. Batteries depend on cobalt, lithium

---

1. One metric ton can be referred to either as a tonne or as 1 MT.

and nickel; the magnets for electric generators and motors rely on neodymium and other rare earth elements; and the lines that connect the diverse components of the green economy are made mostly from copper. The US White House (2022) has announced that it expects global demand for such critical minerals to skyrocket by some 400–600 per cent over the next several decades, while the demand for the even more specialized minerals (e.g. lithium and graphite) required by electric vehicle batteries is expected to increase by as much as 4,000 per cent. Investors are now scouring the earth, the deep-sea bottom and even the heavens above in search of these resources. This push for new non-renewable resources is introducing the challenges of natural resource management to a whole new group of policy-makers – those in states with no previous experience in natural resource management, and those who are responsible for managing the global commons.

These challenges extend beyond the problems associated with securing the natural resources needed in a post-carbon economy. We, the global community, have long recognized the broader constraints to growth on a planet with limited resources.[2] More familiar renewable resources, such as farmlands, forests and fishing grounds, suffer from increased pressure of exhaustion. Despite increased improvement in agricultural productive capacity, we are still unable (or unwilling) to feed the world. Worse, conditions will only become more diffi-cult in the future, as the world's population grows, whereas the amount of agri-cultural land will remain (largely) constant.

These trends should force us to rethink the way that the world community ought to manage its natural resources in the face of three serious challenges. First, it must be prepared to *replace its reliance on non-renewable energy sources with more renewable forms* (e.g. wind/solar/hydro). At the same time, however, it needs to encourage *a shift from one type of non-renewable resource* (carbon-based resources) *to another type of non-renewable* (but recyclable) *resource*, with a significant rise in the extraction of silver, cobalt and other rare minerals used in the electrical value chain. Finally, it needs to ensure *better management of renew-able resources*, to protect against over-exploitation and achieve sustainability. These three challenges will force the global community to explore and develop new types of resources and markets. In doing so, it will need to proceed with caution, so that it does not repeat the mistakes of the past.

We recognize that mainstream approaches to natural resource management (NRM) have much to offer. They can muster an astonishing amount of capital and competences to bring scarce and often inaccessible resources to market.

---

2. This argument can be traced back to Malthus (1993 [1798]), if not earlier. Important headliners since then include: Sears (1980 [1935]), Vogt (1948), Thomas (1956), Bookchin (1975 [1962]), Carson (1962) and Meadows *et al.* (1972).

When properly designed, these approaches can address many of our most pressing environmental and climatic concerns. In a nutshell, today's mainstream management regimes can be both economically and environmentally sustainable. The problem is that these NRM regimes are not *politically* sustainable: they rely on a private taking from the common wealth, and they generate untenable inequalities. Not only are today's NRM regimes unfair but they undermine the very sort of (local) political support we will need if we hope to access and secure the natural resources necessary for our future. After all, who will want a dam built in their backyard if the economic gains from that dam go elsewhere (e.g. in the form of dividends to faraway shareholders)? It matters little that our current path is both economically and environmentally sustainable if it ends in a political dead end.

There is a better path forward. In staking out that path, we offer a different kind of book. We leverage our academic experience and expertise to propose a new approach to managing natural resources. In short, we play the role of advocates, in addition to being analysts. We adopt this unconventional role because we think that the world community faces significant challenges, and our existing approaches to managing scarce natural resources are both unjust and unsustainable.

This introductory chapter contains three parts. First, we introduce the nature of the challenges facing the global community. Most of these challenges will be familiar to our readers, in that they deal with the constraints on growth in a world with limited resources. But the costs of these trade-offs have grown in the context of climate change, and we are now forced to explore new resource frontiers and encroach on other forms of nature – those that have previously lain beyond the grasp of technology and markets. In developing these new markets, we will face a number of political challenges concerning the access and control (or ownership) of nature, and how this control is allocated.

In the second part we consider mainstream approaches to natural resource management. This part includes a short review of the different academic and policy approaches to NRM, and a brief assessment of their accomplishments and failures. The results are unambiguous: we have made remarkable strides in improving (economic and environmental) efficiencies in the way we exploit our natural resources. In encouraging these efficiencies, however, we have allowed private interests to abscond with significant value that they have not themselves produced. This has exacerbated political and economic inequalities around the world, which – in turn – undermines support for the kind of reforms that might increase productivity.

In the third part of this introductory chapter, we propose an alternative, more sustainable, approach to NRM. This approach starts by recognizing how nature makes for an awkward commodity, and that the process of bringing nature to market is an inherently political one. Because much of the commodity value of nature is produced by nature itself, as harnessed by political sovereignty (not individual initiative and entrepreneurship), this value belongs to the community and therefore ought to be administered by its democratically elected representatives in the community's best long-term interests.

Our proposed approach is neither new nor revolutionary; it is the baseline for how Norway has managed much of its natural resource wealth over the past century. It has also been practised, for centuries, on land markets in a number of local and national contexts. We believe that this approach can be extended to other countries and contexts, as well as to other natural resources. Although these ideas are not new, they are now able to draw greater attention and currency in today's climatic, ideological and political context. We believe there has never been a more opportune time to introduce a more just approach to NRM. We hope that we can convince the reader of this pressing need.

The challenge

Our management of the earth's natural resources is one of the most pressing challenges that we, as a global community, face. It is obvious that our planet's resources are finite, and these natural limits must affect the way we develop in the future.

We, as authors, are concerned about climate change, resource exhaustion and environmental degradation, but it is not our primary concern. It is more important for us to shine a light on the global poverty, inequality and injustice that mainstream NRM regimes produce. In our effort to address the global climate crisis, we cannot repeat these injustices and continue to ignore the needs of millions of people who will consequently suffer from a lack access to food, shelter, clean air and water. As we prepare for the future, we need to address both threats: the environmental and the distributional. Luckily, we can fight both battles with the same stick.

The challenge we face concerns finding a balance, along two disparate axes. The first axis is natural, and concerns the need to balance the limits to our use of existing natural resources and the untapped potential of nature that lies in waiting. We have inherited an unfathomably large and complex natural system, but we have barely scraped the surface of its potential. As we approach the limits to this surface area, we are pushed deeper into nature, in search of new resources. The first part of this section aims to counter some of the pessimism endemic to resource management by pointing to the potential bounty of the nature that remains.

The second axis is political, and revolves around the issue of stewardship. As we shall see, the question of ownership and control is central to the way we think about allocating access to scarce nature (in part, to avoid what is called "the tragedy of the commons"). Resolving this question involves decisions with enormous distributional consequences: decisions about enclosure, access, commodification and value creation. As we embark on new resource frontiers, we will face new rounds of these kinds of decisions, and we need to consider their distributional consequences.

As a matter of history, political convention and convenience, this stewardship is operationalized at the nation state level, allowing different states to manage their natural resources in very different ways. This is clearly unjust, in that the allocation of natural resources is unequally distributed across nation states; but these are the cards we have been dealt. Hence, there can be no avoiding the fact that the heart of our struggle lies in the sovereign state, whose political authority is absolute within the boundaries of recognized territory, and central to any decision about how the world governs common, or unclaimed, territory in the future (e.g. the high seas and the seabed below them, the skies above, Antarctica and the deep earth). After all, the United Nations' resolution on "permanent sovereignty over natural resources" (UN 1962) clearly and explicitly recognizes the sovereignty of peoples and nations over their natural wealth. The political authority of states is sovereign: this is the political authority that decides how we allocate access to scarce resources, and this is the authority that must be held accountable for the consequences of that allocation.

Of course, this sovereign authority is tethered to a world whose political and ideological tides are in constant flux. The scope of sovereign power can vary a great deal from one generation to another, as the power of states, versus markets, ebbs and flows. Policy-makers in the 1960s and 1970s enjoyed much greater autonomy than their successors in the 1990s and early 2000s, when the norms and rules of international exchange imposed stricter limits on sovereign authority. This tide is again changing, and today's voters are weary of unfettered markets; they expect more from political authority. This is why we think that now is the time to introduce a better, more sustainable, approach to managing our natural resources.

Nature's limits and potential

The scarcity of nature is especially evident in the market for oil, where consumption over time leads to the inevitable exhaustion of a natural resource. It is less evident, but equally true, that scarcity threatens our access to the renewable resources, in that even renewable resources can be ruined by mismanagement and degradation.

In both cases (renewables and non-renewables), access to nature is fixed in quantity and unequally distributed across the globe. In other words, some places are blessed with fertile land, sun, waterfalls, oil or cobalt, while others are not. We cannot increase the total amount of these resources; we can only use them more efficiently.

Astrophysicists tell us that 90 per cent of all our lithium was created within 20 minutes of the birth of our universe, in big bang nucleosynthesis (BBN). Those elements that are heavier than lithium were created in stars, which began to form some 180 million years later. Iron and related elements (such as chromium, manganese, copper and nickel) are created from the ejecta of supernovas, in which oxygen and silicon fuse (and continue to fuse). Gold is the product of neutron stars colliding, while tin and lead are the offspring of red giants (Doepel & Urama 2021). The value of these natural resources, whether it is lithium or lead, was created at the beginning of time, in a process that belongs to no one. These are gifts to humankind that cannot be reproduced or repeated, even though they can be recycled.

Comparatively speaking, petroleum is relatively young, and reproducible (in principle). Petroleum, like other fossil fuels, is formed from plants and animals (especially algae, plankton and zooplankton) that died millions of years ago. When a large quantity of this organic material ends up in a confined area (geologically speaking), and gets buried under sediment, and exposed to extreme pressure and high temperatures, the result is a fluid mix of liquid and gaseous hydrocarbons, inorganic chemical elements and physical impurities. The qualities that we value in petroleum, as a natural resource, are the result of this chemical and physical process that has taken place over millennia, completely independent of human action. This gift from nature will continue, but it will be a very long time before today's organic material can be turned into hydrocarbons.

Other gifts of nature are the kind of gift that keeps on giving, however. The marvels of photosynthesis and the hydrological cycle provides us with water, food, forests and wildlife that grow and reproduce value entirely on their own. The power of the wind and the heat of the sun can be relentless, if not always constant. In this realm, nature is a perpetual producer, but this productive power, like that of the minerals, ores and fossil fuels, is one that is unequally distributed around the world.

Our natural stores are clearly limited. To demonstrate this, Figure 1.1 provides an overview of how the earth's surface area is divided, by types of land use. Here we see that most of the earth is not (currently) suitable for human habitation, as over 70 per cent of the earth's surface is covered by ocean. Ninety per cent of the ocean (and 50 per cent of the earth's surface) is covered by deep sea (over

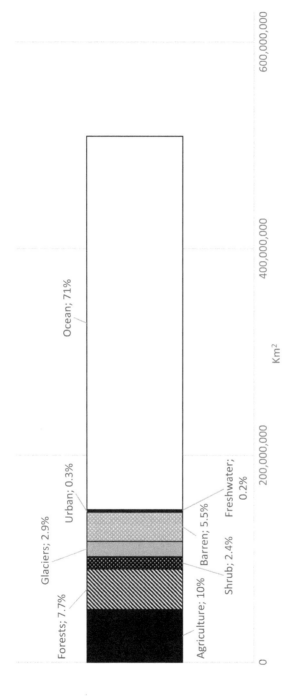

Figure 1.1 Global land use types on the earth's surface area
Source: Ritchie and Roser (2019).

200 metres), and only 0.0001 per cent of the world's deep seafloor has been investigated. We use less than half of 1 per cent of the earth's surface for urban development, and about 20 per cent of the earth's surface area is considered habitable (made up of agricultural land, forests, shrubs and grasslands). A remarkably small share of the earth's surface (0.2 per cent) is covered by fresh water.

It is a challenge that so little of the planet is habitable given our own remarkable capacity to procreate. Every year 140 million babies are brought into this world, while only 58 million people leave it in death; the difference (82 million) contributes annually to the total stock of people living on our earth. As a result, the world's population has exploded since the start of the twentieth century (see Figure 1.2). By 2100 the UN Population Division expects the world's population to reach 10.9 billion people. This increase in mouths to feed, heads to cover and bodies to clothe will surely put a strain on the world's storehouse of natural resources.

At the same time, it is important to avoid panic. The world's population growth rate has been falling dramatically since 1968, and this will – over time – deliver a new demographic balance in the future. In addition, the biggest challenge lies not in the limits to growth but in the difficulty of reallocation. In many cases we have enough of these scarce natural goods; the problem is that they are unequally distributed. Whichever future path we choose, though, we will still need to navigate the challenges associated with scarcity in nature.

Technology pushes constantly on the boundaries of accessible nature. Global mining ventures are already lining up to harvest the minerals that lie on the seabed beneath international, deep-sea, waters. We can expect that an even larger number of venture capitalists are calculating the potential rewards from wind turbines and kites suspended in the lower atmosphere; harvesting the minerals on asteroids passing by; or tapping the enormous thermal energy that lies at the core of our planet. In recognition of our growing need for new resources, and the potential of future technology, we will begin to wade deeper into the earth's oceans, subsurface and atmosphere. These are the new frontiers of nature, which tempt many of us, because they appear free for the taking.

To demonstrate the potential scope for natural exploitation, on this larger scale, consider Figure 1.3. In this figure, our current engagement with nature is mostly limited to the thin black circle representing the earth's surface area – the same surface area depicted in Figure 1.1. Beneath us, untapped, lie the several layers of earth: the upper and lower mantle, the inner and outer core. Above us, the Kármán line, at 100 km above the earth's mean sea level, can be used as an imaginary boundary between the earth's atmosphere and outer space. Above the Kármán line lie many thousands of kilometres of open space, stretching out to the orbit of the moon. All of this natural territory is within grasp, some of it within our lifetime. Exploiting this new space will obviously introduce a number of political challenges (see, e.g., Deudney 2020).

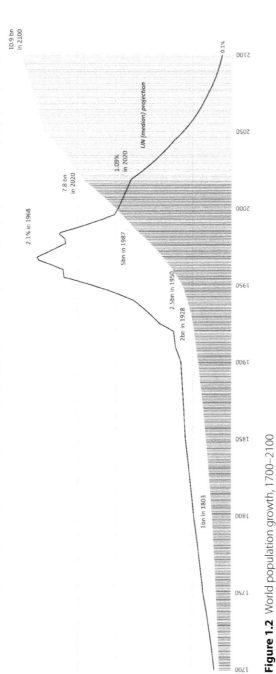

Figure 1.2 World population growth, 1700–2100

Note: The world population growth rate is depicted as a line; the world population is in histogram form. After 2019 the data are projections based on UN median fertility variant. See the original sources for more information.

Sources: Roser (2019) and UN (2019a, 2019b, 2019c, 2019d).

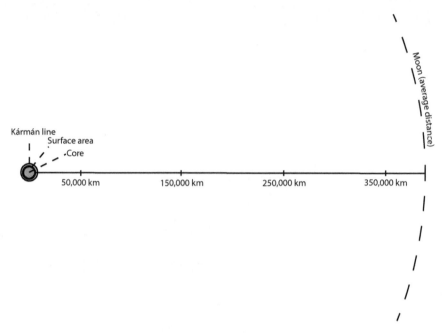

Figure 1.3 The final frontier
Note: Roughly to scale. Core includes both mantles and core (inner/outer). The core extends from the centre of the earth to the earth's crust, located 35 km below mean sea level. We use the IUGG's mean radius, or 6,371 km from the centre to the three radii points: two at the equator, one at a pole. The Kármán line is a placeholder marking the edge of the earth's atmosphere, set arbitrarily at 100 km above sea level.
Source: International Union of Geodesy and Geophysics: www.iugg.org.

For the most part, nature remains in common stewardship. The *vast* majority of our natural space is not claimed by private owners, but belongs to us as "common heritage of [hu]mankind" (to borrow from the United Nations Convention on the Law of the Sea, UNCLOS, which came into force on 14 November 1994; see UN 1982: preamble). Everything beyond the small ring of the earth's surface in Figure 1.3 remains unclaimed, common space/territory. As we extend outwards and downwards from the earth's surface, there will be growing pressure to enclose more and more of this common space – taking it out of common ownership (where it is currently "unused"), and privatizing it, so that we can exploit this nature more effectively.

This sort of unclaimed natural frontier is not limited to the space beyond the earth's surface area. If we take the same division of surface area as found in Figure 1.1 but divide the land and sea masses into common territory and territory that is claimed by sovereign states, as is done in Figure 1.4, then we find that the share of common/sovereign nature is, roughly, split evenly: 46.7 per cent

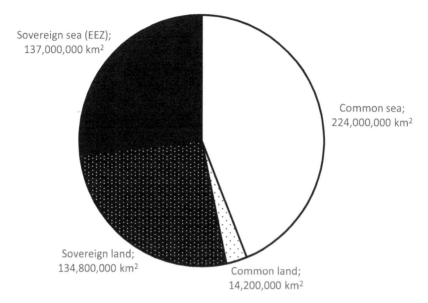

Sovereign sea (EEZ);
137,000,000 km²

Common sea;
224,000,000 km²

Sovereign land;
134,800,000 km²

Common land;
14,200,000 km²

Figure 1.4 The global allocation of nature
Note: In this depiction, "common land" is limited to the surface area of Antarctica.
Sources: Ritchie and Roser (2019) and Sea Around Us (2016).

remains in common hands; while 53.3 per cent has already been "claimed" by sovereign authorities. This sovereign nature is roughly divided between land and sea claims (so-called exclusive economic zones, EEZs, which were first prescribed by the 1982 UNCLOS). Hence, over 60 per cent of the world's oceans remain in common hands, while only about 10 per cent of the world's land surface area has remained beyond the reach of sovereign authorities.

Within each of these sovereign claims we find a remarkable array of approaches to managing natural resources. Each sovereign state decides for itself how to allocate access to nature that lies within its sovereign territory. Accordingly, there is much common nature remaining within individual sovereign states. At the same time, these states negotiate with other sovereign states about how to access the remaining (globally common) nature. The resulting decisions are difficult and controversial, as they transfer public/common resources into private property and create significant value in the process.

One of the complicating factors in these decisions is that human survival depends upon access to natural resources. We simply cannot survive without food, clothing, shelter, air and water – all of which are derivatives of natural resources. In recognizing this dependence, public access to these necessary resources has been secured by a number of covenants, spanning centuries: from the English Charter of the Forest (in 1217) to the UN's International Covenant on Economic, Social and Cultural Rights, which came into force on 3 January 1976 and which declares: "In no case may a people be deprived of its own means of subsistence" (UN 1966: pt 1, art. 1, ch. 2).

Because land and forests provide us with most of what we need to survive, their private enclosure forces people to find alternative means of accessing food, shelter, energy and the like (either by selling their labour in exchange for resources that were once free to take, or by stealing them from those who now claim ownership). In much of the developed world we have come to accept the enclosure of land, and the need to pay for the food, energy and protection necessary for our survival. What was once free for the taking is now a commodity to be bought and sold at market. In this political context, people need paid employment (or some other means to secure payment) if they are to survive and/or afford life's necessities.

In other countries and at other times, and with specific types of land, this enclosure process has taken on different forms, or is still unfolding. For other natural resources, beyond land, the process has developed along different routes, or not at all. For example, it is the state that usually owns subsurface oil and minerals (in most countries), but it does so as a collective representative for its denizens. Other natural resources, such as the sun, wind and oceans, remain unowned. With these resources there is still widespread acceptance of common "ownership", and many of us find it difficult (or scary) to imagine how these resources might be "enclosed".

Current approaches

There is an incredible amount of work dedicated to natural resource management. Most of this work occurs at the resource level and is concerned with environmental and economic issues. Nearly all of it tends to leverage market forces.[3] In particular, mainstream approaches to NRM rest on two underlying

---

3. Our literature review addresses what might be called the legalistic approach to NRM, whereby the focus is trained on the challenges of managing resources when the nature of the good, and its ownership deed, is complex or uncertain, and when this uncertainty can lead to what is called a "tragedy of the commons". As this work focuses on the allocation of scare resources, it tends to be dominated by economists. This is not to ignore other management traditions, anchored more in the science and engineering fields, that focus on resource utilization (consumption/ non-consumptive purposes) or the need to optimize the use of a given resource, from either an economic or an environmental perspective. These other fields of management are not committed to particular ownership and/or allocation regimes.

assumptions, borne of the marketplace, both of which are problematic. The first is an argument that privatization of nature is necessary to avoid waste and to increase efficiencies. This, in itself, is not so much a problem as the underlying assumption that the privatization process is natural, necessary and somehow apolitical. The second assumption is a derivative of the first: that the market for natural resources is similar to other commodity markets, and hence follows the same basic laws. Let us take a closer look at these two problematic assumptions.

Privatization

The privatization argument has deep roots and can be traced back to Aristotle: "For that which is common to the greatest number has the least care bestowed upon it. Everyone thinks chiefly of his own, hardly at all of the common interest; and only when he is himself concerned as an individual" (Aristotle 350 BCE, bk II, pt III). In the seventeenth century this argument was carried forward by John Locke, who popularized a labour theory of property (described in more detail below). Today the placeholder for this argument rests with a remarkably influential article by Garrett Hardin (1968), entitled "The tragedy of the commons". In a nutshell, a "tragedy of the commons" approach holds that natural resources will be overused (exhausted) and abused (polluted) when held in common. State intervention in or ownership of the commons are seen as non-starters, because public bodies are *assumed* to be inefficient, and people are *assumed* to prefer marketization. In Hardin's remarkably belli-cose words: "The alternative of the commons is too horrifying to contemplate. Injustice is preferable to total ruin" (1968: 1247).

In its most extreme form, this argument is used to predict widespread socio-economic problems when countries fail to introduce private and formal property rights regimes, especially in contexts that are rich in natural resources.[4] In this light, privatizing the commons ensures that individuals will put their own pri-vate property to the highest and best use; when this is done it is assumed that the larger community will become better off. Consequently, the only reasonable path forward is to privatize and commodify nature. As the survey on water by *The Economist* (2003) could declare:

> Water, the stuff of life, ought to be the most precious of all gifts. Yet throughout history, and especially over the past century, it has been

---

4. The contemporary foundation for this argument lies in a so-called "property rights approach" (e.g. Alchian & Demsetz 1973; Demsetz 1967, 2002), but its application in countries rich in natural resources can be found in influential works such as Barbier (2005: 122–40) and De Soto (2020).

ill-governed and, above all, colossally underpriced. Indeed it is often given away completely free ... [T]he best way of solving it [providing universal access to clean water] is to treat water pretty much as a business like any other.

This rather naive focus on privatization has been tempered in recent years. Although support has not completely disappeared, the "tragedy of the commons" approach now enjoys fewer proponents in the wake of Elinor Ostrom's Nobel-Prize-winning efforts.[5] Because of Ostrom, it is increasingly recognized that collective governance of the commons is possible, and that the challenges we once attributed to the tragedy of the commons (and the free rider problem) are largely exaggerated. In effect, Ostrom extended our vocabulary beyond the simplistic binary concepts of "market" and "state", and provided some wriggle room for "the community". For Ostrom, goods are not simply "public" or "private"; they can also be "common-pool resources" (CPRs), sharing the characteristics of both public and private goods (Ostrom 2009, 2012).

We do not need to climb into the details of how CPRs can be managed (and there is a very rich literature here).[6] Our point is to note that it was once commonplace to define types of property on the basis of *the type of good*: some goods naturally lend themselves to private or common property regimes. It was then assumed that the best way to improve the efficient use of goods/resources that were difficult to exclude (public goods and CPRs) was to privatize them – i.e. make it possible to exclude others from using them. Ostrom's work changed this focus, by recognizing that "common-property resources are not automatically associated with common-property regimes – or any other particular type of property regime" (Ostrom 2003: 249).

Although Ostrom opened up a door for political agency, it is not a very wide one. By focusing on CPRs, rather than the commons in general, Ostrom limits her focus to natural or man-made resources that are rather limited in scope.[7] Ostrom's (1990) work challenges the pessimistic conclusions of the "tragedy of the commons" approach and shows that the commons are indeed governable (at least at the subnational level, where her focus is trained). Following Hardin, Ostrom is not interested in justice, per se. Like nearly all

---

5. See, for example, Ostrom (1990, 2003, 2009, 2012).
6. For useful overviews, see Isaac *et al.* (2010), Acheson (2011), De Schutter and Pistor (2016) and Sikor, He & Lestrelin (2017).
7. See Obeng-Odoom (2021: ch. 3) for a critical examination of how Ostrom's "common pool resources" differ from "the commons".

the others working in this area,[8] her focus is trained on issues of efficiency and ecology.

In short, privatization remains the world's go-to solution for managing natural resources, even if our enthusiasm has been somewhat dampened by the work of Elinor Ostrom. Although we now recognize the potential of middle-range solutions to the problem of the commons, there is remarkably little work done on how and where private interests should be brought into the management mix; we simply assume it is best to enclose the commons into private bundles of rights.

Markets

This brings us to a second problematic assumption: current approaches to NRM assume that the market for natural resources is like the market for all other goods and services, in which supply and demand meet in equilibrium, in response to varying price signals. To understand why this is a problem, we need to reflect briefly on how markets are supposed to work, in theory.

In ideal markets, the price of a good/service rises automatically in response to an increase in demand for that good/service. This (higher) price incentivizes private investors/producers to enter into the market, produce new goods and services and reap the advantage of higher prices. Profit, then, is the legitimate reward for the risk and insight employed to fill the demand/supply void. In response to higher prices, the supply of goods rises to meet the increased demand, and the market clears. As more producers enter the market, chasing after these higher returns, the resulting competition will erode any extraordinary returns, and the price of the good will return to equilibrium, but now with a supply that meets demand. This is the textbook market model we all learned about in school, and it is described in more detail in Chapter 3.

In this ideal form, the market is assumed to include several built-in correction mechanisms. In particular, we assume that producers have access to the factor (capital and labour) inputs they need to increase supply. If either factor is in short supply, it can be easily substituted by the other. As a result, there can be no bottlenecks in supply, as any shortage is quickly remedied with substitution strategies. In addition, this ideal market model assumes there are no barriers to entry for new producers. Anybody and everybody has access to the inputs they need to produce the goods in question. Hence, when the price of a good increases (say, due to increased demand), any and all producers are free

---

8. Two exceptions to this rule are Pistor and De Schutter (2016) and Obeng-Odoom (2021).

to enter into the market to fill the gap. Finally, this ideal market is characterized by competition and populated with a myriad of producers and consumers, none of whom functions as a price maker (monopolist/oligopolist) or price taker (monopsonist/oligopsonist).

It is this ideal market approach that lies beneath most contemporary NRM regimes: we adopt this market approach to secure the efficient extraction and use of scarce natural resources. This efficiency gain is derived from the fact that natural resources, *in situ*, do not have a price; they remain as the heavens, mountains, rivers, forests, etc. – beautiful, yes, but without market value. This absence of (market) value is sometimes because natural resources are abundant and free (think of the air); sometimes because it is unclear who actually owns the resource (think of the sun); and sometimes because they are difficult to locate or extract (think of minerals or petroleum). For all these reasons, resources in nature are undervalued by the market – and for this reason there is little incentive to use them efficiently. To create economic value, and to use these resources more efficiently, policy-makers "enclose" nature into bundles of rights that can be allocated to private interests/producers. Producers then turn these natural resources into commodities, creating economic value. When the rewards for natural resource extraction prove to be extraordinarily high, we attribute this gain to the innovation and risk-taking of the private producers, and reward them with windfall profits.

To summarize, then, the most common approaches to NRM provide our policy-makers with four related incentives to privatize access to, and to commodify, natural resources.

(1) We hope to *create value* by taking "value-less" natural resources and converting them into valuable commodities. We do this by means of an appropriation process that "encloses" these commons into legal entities and then allocates access.

(2) We assume that this enclosure allows for a *more efficient utilization* of these natural resources, now as commodities. This assumption is based on a familiar belief that market forces and private ownership are best suited to settling issues of scarcity and reward, and because we need to overcome the challenges often associated with the "tragedy of the commons".

(3) This process *allocates rewards* through market mechanisms in a manner that appears to be objective or neutral. The resulting increase in value goes to those private interests that are able to "flip" these natural resources, now commodified. It is this private initiative that is regarded as creating value out of nothing. Any resulting "windfall" is seen as a just reward for the risks, insight and ingenuity of the private interests that are able to satisfy unmet demand in the market.

(4) In return, we are able to *secure new financing and economic activity*. As access to these resources is sometimes auctioned or sold off, the resulting funds can be used to fill government coffers. As these gains tend to be one-shot, more significant economic rewards can come from the expectation that the commodified resource will generate additional economic activity (jobs, tax revenues, increased gross domestic product [GDP], knowledge/experience, etc.).

We think this is a fair and accurate depiction of the mainstream approach to NRM. The result is a convenient, and not unreasonable, way for policy-makers and academics to think about, and to justify, a resource management model that encourages the privatization of natural resources as a means to increase their efficient exploitation, to the benefit of the larger community.

Results

The results derived from the mainstream approach to NRM are impressive. Humankind's capacity to find, capture, process and finance the recovery of scarce natural resources is absolutely amazing. Engineers have developed, and continue to develop, astonishing and efficient means for locating and accessing natural resources, even when these resources are found in some of the most inaccessible, unstable and inhospitable places. It is nearly impossible to look at, or read about, the Three Gorges Dam, the "Troll A" offshore natural gas platform or the promise of asteroid mining and not be impressed by the sheer techno-logical and financial muscle on display.

All the while we have become increasingly aware of the need to access these resources in an environmentally sustainable manner. After all, most of our regu-latory attention has been focused on encouraging a shift from non-renewable to renewable sources of nature, while improving the efficiencies and environmental protections associated with the use of renewable natural resources. The rapid growth in new solar and wind technologies attests to this awareness. Indeed, the global share of renewable energy resources was nearly 17.5 per cent in 2016, and it is growing quickly (World Bank 2020a: 63). Further evidence can be found in the environmental regulations increasingly placed on the extraction of more traditional resources. Clearly, more can (and should) be done, but we are very much aware of the environmental challenges to harvesting and using our natural resources, and policy-makers are choosing to manage these resources in a more environmentally sustainable manner.

In concentrating our focus on economic and environmental efficiency, how-ever, we have largely ignored the distributional consequences of our management regimes. Mainstream NRM approaches have encouraged a growing concentration of ownership, wealth and power. This growing inequality is fuelling public resistance to new technologies and markets that will be necessary for our future survival: witness the rising opposition to land-based wind turbines.

Although natural resources belong to the commons, the wealth they generate tends to go elsewhere. As the UN Secretary-General, António Guterres, noted in a 2021 speech to the Global Roundtable on Transforming Extractive Industries for Sustainable Development, mineral wealth seldom translates to common wealth. Although mineral-rich countries account for a quarter of global GDP, half the world's population – nearly 70 per cent of their people – live in extreme poverty. Worse, the situation seems to be deteriorating: of the world's 72 low- or middle-income countries, 63 have increased their dependence on extractive industries over the past two decades (Guterres 2021). The money flowing into these countries (chasing down those valuable natural resources) brings additional challenges. This difficulty has many names and takes many forms. Whether we refer to it as a resource (or oil) curse, or a paradox of plenty, the problem is one that has long haunted resource-rich countries (Venables 2016).[9]

This is not a new concern or observation. We have simply become numb to the fact. As early as 1711 Richard Steele noted in a contribution to *The Spectator*, the magazine he had co-founded: "It is generally observed, That in Countries of the greatest Plenty there is the poorest Living" (Steele 1711: 680). Over a century later this relationship was the topic of a book often heralded as "the best-selling book ever on political economy,"[10] *Progress and Poverty* by Henry George 1992 [1879]. For centuries we have recognized that significant value lies in the commodification of natural resources, but that the resulting wealth seldom finds its way back to the people who own them. As Fred Harrison (2008: 118) notes, "Nature's resources do no curse anyone. Rather, the curse flows from bad stewardship of the public domain."

We think this is our most pressing challenge. As environmental, demographic and climatic changes force us to exploit new resources, we will need to address the distributional consequences of enclosure, allocation and commodification. As the markets for water, wind and solar energy develop, they will encroach upon our very human need to drink, breathe and stay warm. In allocating private access, control and/or ownership over these resources, as we have already done with land (in much of the world), we will be forcing much of humankind into an increasingly precarious relationship to the market.

---

9. See Chapter 7 and Box 9.1 for further elaboration on these concepts.
10. See, for example, Robert Schalkenbach Foundation (n.d.) and Blaug (2000: 270).

An alternative approach: becoming aware of the Natural Dividend

Most of our current approaches to NRM assume that the market for resources works like the market for other goods and services. We think this assumption is a costly mistake; these markets are unique, and they ought to be managed accordingly. Evidence of this mistake is clearly available to those who look for it: natural resource markets tend to be characterized by extraordinary market concentration and astonishingly high profit levels. Wars have been fought, regions colonized and fortunes amassed from the access granted to scarce natural resources. It is not by chance that the largest companies in the world, until very recently, were concentrated in the oil and energy sectors. These are markets in which oligopolistic producers are able to leverage their market power to secure rents that are not of their making.

We argue that these approaches are unfair in at least two (related) ways. First, market-based approaches divert attention away from the most significant sources of value in the commodification of natural resources. It is not private initiative that creates the massive rewards that often characterize these sectors; these rewards are derived from rents that are produced by the resources themselves (differential rents), the way that we allocate access to them (regulatory rents) and by the nearness to community-provided infrastructure (locational rents).[11] These three types of rent constitute what we call the *Natural Dividend*. When we ignore the nature and source of these underlying rents, they are easily captured by private interests, which abscond with them under the cloak of profit.

Second, and relatedly, market-based approaches focus myopically on efficiency. In doing so, they ignore the role that political authority plays in creating and facilitating an unjust distribution. In particular, market-based approaches allocate reward to private initiative, while conveniently ignoring the value created by nature and its regulation – independent of private initiative. This is clearly unfair. By documenting the source of value creation in natural resource markets, we intend to show how private initiative is only part of the value creation process. More specifically, the creation of extraordinary value is the result of nature itself and the allocation process that limits/broadens access to that nature.

As we begin to reposition our relationship to nature and consider how to exploit new types of natural resources, we need to be more aware of the distributional consequences of how we allocate access to these resources. Each of the varied responses to the challenges of environmental degradation and climate change promises to increase the relative scarcity of natural resources. As we shift

---

11. Rents can also be created by producers forming oligopolies and cartels (i.e. creating scarcity). When this happens, political authorities tend to notice the extra value produced, and prohibit its capture by way of anti-trust regulation.

the world's consumption from one set of scarce natural resources to another, we must do a better job of managing the distributional fallout from our NRM regimes. In short, we need to develop management regimes that are not only efficient and safe, but also just.

In making this argument, we should clarify its limits. This book is different from others in that we focus on the middle ground, ideologically speaking. The underlying conflict that propels this study – the conflict between private and common interests – is as old as civilization. Although the push for privatization has been unrelenting in the recent past, it would be naïve to think the conflict has been resolved or settled. When we step back and take a broader historical view, we see that the favoured solutions (private/collective) tend to swing back and forth, from century to century, like a pendulum (Schlatter 1951). We believe that this balance of power has already begun to change, but right now we find ourselves in a political context that still prioritizes the private over that of the collective. Like it or not, we take this as our point of departure.

The efficiency gains we associate with privatization can occur at different levels and in different ways, however, independently of the baseline management regime. Consider a hypothetical analogy from the backyard. A large family own a plot of land in the countryside and hopes to find water to fill a well. They do not know for sure if there is water lying beneath their plot of land, but they decide to look for water, and then tap into it (should they find it). The family have two options: they could do this themselves (recognizing a relatively steep learning curve and initial capital investment), or they could hire it out to an experienced private contractor. As they have no use for the drilling machinery (or the acquired knowledge) after the water is found and recovered, the family decide the most sensible choice is to hire a private drilling contractor. In hiring the contractor, the family are provided with two contract options. In the first option, the family shoulder all the risk, by agreeing to pay for all necessary materials plus an hourly fee for each hour of work. In the second option, the contractor shoulders the risk by offering a fixed fee (plus the cost of all necessary materials) to find and deliver the water. In either of these scenarios, it is completely unthinkable that the family agree to terms by which the contractor is granted ownership in the underlying water resource. The contractor is providing a service and will be rewarded for that service – but the underlying resource remains owned by the family.

In this example, it does not matter that the owner is an individual or a family; as owners, they act as one in their negotiations with the contractor. In deciding on the most efficient solution to their water needs, the family has to balance the short-term economic benefits against the long-term benefits of securing a drilling rig and the expertise necessary to drill wells in the future. In deciding to choose a private contractor, the family recognize that an experienced contractor could do the job more efficiently, but they jettison the opportunity to learn the trade and pursue future wells at a reduced price. The efficiency gains from privatization lie here in the service provided, and the timeline prioritized, not in the underlying ownership of the resource.

Let us be clear: this is not a book about extending the commons to new areas; we take common ownership as an historical point of departure, not a goal in itself.[12] Rather, our concern is with the source and distribution of value produced by common resources. The responsibility for deciding whether private or public entities should be allowed to exploit these shared resources rests with local and legitimate political authorities, in response to popular pressures and opinion. Similarly, it is not our desire or intent to demonize private interests. Private interests deserve a just return on their investments of capital and labour. Rather, ours is an argument for ensuring that the distribution of returns go to their rightful owners. Although we are concerned that private interests are currently able to abscond with publicly created value, we recognize that these interests play an important role in bringing resources to market.

In short, our objectives are relatively modest. We take the dominant approaches to NRM as our point of departure: where authorities choose to employ private interests to commodify our common natural resources. We then suggest a better way of managing these resources, given that point of departure, to ensure a more politically sustainable outcome. This approach is neither new nor inefficient; we can find traces of it in numerous countries, stretching over decades (even centuries) across several different resource markets.

Overview

We intend to draw people's attention to their collective ownership of natural resources, and initiate a discussion about how the regulation of these scarce resources will produce rents, which belong to the people. As we reform our management responses with an eye on securing environmental sustainability, we must also discuss how the (potentially significant) rewards from these management regimes are to be distributed. Obviously, private individuals and companies should be compensated for their efforts, their capital and their willingness to take risks. But private interests should not be allowed to access the rent that is generated from these regulations. When this happens, it can undermine political and social support for the needed regulations. In other words, any regulatory regime needs to be sustainable environmentally, economically *and* politically.

---

12. There are already a number of authors who argue vociferously for extending the commons (e.g. Linebaugh 2008; Bollier 2014; Standing 2019; Hayes 2020; Barnes 2021; as well as several contributions in Bollier & Helfrich 2012). Even the Pope has got in on the action (Francis 2015).

This book aims to demonstrate the existence of a Natural Dividend. Natural resources, and our regulation of them, can and often do produce significant value in the form of rents. These rents belong to the community; they are our shared Dividend. We recognize that not every natural resource will generate a significant Natural Dividend, and that the scope of the Dividend will vary with market conditions over time. Our point is simply to draw attention to the need to design NRM regimes with this potential in mind, so that private actors are not able to walk away with that Dividend when it does arise. We also recognize that any attempt to capture the Natural Dividend will be politically contentious; much negotiation will necessarily occur over determining when and where the Natural Dividend develops and how it is best captured. To prepare for this possibility, political authority needs to develop management regimes that recognize the existence of the Natural Dividend, and allow for its capture, when and where it develops.

To do this, the first part of the book offers a new and different approach to thinking about nature: to whom it belongs, how it is valued and how it becomes enclosed and commodified. In doing so, we argue that nature, and our regulating access to that nature, creates substantial (market) value. Chapter 2 begins with the obvious: that nature, initially, belongs to us all in common. This argument requires that we distinguish between nature and natural resources and explain how value is created as nature becomes commodified. Chapter 3 introduces the Natural Dividend. This Dividend is produced by nature, and by regulating access to that nature. In both cases, the source of the Natural Dividend lies with the original owners of the resource (the community), and the political authorities that represent it. As we shall see in subsequent chapters, many of the exorbitant returns we find in the market for natural resources are a result of this Natural Dividend, not the acumen of private interests. Hence, political authorities need to manage these resources to ensure that this Dividend is not captured by private interests but remains with its rightful owners: the public.

The main body of the book, Chapters 4 to 7, considers how this framework can be adapted to manage our natural resources in a world of increased scarcity. Our empirical focus is equally divided between food and energy markets. These chapters compare national approaches to natural resource management on (or in) the land, the sea, the sky, and the inner earth. For each of these resources we then focus in on a particular resource market as a case. Our choice of cases is not meant to be exhaustive or representative; we chose these cases mostly for their illustrative value. This is because every natural resource has the potential to generate a Natural Dividend, and the process of enclosing, allocating and commodify is remarkably similar across resource types. In particular, Chapter 4 looks at the markets for farm and forestry land; Chapter 5 examines the markets for marine resources, but with a particular focus on salmon farming; Chapter 6 explores the emerging markets in the sky (for renewable energy, especially solar and wind power); Chapter 7 considers the markets for subsurface resources (petroleum and minerals).

The closing section of the book peers even further into the future, by considering resource management in the world beyond sovereign territory. Increased scarcity and new technology are pushing the resource frontier into the polar regions, into (and under) the deep international waters that lie beyond sovereign territory, and into the atmosphere and space above us. As the resource frontier is extended it is necessary that we protect humankind's common rights over these resources. Chapter 8 considers the institutions that manage these resources today, and how they might employ a better regulatory framework to protect our Natural Dividend in the future.

Chapter 9 concludes by pointing to four lessons that can be learned from reading this book. Among these is the need to proceed with caution. In recognizing the important role played by political authority in creating the Natural Dividend, we must also recognize the need to ensure that political authority is made accountable. In short, securing the Natural Dividend is only the first step; we must also ensure that the Natural Dividend is managed fairly and well, and in ways that can lift the resource curse. In recognizing the existence of the Natural Dividend, and how it can be secured, we are left to ponder why these regimes are not more common. We close by arguing that the time is ripe to introduce more just NRM regimes and we consider some of the expected hindrances to a just transition.

In short, we offer a very different way of viewing our relationship to nature. This view, though unique, is not untried. Throughout the book we point to several examples of how such a regime is being (or has been) used, in particular markets, scattered through time and space. We draw attention to these examples and focus on the need to protect our common heritage with a management model that allows communities to secure the benefits we can and should expect from our scarce, but shared, resources. This is our Natural Dividend.

2

WHO OWNS THE SUN?

This chapter argues that nature belongs to us in common, and that the value produced by nature remains with the commons even after it has been enclosed and that enclosure has been allocated for private use.

This is both an easy and a hard argument to make. It is an easy argument when applied to those forms of nature that remain abundant. After all, few people are willing to argue for the exclusive or private ownership of the sun or the wind, such that others cannot enjoy their benefits (or wrath); or that the value-creating potential of nature – such as photosynthesis, thermodynamics or the hydro-logical cycle – should be, or can be, privatized. It is clear that these gifts of nature belong to us all, in common.

It is a more difficult argument to make in a context in which access to nature and natural resources is scarcer and commodified. This context is most evident in the market for land, where private rights to property have existed for cen-turies, and where plots of land are bought and sold on open markets. Although we can agree that the origins of land ownership are found in the commons, there is much land that has already found its way into private hands. It would be dif-ficult (and probably unfair) to bring this land back into the commons. But, even in those areas where we have granted exclusive access to nature, we can still (and should) ask: how much of nature's underlying productive power (and the value it generates) is transferred with a private title to nature?

Consider the question we use to title this chapter: "Who owns the sun?" In many ways, it is an absurd question. No one owns the sun. Or, alternatively, the sun is ours to share. After all, the sun was created in a process that is completely independent of (and prior to!) human influence: no person made or produced the sun. More importantly, the sun is absolutely essential to our survival on the earth: without it we would die. Should the sun fall under private ownership, its owner would have monopoly power over our very existence; we would be forced to pay anything, and everything, for a ray from the sun. Besides, the sun is available for everyone to use: its warmth and light are abundant, if unequally distributed across the globe. Who would want to pay for the sun when they can use its power freely?

No one owns the sun, but all of us take the sun's light and energy and use it to see and get warm, and some even use it to power their homes. This power of the sun is a gift of nature and is free for the taking. This is not a problem, in that each of us can use sunlight without detracting/subtracting from the amount of sunlight that is available to others (it is a true non-rivalrous good in this regard). In these cases, sunlight remains as nature: it is not commodified, or sold in a market. To the extent that solar energy can be seen as valuable, it is a form of common wealth.

But there are also those who take the sun's power (freely), use it to create energy and subsequently sell that energy on the market. These people are taking the power of the sun and commodifying it. Although the nature (sunlight) going into this process is free, the energy coming out (e.g. electrical power) has value as a commodity. In the process of commodifying solar energy, a common wealth is transformed into private riches.

This commodification process is the focus of our book, and it drives us to ask three important questions.

(1) Who is it that grants this solar entrepreneur the right to harvest and sell the sun?
(2) How much of the energy produced was the result of the entrepreneur who captured the sun's energy (this would be her rightful reward)?
(3) How much of the energy produced is the result of the sun itself (whose reward belongs to no one, or to the commons)?

This is the crux of the matter, and it lies beneath any and every attempt to commodify nature. After all, who owns the air? Who owns the wind? Who owns the atom? Or the sea? In these forms, nature belongs to all of us in common: it is owned by no one, and such value it produces remains as part of the common wealth. Yet each form of nature has the potential to become a commodified and valuable natural resource, whose value can be captured, enclosed and privatized. This capture may be necessary – for reasons we go on to discuss – but in allowing its enclosure we need to be aware of the significant distributional consequences that result.

There is nothing particularly unique about the sun, air or water in this regard. These same questions and concerns were once asked of land, and our initial reaction to private ownership of land was the same as it is with our (contemporary) reaction to owning the sun. After all, the land provides us with all of the things we need to survive: food, shelter, energy and water. As with the sun, we cannot live without access to the land's bounty. Like the sun, land was originally abundant and free for the taking; people could roam the earth and enjoy its bounty, without detracting from the use or enjoyment of others. Indeed, a person might even fence off a piece of this earth, and call it her own, knowing that doing so would not inhibit others from doing the same. If you asked a fifteenth-century dweller "Who owns the land?", her response would probably have been like ours with regard to the sun: "Nobody (except perhaps God) owns the land: it is there for us all to enjoy." In this context, the idea of private ownership would be frightening, as it would allow an individual "landowner" to have exclusive (or monopoly) control over the nature we need to survive.

For better or worse, most of nature still lies beyond the grasp of private ownership. In the future we may decide that it is necessary to allocate private access to these common resources – for example retrieving minerals from a nearby planet or asteroid – but that decision is still a long way off. But even the nature that remains within our grasp lies mostly beyond the reach of private owners. As we shall see in subsequent chapters, most forms of nature remain unowned, are publicly owned or belong to the local community.

Increasing scarcity will force this to change, and we need to be prepared. We have already seen this change in our approach to managing land, as it became scarcer (relative to a growing population). We expect the same sort of scarcity to develop in other natural resources, forcing us to rethink the way we allocate access to them. As demand for these scarce resources increases, we may find it necessary to concentrate ownership/access in order to secure greater efficiencies and economies of scale. Should this happen, we may find that private owners can leverage their monopoly control over scarce and essential resources and take from the common wealth.

This is not an argument against enclosure or privatization; there are many good reasons to enclose nature. But doing so excludes access to essential (and previously shared) resources, and this creates a number of political and social challenges. Another set of challenges develops when this exclusion results in extraordinary, unearned, gains. When these gains are the result of natural and political processes that are unrelated to the "owner's" efforts, the community (or, more correctly, its legitimate political authority) needs to decide how these gains should be allocated.

In this chapter we lay the groundwork for an argument that nature's bounty belongs to us in common, even if we enclose parts of it for private use/exploitation. It does so in two steps. In the first, we describe how we approach nature in its original form: as abundant, essential and accessible to everyone. In this state, it is easy to recognize common ownership in nature. The second section then turns to the process of enclosing, allocating access to and commodifying nature. This process is political and reflects the needs of the community to limit access to scarce but essential resources. In limiting access, the community creates significant (market) value.

Nature in common

Nature is the absence of human meddling. It is the earth, air, water and sun that constitute the essential, life-giving components to our planet. In its original form, nature exists as a means of subsistence, equally accessible to all of us. This allows us to value nature in any number of different ways (and independent of markets): as the source of life (providing food, water, air, energy, etc.); as a source of inspiration and fear; and even as a refuge from the human world surrounding us. Most significantly, nature exists independent of us; it is not of our making.

In the raw, nature is characterized by two qualities: its resources are essential for our survival; and they appear to be provided in great abundance. Over much of history it has been these two qualities that have been used to argue that nature belongs to us all, as common wealth.

Nature as essential

Nature provides us with the resources that are absolutely essential for our survival as human beings: air to breathe; water to drink; food to eat; and the clothing and shelter we need to protect us from the elements (see, e.g., De Schutter & Pistor 2016; Hall 2016). This is most obvious if we think about water: without water to drink, any one of us would die within a matter of days. It may take longer to die from starvation, exposure to the elements, or from air poisoning – but food, shelter and clean air are also essential to our survival. This recognition is a constant: it is as true today as it was two millennia ago.

Imagine you fall off the end of a cruise ship, *à la Captains Courageous*, and end up alone on a large, fertile but deserted island. In your effort to survive, you would not hesitate to take the food, water and shelter provided by the island; you would not be concerned about rightful ownership; and you would not exert any effort to enclose the bounty of nature and claim it as your own. You would take what you need, and you would be right in doing so.

This is the sort of thought experiment that political and legal thinkers have considered for centuries, and such a simple intellectual device forces us to recognize that our right to access nature is shared equally by everyone, and that such rights exist prior to (and independently of) the creation of society and political authority. As Henry George wrote in his *A Perplexed Philosopher* (2006 [1892]: 31): "The right of each to the use of land is still a direct, original right which he holds of himself, not by the gift or consent of the others."

In the state of nature, as on the hypothetical island, *essential* resources are provided by nature, free of charge; they are there for the taking. For most of human history, and for many of the world's poorest inhabitants, access to food, water and energy (e.g. firewood) is inextricably linked to the land. Consequently, restricting access to land has been the equivalent of restricting access to these essential resources.

When nature is enclosed (and access restricted), we need to find other ways to secure these essential resources. Markets provide the default delivery mechanism, but these are far from just. There can be no fair deal between a buyer desperate to secure an essential resource and a seller who has an exclusive (read: monopoly) grip on that resource. Worse, many people lack access to functioning labour markets and/or the public supports that will allow them to enter the market to buy food and water. Without access to natural resources, people need money; without access to money, people cannot survive. It is that simple. Although there may be good reasons for limiting access to scarce natural resources, they become morally problematic when those resources are essential to human survival.

Nature as abundant

The second defining characteristic of nature in the raw is its apparent abundance. This appearance is both nature's promise and its bane. It is also, mostly, an illusion.

Nature's promise lies in what might be called the "gifts of nature": it provides us with a renewable, and unending, source of essential value. As much of nature is renewable (when properly managed), it has the capacity to produce this essential value forever. After all, why would I need to own a piece of land if I can go out and take what I need directly from nature? Why should I try to enclose the sun if I can warm myself freely (and doing so does not affect others from also seeking the warmth)? Why should I restrict others from fishing if we can all fish in a vast and abundant ocean? When nature remains in the raw, and appears to be abundant, we can access its bounty freely and without quarrel.

Over time, we have come to learn that the appearance of natural abundance is deceiving, in at least two ways. First, not all of nature's resources are renewable. Non-renewable resources, such as minerals and petroleum, are clearly scarce in that they are not (feasibly) reproducible. These resources exist as a fixed pool (let us ignore the recycling of minerals for now), which is drained by consumption. After all, if one person (or generation) consumes all of the resource, there is none left for others.

Second, even renewable resources can be depleted and poorly managed. This can happen in any number of ways. Existing resources can be diminished by pollution and neglect: polluted farm and forest lands must be taken out of production (think Chernobyl); unprotected animals and plants can and do become extinct (think Tasmanian tiger). In addition, the abundance of nature can shrink, relative to a growing population. Indeed, the very appearance of abundance makes nature susceptible to the tragedy of commons introduced in the opening chapter.

Because it seems as if there is an abundance of land, or fish in the ocean, individuals might take more from nature than its capacity to provide. In short, nature is often not as abundant as we think, and the absence of regulation can fuel nature's demise. Worse, as people become aware of the potential scarcity, there is a rush to claim/seize control of these essential resources, threatening disorder and conflict. Political authority responds to this threat by restricting and allocating access to essential resources in ways that must appear to be both fair and efficient.

Abundance in practice

Nature as commons is our default position. Since Cicero, at least, we have recognized that "by nature nothing is private".[1] Traditional sources of authority tend to hold that nature belongs to us in common and should be made freely available. Many of the world's indigenous cultures and religions recognize that the current generation does not and cannot inherit or own the land; we only borrow it from our children. A classic example of what might be called an indigenous approach to resource management was voiced by Massasoit, the seventeenth-century leader of the Wampanaog confederacy, who tried to describe to the English settlers his people's relationship to nature: "What is this you call property? It cannot be the earth, for the land is our mother, nourishing all her children, beasts, birds, fish and all men. The woods, the streams, everything on it belongs to everybody and is for the use of all. How can one man say it belongs only to him?"[2]

This common approach to owning the earth can be found in most of the world's religions, but it is often framed in terms of ownership by an omnipotent God, managed by his/her representative on earth, for a limited period of time. In these approaches, God owns the earth, and we are merely temporary stewards. Hence, in the Old Testament we are told that the earth belongs to Yahweh: "The land shall not be sold for ever: for the land is mine, for ye are strangers and sojourners with me" (Leviticus 25:23); similarly, the Quran holds: "Unto Allah belongeth whatsoever is in the heavens and whatsoever is in the earth" (Surah Al-Baqarah 2: 284).

---

1. Cicero, *De officiis*, I.8. 21. This is Grotius' (1916 [1608]) translation from his *Mare Liberum*. In our version of Cicero, it is less elegantly translated: "Private possessions, indeed, are not so by nature" (and it is in verse I.7). See Cicero (1887 [44]).

2. It is not possible to document this quote, although it is famous and consistent with many indigenous beliefs; see Hutto (2017).

More earthly lawgivers tended to agree, as was evident in the Magna Carta and the Law of the Forest (1215–17). When the Romans invaded Britain, they introduced Emperor Justinian's four categories of ownership, only one of which was private (*res privatae*). The *res communes* (open access, including the air and the sea) was considered the natural property of all humanity; the *res publicae* (state property, including rivers, parks and public roads) belonged to all citizens; the *res universitas* (community property) included public amenities, such as public baths and theatres; and the *res nullius* belonged to no one, and referred to wasteland, cattle pasture, woodland and wild animals (Thomas 1975; Hayes 2020: 29).

Even the liberal foundations for private property were built upon land that was originally assumed to be held in common. Seventeenth-century legal and political philosophers, such as Hugo Grotius (2016 [1625]) and Samuel von Pufendorf (1729 [1672]), started from the tenet that God had given the earth (along with all its plants and animals) to mankind (Genesis I 29–30, IX 2). From this common wealth, people agreed – among themselves – to divide tracks of land into private holdings, while leaving the remainder free for others. Thus, for both Grotius and von Pufendorf private property in land was the result of human consent in the state of nature. Locke (1960 [1688]), most famously, began at the same place, but grounded private property in natural law (to ensure that private property, once consented to, could not be revoked). Locke argued that it was by working the land, not by the consent of others, that common land could be turned into private property (so long as there was sufficient land remaining for everyone else). We return to these arguments in Chapter 4.

As we shall see, Locke's approach to property ownership came to dominate in the West. But, even as it did, it remained contested. In 1797, for example, Thomas Paine would argue:

> It is a position not to be controverted, that the earth, in its natural uncultivated state was, and ever would have continued to be, THE COMMON PROPERTY OF THE HUMAN RACE. In that state every man would have been born to property. He would have been a joint life proprietor with the rest in the property of the soil and in all its natural productions, vegetable and animal.
> (Paine 2017 [1797]: 28, emphasis in original)

A century later Henry George took up the same battle cry:

> The equal right of all men to the use of land is as clear as their equal right to breathe the air – it is a right proclaimed by the fact of their existence. For we cannot suppose that some men have a right to be in this world and others no right. (George 1992 [1879]: 338)

Even in our own time we find traces of this argument in the 1982 UN Convention on the Law of the Sea, which recognizes that much of the earth's surface – lying under the oceans, which are owned by no country or organization – remains in common custody:

> Desiring by this Convention to develop the principles embodied in resolution 2749 (XXV) of 17 December 1970 in which the General Assembly of the United Nations solemnly declared inter alia that *the area of the seabed and ocean floor and the subsoil thereof, beyond the limits of national jurisdiction, as well as its resources, are the common heritage of mankind*, the exploration and exploitation of which shall be carried out for the benefit of mankind as a whole, irrespective of the geographical location of States ...   (UN 1982, preamble, emphasis added)

One reason that there is continued interest in holding nature in common, despite a long history of (and widespread use of) enclosure, is the recognition that nature continues to provide us with essential resources, and that enclosing or privatizing nature can threaten our access to these essentials.

Nature as commodity

So long as we think there is enough water, air, sun, inner earth and upper atmosphere to go around, we will think it is free for the taking. We continue to accept common ownership in most forms of nature, at least in principle; and most of the nature that is available to us remains in common hands (unclaimed). It is only after we begin to recognize the potential scarcity of nature that we find a need to make claims upon it. There are many good reasons for enclosing land (and nature, more generally) – for example to increase its efficient use – but doing so introduces a number of social and political challenges.

After all, in enclosing nature, we restrict access to it. No longer part of the commons, enclosed nature has been parcelled and made scarce. When this enclosed nature falls into private hands, we can clearly see how private wealth comes at the expense of common wealth. This paradox was first noted by the eighth earl of Lauderdale, James Maitland (1759–1839). Subsequent social scientists refer to the "Lauderdale paradox" to mean that private riches and public wealth are inversely related to one another (see Box 2.1). As scarcity is necessary to create value in exchange, the growth of private riches depends on taking that public or common wealth that was freely abundant, and making it scarce.

BOX 2.1 THE LAUDERDALE PARADOX

The Lauderdale paradox refers to an argument developed by James Maitland, an earl of Lauderdale. In 1804 Maitland first published *An Inquiry into the Nature and Origin of Public Wealth and into the Means and Causes of Its Increase.* In this work, Maitland questions the common understanding of public wealth as the aggregation of individual riches and argues that private riches grow from the taking of public wealth.

To minimize confusion, Maitland's employs the word "riches" to describe private fortunes, and "wealth" when referring to public opulence (Maitland 1819 [1804]: 7). Value (exchange) is then explained in terms of desirability and relative scarcity (15–16, 35–6). Maitland goes on to define public wealth as *"all that man desires as useful or delightful to him"* (57, emphasis in original), whereas private riches are *"all that man desires as useful or delightful to him; which exists in a degree of scarcity"* (58, emphasis in original).

On closer examination of the nature of public wealth, Maitland recognizes an inverse relationship between public wealth and individual riches: "[T]hat an increase of riches, when arising from alterations in the quantity of commodities, is always a proof of an immediate diminution of wealth; and a diminution of riches, is evidence of an immediate increase of wealth" (57).

This argument is advanced by way of a thought experiment and several references to actual historical examples. Maitland asks us to consider a man who would make water scarce. In nature, water is abundant and owned by all: it is a perfect example of public wealth. By enclosing the right to access this abundant water, and in making it scarce, the man would clearly succeed in increasing his individual riches, as the water would remain desirable, but would become suddenly – as a simple function of the enclosure – more scarce (42).

The earl of Lauderdale recognized that this sort of private taking from the public wealth was a disgrace – "The common sense of mankind would revolt at a proposal for augmenting wealth by creating a scarcity of any commodity generally useful and necessary to man …" (41) – and that this paradox was not just idle speculation, as when Dutch and American colonists burned their crops (52) or inhibited their harvest to reduce supply, thereby increasing their individual riches (52–3). "So truly is this principle understood by those whose interest leads them to take advantage of it, that nothing but the impossibility of general combination protects the public wealth against the rapacity of private avarice, for, wherever combination has been possible, mankind have found, in the diminution of their wealth, the fatal effect of this disposition" (52).

In the first section (above), we began by assuming that nature was abundant and essential, and we pointed to traditional approaches that recognize the need for common access. It should not be controversial to recognize that nature began in the commons (at some point, back in time) and that we are slowly transitioning away from this point of departure.

This section considers that transition from common to private access and looks at the distributional consequences of privatizing access to nature. We begin by noting that it is awkward to speak about ownership of nature. We also realize that there are a plethora of national approaches to "owning" nature, and these vary significantly across time and resource types. After all, governments do allocate exclusive access to nature, and we sometimes (if misleadingly) think of this as ownership. To avoid confusion, and to underline the transitory and restricted tenure of our control of nature, we refer to "concession holders" or "concessionaires" rather than to "owners".

The traditional response to the threat of increased scarcity in nature involves three main steps: enclosure, allocation and commodification. In deciding to enclose nature, and then allocating these enclosed lots to a privileged few, political authority creates a new type of value, which the concessionaire is able to pocket when the resource is eventually commodified.

Enclosure

Enclosure entails a legal appropriation[3] process that creates private rights for accessing natural resources that originate in common property. This process is inherently political and conflictual, and potentially immoral.

The first step in this process might be called the "original appropriation". This happens when nature, unbound and untitled, is enclosed and allocated by a legitimate political authority. This allocation might be carried out by means of a gift, grant or sale (e.g. by auction). Over time this original allocation is forgotten, and the private concession of nature makes it appear like a commodity, similar to other things bought and sold in the market.

Because the enclosure of nature impacts our ability to survive (and challenges long-held perceptions of right and wrong), our discussions about "original

---

3. We are uncomfortable with this term. "Appropriation" refers to the act of taking something for one's own use, usually without permission. But "enclosure" is done by legitimate political authority, and hence enjoys the requisite "permission". "Expropriation" is equally troublesome, as it means to deprive someone or something of possession or proprietary rights. In effect, we are looking at expropriation from the commons but a sort of permitted appropriation to private interests. In view of this, we think "legal appropriation" is the most appropriate term.

appropriation" and the actual history of enclosure are both filled with conflict.[4] This enclosure process is most established (and perhaps most familiar) in the market for land, for which we have developed a number of physical and legal boundaries that facilitate exclusion – i.e. that provide a legal basis for keeping others from using the land. But a very similar process of enclosure can be found in the way political authority allocates concessions to mine minerals, drill for oil and/or farm the wind, sun and sea. In these cases, enclosure is less physical and more administrative and legal – but it is an enclosure nonetheless. As with the market for land, the power of enclosure lies not in the fence but in the legal authority to control the resource, and to exclude others from accessing it.

In practice, the way we allocate access to nature varies significantly, and the legitimate authority for this allocation lies with sovereign nation states. At the end of a long and complicated historical process, and as reflected in the Peace of Westphalia (1648), most of the world's land mass has been divided up into sovereign territories, with any remaining "open" space left to common stewardship. The management and regulation of this common area has always been, and remains, contentious, as we are unable to agree whether this residual space should be seen as *res communes* or *res nullius*. As we shall see in Chapter 8, these shared areas are governed by international agreements that vary in scope when applied to land (Antarctica), the open seas and the skies above.

Contemporary political authority rests in the physical control over distinct patches of territory associated with sovereign states, and defended by a subtle combination of consensus and force. After all, there is no international "Law of the Land" governing the acquisition, use and disposition of land territory. There are only a plethora of national laws, varying over time, and reflecting ever-changing perceptions of justice. In these national histories, the issues of property and ownership often lie at the bottom of much political, sometimes revolutionary, struggle. As a result, access to nature and the power of property ownership is distributed in a remarkably varied manner, and the allocation of access to nature – its "excludability" – is the result of a political act; it is not a function of nature, natural law or some omnipotent God (or her invisible hand).

Legal access

Controlling access to our common resources is inherently contentious. There are at least two reasons for this: (a) we cannot agree about the source of value (and to whom it belongs); and (b) it is common (albeit misleading) to confuse the right

---

4. The story of the English enclosures is well known, and well told; see, for example, Thompson (1991 [1963]), Linebaugh (2008, 2010) and Hayes (2020). For a broader history of similar land grabs, see Alden Wily (2013).

to *access* nature with the underlying rights of *ownership*.[5] The question of value is discussed in the section that follows; here we discuss the thorny issue of access.

How does political authority allocate access to enclosed nature? To answer this question, we might start by recognizing the remarkable lack of consensus over what ownership in property actually means. This meaning varies widely, across time, political space and resource type. Perhaps David Hume (2006 [1748]: 197) said it best when he noted that "[t]he questions with regard to private property have filled infinite volumes of law and philosophy, if in both we add the commentators to the original text; and in the end, we may safely pronounce, that many of the rules there established are uncertain, ambiguous and arbitrary".

There is, after all, a significant difference between the rightful ownership of something that is created, something that is transferred and something that is acquired from nature.[6] It is one thing to own a chain saw, and a completely different thing to own a forest. Indeed, when we look more closely at how access to nature is allocated, we find that *ownership* rights are almost never transferred: they remain (mostly) with sovereign political authority, and can be restricted/rescinded at any time. In practice, what we think of as ownership of nature is actually a form of permission/licence granted to the user, often with explicit restrictions on use and for limited periods of time.

In most contexts, individuals cannot actually "own" nature. Its ultimate ownership rests with the sovereign government, which has the legal authority to decide how all access to nature within its territory is allocated, and that government can (and does) rescind that access in the name of the community it represents. This access tends to be limited and reverts back to the state when any doubt arises about formal legal control (escheat[7]). What we think of as "private property" in nature is really an abstract bundle of rights that governments grant

---

5. There is a growing recognition of this tension, even within the legal tradition, as evident in the renewed interest in the legal paradigm known as "nature's trust", whereby "[g]overnment, deriving its authority from the people as a whole, must act as fiduciary to protect the natural resources held in trust from damage, as well as from dangerous privatization" (Wood 2014: xviii). See also Weiss (1984) and Farley *et al.* (2015).

6. Following Honoré (1961: 113): "Ownership comprises the right to possess, the right to use, the right to manage, the right to the income of the thing, the right to the capital, the right to security, the rights or incidents of transmissibility and absence of term, the prohibition of harmful use, liability to execution, and the incident of residuarity: this makes eleven leading incidents." For a description of the tension between commodity and commonwealth views of property, see Wood (2014: 312–18). For a description of the recent change in perceiving property as a right to a thing (*in rem*) to property as a bundle of rights in resources (*in personam*), see Merrill and Smith (2001).

7. *Hjemfallsrett* in Norwegian. Escheat refers to the reversion of property to political authority when there are no legal heirs. When used in concession agreements, the principle of escheat ensures that the underlying resource returns to the rightful owner (the public) at the end of the concession period, along with any improvement that may have been made during that concession.

to individuals or communities. It is these rights that determine who can use the natural resource, who can manage the resource and whether the use/management rights can be transferred to others (USAID 2006: 3). In the market for land resources, we call this abstract bundle of rights an "estate", but the same sort of bundle of rights can be (and is) applied to accessing fishing grounds, mineral deposits, drinking water, wind and solar channels, etc.

At the most general level, it is common to distinguish between four basic categories of allocation regimes, and the origins of these regimes can be traced back to the Roman code, as mentioned earlier.

(1) *Private property* exists when exclusive rights of access are assigned to individuals or private interests.
(2) *Common property* exists when exclusive access rights are given to a group of individuals, a community, an association or other groups.
(3) *Public property* is the default setting, when nature and natural resources are owned and managed by the government. As noted in the text, sovereign governments remain the de facto "owner" of nature.
(4) *Open access* is the residual category, when the rights to accessing nature are ambiguous and not explicitly assigned. This is sometimes referred to as nul property.[8]

Of these four types of allocation rights, three rest solely with sovereign authority. It is the political authority in sovereign states that decides how much of nature will be held in common, public and/or private hands. As we have already seen, only a small portion of the world's land surface area remains in open access form – i.e. Antarctica – but, beyond these sovereign claims, a large share of the remaining nature (above and below the land, or out to sea) still belongs to us in common.

In granting these bundles of rights, governments authorize who will be allowed to access the nature; how long this access will be granted (e.g. for an indefinite period or limited period); and whether these rights are alienable/transferable (e.g. can they be sold, transferred and/or inherited?). This authorization is necessary so that one person or company cannot take advantage of another person's property without their consent. As nature belongs to us in common, our representatives in government authorize this private "taking". They do this to keep the peace and protect the resources (from either inefficient or over-exploitation), for the benefit of the community they represent.

The way this is done varies a great deal across time and countries and their requisite legal traditions. It is important to underline the significant variation

---

8. "Nul" is short for *res nullius*, which is Latin for "thing of no one".

that exists across national management regimes. Indeed, in the pages that follow we trace this variation across different forms of nature. States are free to choose the form of this authorization, and tend to employ a number of different legal instruments, including concessions, licences, production-sharing agreements, joint venture arrangements and other forms of authorization. What these forms of authorization share is a recognition that the state maintains the ownership rights and control over the resource through its regulatory powers, while recognizing the need to provide just and reasonable compensation to the concession/licence holder, who (usually) carries the financial risk associated with bringing the resource (and/or its product) to market.

In general, however, governments grant individuals (and/or communities and companies) access to the productive capacity of nature, the ownership of which remains in the commons. For the sake of convenience, we will call this authorized access holder a concessionaire, even though the terms of a particular concession agreement, licence, joint venture or production-sharing agreement (for example) are bound to vary (see Box 2.2). When sovereign governments allocate private access to nature, the concessionaire is permitted to access our common nature and make improvements, and the concessionaire enjoys a legal

---

BOX 2.2 CONCESSION DEFINED

The World Bank (n.d.e) defines concessions as follows:

> A Concession gives a concessionaire the long term right to use all utility assets conferred on the concessionaire, including responsibility for operations and some investment. Asset ownership remains with the authority and the authority is typically responsible for replacement of larger assets. Assets revert to the authority at the end of the concession period, including assets purchased by the concessionaire. In a concession the concessionaire typically obtains most of its revenues directly from the consumer and so it has a direct relationship with the consumer. A concession covers an entire infrastructure system (so may include the concessionaire taking over existing assets as well as building and operating new assets). The concessionaire will pay a concession fee to the authority which will usually be ring-fenced and put towards asset replacement and expansion. A concession is a specific term in civil law countries. To make it confusing, in common law countries, projects that are more closely described as BOT [build–operate–transfer] projects are called concessions.

---

and moral right to the rewards that are produced by those improvements. This is both clear and just. It is less clear whether this right to access includes the right to pocket the value created by natural and collective processes that are *not the result* of these improvements.

In short, sovereign governments grant exclusive rights to access nature. In doing so, governments have decided that it is beneficial for the community it represents to limit (exclude) access to nature. This might be because political authorities believe a private and professional operator can harvest the resources more effectively; to prevent the wasteful over-investment that arises when private interests compete over scarce resources; or because the political authorities want to allocate access in a way that will minimize potential conflict over scarce resources. Whatever its reasoning, political authority decides to allocate access to nature in the form of a title, licence or concession – but it has *not* transferred ownership of the productive value associated with the underlying nature. We argue that this productive value remains with the people (more accurately, their representative: sovereign political authority), and it cannot and should not be transferred.

Commodification

We have now arrived at the third phase of transitioning from common to private wealth. Once nature is enclosed, and access has been allocated by political authority, the concessionaire has a right to bring these resources to market and exchange them for money. This is the essence of the commodification process.[9] But the commodities produced by nature are different from those produced by humans in at least two ways: (a) with natural products, much of the market value does not find its way back to the original producer; and (b) the supply of nature is indifferent to demand and restricted by the enclosure and allocation processes just described.

We have already recognized that nature is not of our making; it exists independently of our efforts. This section aims to demonstrate that this independent nature can create value, which can be subsequently commodified and sold on the market. In particular, we hold that the market value of natural resources

---

9. The commodification process is distinct from the process of enclosure and allocation, as described in the preceding sections. Although enclosure is necessary for commodification, it is not sufficient: after all, much land is enclosed as public property, but is not commodified (e.g. it might remain as a park, or commercial access is not allowed). The concession holder needs to bring the resource to market before it can be commodified. Given that the concession was costly (it costs political, social or financial capital), it is likely that the concession owner will need to reclaim these costs, and commodification is the easiest way to do this.

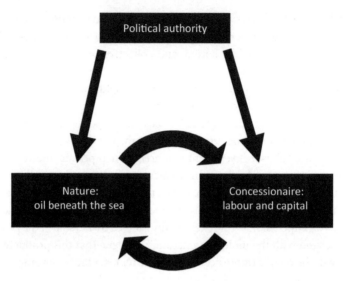

Figure 2.1 Market value creation in nature
Source: Authors.

is determined by three different players (when we set aside the question of demand): the entrepreneurial activities of the concessionaire and/or her contractor; the productive forces of nature itself; and the political authorities that regulate access to nature. The latter two players tend to be ignored in most contemporary NRM approaches – but they take centre stage in our account.

None of these three players, alone, can create (market) value. Their own individual efforts remain largely "value"-less without the help of the other. Imagine a pool of oil lying deep below the ocean bottom. This oil, lying untouched in the raw, has no market value; it has only the potential to become valuable. The same can be said of the labour and capital inputs we attribute to the concessionaire: without access to the raw materials (provided by nature), labour and capital inputs are worthless, except as potential value. Consequently, nature and the concessionaire need to be brought together if they are to produce something of (market) value. It is political authority, as gatekeeper and regulator, that facilitates this relationship, by allowing the concessionaire to access nature. This relationship, which can be characterized as complex and interdependent, is depicted in Figure 2.1.

In making this argument, we hope to avoid the quagmire that is the valuation problem in contemporary economics.[10] This is not easy, in that so much of the

---

10. See Mazzucato (2018), Farber, Costanza and Wilson (2002) and Burkett (2003) for introductions to the literature. The theory of value was also a central topic of disagreement between Marxists in the last quarter of the twentieth century; see, for example, Steedman and Sweezy (1982).

way that we think about value is already framed by the market (and contemporary approaches to economics), and much of what we value in nature (e.g. fresh air, clean drinking water, beautiful sunsets) is deemed worthless by the market. It is for this reason that political authority is often willing to give nature away, free of charge.

We have sidelined demand as an important determinant of market value, by holding it constant (*ceteris paribus*). When this is done, there are then three remaining contributors to the market value of natural resources. First, there is the underlying productive value of nature, which we call the "gifts of nature". Second, there is the value added by the formal political process (enclosure, allocation, regulation) that ensures legal custody of (and monopoly control over) the resource, but also makes the resource scarcer for others. Finally, there are the improvements made by the concessionaire: the capital and labour power invested to bring that resource to market. Although these (capital and labour) investments may or may not improve the productive capacity of the underlying nature, they remain instrumental in bringing the resource to market. Let us take a closer look at each of these three contributions.

The gifts of nature
Nature, on its own, has the potential to create significant value. For example, in its 2018 *Living Planet Report*, the WWF (2018: 6) estimates that nature provides services for humanity worth around $125 trillion a year. We have already crossed this bridge in recognizing that nature produces resources that are essential for human survival (essential = valuable). But nature also produces energy and resources that can be traded as commodities, and for which the path from nature to markets is relatively short, direct and uncomplicated. The problem is that the *source* of this value (created by nature) is usually unacknowledged in mainstream approaches to NRM: we are unwilling to distinguish between the value created by nature and the value created by human efforts that are applied to nature. As a result, this value is easily (and, we argue, unfairly) captured by the concessionaire.

Nature provides – and it does so freely. Indeed, it is this unique source of potential value creation that makes natural resources such an attractive commodity. This gift of nature[11] is most clearly evident in the case of land, and it is the reason land was granted such special status in the productive pantheon of classical economics: it is one of three original factors of production. Nature's

---

11. This notion of "nature's gifts" has a long history, and we are uncertain of its origins. The earliest reference may be Turgot (1898 [1770]: 9), who is probably best known for this framing. But see also Malthus (1903 [1815]: 16) and Marx (1967 [1867], vol. 1: 206).

incredible facility to create value on its own, and/or in combination with human labour, lies at the heart of modern economics, as captured by the French physiocrats. Their leading spokesperson, François Quesnay, held that "the land is the unique source of wealth" (Quesnay 1963a [1767]: 232).[12] But Robert Turgot was more elegant when he argued that "[t]he earth ... is always the first and only source of all wealth; it is that which as the result of cultivation produces all the revenue; it is that also which has provided the first fund of advances prior to all cultivation" (Turgot 1898 [1770]: 46).

This was only the start of a long train of thought. Nature's capacity to create value lies at the centre of David Ricardo's theory of differential rent (which we explore in more detail in Chapter 4), which became the inspiration for the marginal productivity theory of distribution – the mainspring of neoclassical economics. In recognizing a natural variation in "the original and indestructible powers of the soil", Ricardo (1971 [1817]: 91) provided "the first clear-cut demonstration in economics that some incomes are 'unearned' in the precise sense that they are paid to economic agents without the exertion of any effort on their part" (Blaug 2000: 270–1).

This train continues with Karl Polanyi, for whom nature provides us "the *deus ex machina* of animal and plant propagation" (Polanyi 2001 [1944]: 129), and we find it as a central element in several contemporary strands of ecological economics. These schools of thought – whether they are associated with the "energy theory of value", eco-Sraffian and/or eco-Marxist approaches – ascribe value directly to natural resources (see Burkett 2003 for an overview).

The first of these groups takes the physics of thermodynamics as its point of departure, and points to the need to account for the fact that solar energy is the primary input to the global ecosystems, and *is freely available*.[13] As Gilliland (1975: 1052) shows: "[T]here is no money flow associated with either environmental subsidies or raw energy flow. We do not pay nature for each acre of land taken out of biological production, nor do we pay nature for the millions of years of work it did in making coal or oil."

The owner of a fruit tree (or a pregnant heifer) need only wait, and a new and valuable product (a fruit or a calf) is generated, miraculously. If we cut back on the hubris, we can recognize that nature alone produces the calf (although the farmer can surely facilitate and assist in that process). Better yet, this "original and indestructible power" that Ricardo associated with land can be found across nature, in its many different forms. As French economist Jean-Baptiste Say famously noted,

12. See also Quesnay (1963b [1766]: 207), and his *Tableau économique* (2004 [1758]).
13. For overviews, see Christensen (1989); Farber, Costanza and Wilson (2002); Burkett (2003); and Ayers (2017).

Land ... is not the only natural agent possessing productive proper-
ties; but it is the only one, or almost the only one, which man has been
able to appropriate, and turn to his own peculiar and exclusive benefit.
The water of rivers and of the ocean has the power of giving motion
to machinery, affords a means of navigation, and supply of fish; it is,
therefore, undoubtedly possessed of productive power. The wind turns
our mill; even the heat of the sun cooperates with human industry; but
happily no man has yet been able to say, the wind and the sun's rays are
mine, and I will be paid for their productive services.

(Say 2001 [1803], bk 2, ch. 9: 190)[14]

The wind continues to blow, the sun continues to shine, the tides continue to
turn ... and in so doing they provide natural resources that are never-ending. This
natural capacity to produce value is mostly ignored by contemporary approaches
to NRM. This is a serious problem, in that this value, when it remains unnoticed,
is easily hidden or stolen. We think it is unfair for this value to be pocketed by
private interests that have not contributed to its creation. This value belongs to
all of us, as we own the underlying resource and control access to its exploitation.

An awkward commodity
In most contemporary approaches to economics, the market value of a commodity is framed by Say's law: where the production of a commodity or good
creates its own demand. In a competitive marketplace with flexible prices, producers respond to changing demand (and prices) by producing more or less
of the commodity in question. If the demand of a good increases, then producers are incentivized (by greater profits) to secure the necessary inputs (and we
assume these are easily accessible) to increase supply, until supply and demand
eventually return to equilibrium.

Imagine the announcement of a new royal wedding. Such an event is bound
to fuel a significant increase in demand for royal wedding gift plates. This immediate boost in demand (given a fixed supply) allows producers to raise the price
on royal wedding gift plates; and this potential windfall incentivizes new producers to secure the necessary inputs (labour, tools/machinery, ceramics and

---

14. From the remainder of the passage, we know that Say was not interested just in the fact that is
not possible to own the sun and wind, but that it was not necessary, as these – unlike land – were
inexhaustible. "I would not be understood to insinuate, that land should be no more the object of
property, than the rays of the sun, or blast of the wind. There is an essential difference between
these sources of production; the power of the latter is inexhaustible; the benefit derived from
them by one man does not hinder another from deriving equal advantage. The sea and the wind
can at the same time convey my neighbour's vessel and my own. With land it is otherwise."

paints) to fill the void (i.e. increase the production of such plates). This higher price will last until the increase in supply is sufficient to satisfy the demand. The point of this example is to show that the market for commodities clears, because producers are able to adjust production levels in response to changes in demand, and we assume that these producers have unlimited access to the input goods they need to produce the commodity in question.

In this example, we can see how commodities are produced for sale in the market, and in response to a changing demand. When seen in this light, it is easier to see how natural resources make for an awkward (or, following Polanyi (2001 [1944]), a "fictitious") commodity. This is because the supply (or production) of nature is entirely indifferent to market demand. The wind blows, and the water flows, regardless (and independent) of changing demand for wind- or waterpower.

In *The Great Transformation*, Karl Polanyi (2001 [1944]) argues that land – like labour and capital – is a fictitious commodity, in that its production is independent of market forces: we do not make children to satisfy the demand for labour in the labour market, and we do not create nature to satisfy the demands of the commodities market. Indeed, we do not make nature at all; it is provided to us, and its amount is largely fixed by forces that are exogenous to the market.

> The crucial point is this: labor, land and money are essential elements of industry; they also must be organized in markets; in fact, these markets form an absolutely vital part of the economic system. But labor, land, and money are obviously *not* commodities, the postulate that anything that is bought and sold must have been produced for sale is empathically untrue in regard to them.   (Polanyi 2001 [1944]: 75, emphasis in original)

The supply of natural resources is constrained by the enclosure and allocation processes described above. In allocating exclusive (read monopoly) access to natural resources, political authorities limit the capacity of a competitive market to increase the supply of a commodity in high demand. If the price of aluminium goes up, producers cannot simply increase the production of bauxite (this is fixed by nature), and access to bauxite is severely constrained and allocated by concession. Likewise, if the price of beets goes up, we are not free to begin producing beets; we must first pay a landowner for the privilege of using "her" land, and the total amount of productive land is limited by nature and the process of allocation.

In short, the market for natural resources is far from competitive, and the value of natural resources is generated by *monopoly allocation*. More to the point, in deciding on a management regime, political authorities determine how wide or narrow this access to nature (monopoly allocation) will be. In principle, sovereign governments can decide to grant every citizen equal access to nature (e.g. agricultural, fishing, mineral and wind concessions), or decide that only one person or corporation should be granted a concession to farm all the land, harvest all the fish, mine all the minerals and harness all the wind. Governments might encourage every household to set up a windmill in their backyard, or they might grant concessions to a handful of companies to build enormous wind parks to generate electricity for the community (or for sale to the community). In making these types of decision, sovereign governments determine the relative scarcity (and, with it, the value) of accessing nature.

Hence, when natural resources secure high market prices, it is often attributable to the fact that nature has not provided enough of these valuable resources (to satisfy increased demand); that more nature cannot be produced to meet that demand; and because political authorities further restrict potential supply by limiting access to natural resources through the process of enclosure and allocation. In all these cases, the resulting (market) value has nothing to do with the effort, initiative or risk-taking of the concessionaire.

Returns on labour and investment

The third important contributor to the market value of natural resources is the effort and investment of the concession holder. Since (at least) the physiocrats, we have recognized the importance of labour in securing the value inherent to nature. More famously, John Locke's basic premise was that nature – in itself – provided little that was valuable to man – unless it was mixed with human labour: "For 'tis *Labour* indeed that *puts the difference of value* on every thing; and let anyone consider, what the difference is between an Acre of Land planted with Tobacco, or Sugar, sown with Wheat or Barley; and an Acre of the same Land lying in common without any Husbandry upon it, and he will find, that the improvement of *labour makes* the far greater part of *the value*" (Locke 1960 [1688], II, 338, §40, emphasis in original).

With all due respect to Locke, we do not need to embrace a labour theory of value to recognize the important contribution to market value that labour and capital investments can bring to nature in the raw. After all, many natural resources are difficult to find, access and refine – and significant amounts of capital (and labour) must be risked and invested if these resources are to find their way to market. The digging of mines, the drilling of wells, the building of wind turbines, the irrigation of farmland – all these things make it possible to secure the value inherent in nature (and, without them, the nature could not be commodified). A concession holder recognizes this potential, and invests both labour and capital in order to turn nature into commodities. Clearly, these sorts of investment are worthy of a just reward, in the same way that they are rewarded in the production of more genuine (i.e. not fictitious) commodities.

It is important to note that not all the private investments by concession holders are aimed at increasing the productive capacity of nature, and some of these investments may have a deleterious effect. For example, a farmer may invest a great deal of sweat and equity to bring a crop to market, but these investments add little to the value of the underlying resource (the land). The use of a tractor and pesticides is good for the crop, but does little to improve the land. Indeed, the land can be exhausted by continual and increased production. On the other hand, if the farmer invests in an irrigation system, a barn, a service road, etc., these investments can improve the value of the land.

Our point is that the concession holder deserves a rightful return on these investments, and doing so will incentivize other workers and investors to pursue equally efficient means of extracting/harvesting natural resources. In recognizing this just return to investments of capital and labour, however, we need to separate the value associated with these private investments from the value created by nature and its regulation, and the effect these investments have on the long-term productive capacity of nature. As we shall see in the chapter that follows, this is relatively straightforward, as returns on capital and labour equalize in a competitive market, so it is possible to generate expected returns for similar levels of effort, skill, risk, etc.

Conclusion

This chapter addresses the question of who controls nature and the value it creates. In most of its sundry forms, nature belongs to all of us in common, or it falls under the control of a sovereign political authority that holds it in our name. This sovereign authority regulates access to nature's essential resources, in an effort to protect it from overuse, abuse or conflict. In doing so, we – through our sovereign political authority – create value.

To understand the nature of this value, and to trace its source, we might begin at the end of the commodification train: when nature is brought to market in exchange for money. If we assume a given level of demand, then the market value of the resource is determined by three component parts: the raw potential value produced by nature; the monopoly value created by restricting access to these essential natural resources; and the sweat and equity employed by the concessionaire to truck these resources from nature (in the raw) to the market, where they can be sold as commodities.

The relative value of these three component parts is bound to change, from context to context, but it is important to note that two of the three component parts are *not* the result of the productive efforts of the concessionaire. In short, much of the value of natural resources comes from the fact that they are essential and relatively scarce. This scarcity is partly a function of nature and partly the result of legitimate political authority limiting access to it. We can find no convincing argument as to why this portion of the market value, created by nature and political authority, should be pocketed by private interests that have had nothing to do with its creation. This portion of the market value is our Natural Dividend, and the next chapter explains how it can be harvested in the public interest.

3
THE NATURAL DIVIDEND

The previous chapter presented two arguments. First, we argued that nature, before it is commodified, belongs to us in common, and that the value it produces – nature's gift – also belongs to the commons. Second, we argued that significant market value is created by political authority when it encloses, allocates and facilitates the commodification of nature.

This chapter extends that argument by elaborating on how nature's gift and its management regime generate value in the form of various rents, which together constitute a Natural Dividend. Politically challenging it may be, but it is not technically difficult to secure the Natural Dividend: political authorities need only to do two things. First, they must establish a management regime that recognizes that these natural resources belong to the commons and allocates access to these resources on its behalf. This management regime sets the scope and the distribution of access to the resources (and, hence, their potential value). Second, political authorities need to employ a variety of policy instruments that can secure the Natural Dividend for the public good, and ensure it is not taken. This Divided can be secured in either a political or economic form, and each form employs a different set of instruments.

The Natural Dividend is what economists refer to as a resource rent, which is itself derived from the scarcity (both natural and induced) of natural resources. In particular, the Natural Dividend consists of three component rents: a differential rent; a regulatory rent; and a locational rent. We elaborate on the nature of each of these component rents in subsequent chapters, as they tend to vary in importance across resource types: in Chapter 4 we introduce differential rents; in Chapter 5 we introduce regulatory rents; and in Chapter 6 we discuss locational rents.

This chapter explains the nature of resource rents, in general, and how they can be secured by political authorities. To do this, the chapter is divided into two main parts. The first part introduces the general literature on resource rents and the two main ways by which natural resources are made scarce (and valuable): by way of nature and/or regulation. Although nature can produce a differential rent all on its own, political authorities can produce a regulatory and/or locational rent (or some combination of the two) when they regulate or provide access to that nature. To understand how the Natural Dividend is created, then, we need to rethink the way that natural resources are brought to market. Because we are accustomed to thinking of natural resources as common commodities, like any other, this reframing will require some effort, imagination and goodwill on the part of the reader – along with some additional elaboration on our part as the authors. We are confident that the extra effort exerted will be well rewarded.

The second part then introduces the types of policy instruments that political authorities can use to secure the Natural Dividend, in both political and economic forms. This second part includes a longer elaboration on the utility of introducing a resource rent tax (RRT) regime. The end of the chapter offers a brief caveat before concluding.

"The shitty rent business"[1]

Rent is a very slippery concept. For most of us, rent is the monthly payment we make to landlords for the privilege of living in their apartment or house. Although this payment is for the use of a physical structure (built with labour and capital investments), it also includes a payment for the temporary access to the under-lying land or property. But "rent" is also the term used by classical economists to describe the return from one of the three essential factors of production.[2] In this tradition, the return on labour is called "wages", the return on capital is called "interest" and the return on land is called "rent". Over time, different economic traditions have adopted the term, and employed it in different ways. Today the most common reference to it is probably found among neoclassical economists, who refer to "rent" as an unearned income, or a "prize" that exceeds what is socially or economically necessary (usually the result of some interference in the workings of a competitive economy). As a consequence, much of the normative

---

1. This is in reference to personal correspondence between Karl Marx and Friedrich Engels, as captured in the title to Ward and Aalbers' (2016) article. In particular, Marx wrote to Engels: "Incidentally, another thing I have at last been able to sort out is the shitty rent business. I had long harboured misgivings as to the absolute correctness of Ricardo's theory, and have at length got to the bottom of the swindle" (Marx, in correspondence with Engels: Marx & Engels 1985 [1860–64]: 380).

2. Even here, however, the terminology is slippery, with different economists using the term "rent" in different ways: for example land rent, ground rent, differential rent, monopoly rent, absolute rent, regulatory rent, resource rent, Ricardian rents; etc.

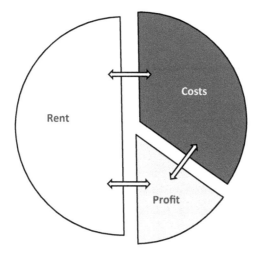

Figure 3.1 Schematic depiction of rent
Source: Authors, based on Moses and Letnes (2017a: 92).

focus of neoclassical economics has been placed on flushing out "rent seekers".[3] In this context, rent is usually framed as the interference of government in some sort of naturally equilibrating market, at the behest of some vested interest.

The Natural Dividend

Our focus is trained on the creation of the Natural Dividend, which combines the classical and neoclassical conceptions of rent. It is important to emphasize that rent is distinct from profit, and it appears only *after* the returns on labour (wages) and on capital investment (profits) have been paid out. This division of value is sketched in Figure 3.1. This is important, as there is often a great deal of misunderstanding about the nature of rent, and its relationship to profit. This confusion may be because it is common (if misleading) to refer to rent as a sort of "super profit".

The Natural Dividend can be broken down into several component parts. In some resources, the extraordinary productivity of the resource site will produce the rent. In others, the rent is a result of regulations that restrict access to these scarce resources. In still others, access to a nearby network, grid or infrastructure can produce the rent. Although these component rents are often difficult to distinguish from one another in practice, the ways in which we manage natural resources

---

3. See, for example, Tullock (1967, 1975, 1993) and Krueger (1974).

can produce some combination of all three rents. Wages, interest and profits can be seen as deserved returns on important inputs of production; the rent, by contrast, is the result of our managing access to scarce (and shared) natural resources.

In other words, rent is an unearned income.[4] Because such things are not supposed to occur in a competitive economy, it may be useful to start our discussion there. Indeed, Henry George noted:

> The law of rent is, in fact, but a deduction from the law of competition, and amounts simply to the assertion that as wages and interest tend to a common level, all that part of the general production of wealth which exceeds what the labor and capital employed could have secured for themselves, if applied to the poorest natural agent in use, will go to landowners in the shape of rent.   (1992 [1879]: 170)

In a competitive market, factor mobility and substitution effects will quickly equalize the profit and wage rates across sectors. The mobility of capital (and labour) equalizes profit (and wage) rates in the course of capitalist competition. It is this competition that is supposed to erode the existence of any surplus profits. But, when natural resources are essential to the commodity being produced, and these are immobile and made scarce or difficult to acquire (for any number of different reasons), the surplus profits can be stabilized for decades, and converted into rents.

After all, in competitive markets, the supply of factors of production is assumed to be unlimited, and highly responsive to price signals. Should a new producer enter the market and sell commodities far below the market price, she can expect a significant profit. But that profit will be temporary, in that other producers will quickly reposition themselves to undercut that initial advantage. Over time, the profits will equalize, a casualty of competition.

Consider a simple supply and demand diagram, as shown in Figure 3.2, where the quantity supplied and demand of goods equalize at point E_*, and produce an equilibrium price (p_*). If a producer in a competitive market is unable to produce the good below the equilibrium price, p_*, she cannot sell it (without losing money). If a new producer is able to undercut that equilibrium price (p_*),

---

4. In this way, the capture of rent is similar to the capture of surplus value in Marx's labour theory of value. The holder of a concession on a natural resource is able to walk off with the Natural Divided because all the components to the commodified value have not been claimed/recognized – and the concessionaire simply pockets the remainder as profit. This is similar to the way that the capitalist is able to abscond with the surplus value of labour in Marx's account; because not all the value that is created by labour is claimed, the capitalist is able to walk off with the remainder (the value added, less the value of labour power), and call it profit.

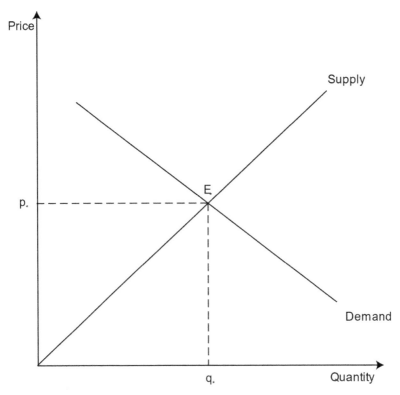

Figure 3.2 Supply and demand in a competitive economy
Source: Authors.

she will enjoy a temporary reward in the form of increased profits, as a result of increased sales at lower prices. But these profits will be fleeting, as new producers enter the market, undermine this advantage and ensure the equalization of profits.

Most readers will be familiar with this figure, as it functions as the workhorse for much contemporary policy analysis. But it is woefully inappropriate for analysing the market for natural resources, as the underlying conditions in these markets are significantly different from the assumptions used to generate the equilibrium (E.).[5] There are, in particular, two important characteristics that problematize any attempt to think about the markets for natural resources as competitive. The first is that highly productive natural resource sites are inherently scarce. This scarcity can be the result of a number of different factors, as

---

5. These conditions do not exist in labour markets either, but this is another argument; see Moses (2021a).

natural resources are scattered unequally across the earth's surface, some are far from existing infrastructures, some of them are non-renewable (and hence depletable) and others are kept off the market by a variety of institutional and/or regulatory devices, or with an eye on speculative gain. It is this scarcity, whether natural or induced, that makes the market for natural resources different from more competitive markets, and it is these unique characteristics – compared to more traditional commodities – that produce the Natural Dividend.

In addition, natural resources are immobile (unlike the other two factors of production, labour and capital). This means that it is more difficult for new resources to enter the market and undermine the surplus being generated under non-competitive conditions. Whereas it may be reasonable to expect an equilibrium return on labour (wages) and capital (interest), the immobility of resource factors makes them difficult or awkward substitutes. When a factor of production is not mobile but linked to a specific owner, it cannot be freely employed in the market to equalize prices. If one capitalist owns a particular resource (farmland, forest, coastal waterway, wind channel, etc.), it prevents other capitalists from accessing that particular resource, limiting its capacity to generate substitution effects. It is precisely because of the scarcity and immobility of natural resources that the surpluses generated in these markets are *not* transitional or temporary (as we might expect under more competitive conditions), but can last for very long periods of time.

The reason that (some) natural resources are able to produce rents is that these resources are highly desirable and yet relatively scarce, as a result of both nature and politics.[6] These resources are scarce in nature, in that the most productive sites are limited in number, difficult to access and/or are non-renewable. But the scarcity of natural resources is also the result of sundry regulatory arrangements (concessions, licences, patents, municipal codes) secured by political authority, as described in the preceding chapter. In some resources, the extraordinary productivity of the resource site can produce the rent. In others, the rent is a result of regulations that restrict who can access scarce resources. In still others, access to a nearby network, grid or infrastructure can produce the rent. In most resources, some combination of these three types of rent contribute to producing the Natural Dividend.

Because access to every natural resource is limited in some way, the agent with licensed access to a resource can secure an extraordinary value from that resource, over an extended period of time, without the risk of competitors entering the market. In effect, our management regimes restrict access to scarce resources,

---

6. Not all natural resources are able to generate substantial rents; sometimes it is simply too expensive to access/produce the resource, relative to the market's asking price. At other times, the way that the resource is managed can be cost-prohibitive, or even encourage over-exploitation. In these cases we can speak of negative rents.

and provide producers with an exclusive privilege, akin to a monopoly right. Under such exclusionary conditions, individuals and firms are able to secure rents because they are protected from competitors who could squeeze out any excess economic surplus – and, in so doing, drive the returns on investments down to normal (equilibrium) levels.

For these reasons, rent can be seen as a sort of "luck of the land (or resource)"; it is not the result of any invested expertise or capital. The Natural Dividend, then, is a sort of "supra-marginal advantage" (Giles 2017: 68), or what Nassau William Senior called "fortuitous profit":

> And for the same reason we term *rent* what might, with equal correctness, be termed fortuitous profit. We mean the surplus advantages which are sometimes derived from the employment of capital after making full compensation for all the risk that has been encountered, and all the sacrifices which have been made, by the capitalist. Such are the fortuitous profits of the holders of warlike stores on the breaking out of unexpected hostilities; or of the holders of black cloth on the sudden death of one of the Royal family. Such would be the additional revenue of an Anglesea [*sic*] miner, if, instead of copper, he should come on an equally fertile vein of silver. The silver would, without doubt, be obtained by means of labour and abstinence; but *they* would have been repaid by an equal amount of copper. The extra value of the silver would be the gift of nature, and therefore rent.
>
> (Senior 1851: 130, emphasis in original)

This understanding of rent was first introduced by James Anderson (1859 [1777]) and became a central part of the economic repertoire through David Ricardo's (1971 [1817]) *Principles of Political Economy and Taxation*. The concept was elaborated upon and problematized by Karl Marx (1967 [1867]) in the third volume of *Capital*, and was popularized by Henry George in his (1992 [1879]) *Progress and Poverty*, where he defined rent as "the price of monopoly, arising from the reduction to individual ownership of natural elements from which human exertion can neither produce nor increase" (167).

As we shall see in more detail in the chapters that follow, much of the Natural Dividend is determined by the efficiency of extracting/producing the resource at a particular site, compared to the least productive site in the market.[7] The

---

7. There are two variables here to consider: the variance in productive sites, and the size of the market. Some markets are naturally restricted by the "perishability" of the good; the market for electrical energy is a case in point.

most productive land, the windiest mountain top, the richest mineral vein, the most fruitful fishing waters, the most sun-drenched desert – these sites, when accessible, enjoy a natural advantage over less productive sites for the location of farms/forests, wind turbines, mines, fishing grounds or solar furnaces. That natural advantage can be further leveraged when these productive sites are located near existing infrastructure (roads/ports/railways/grids). It is these types of advantage that are monopolized by the concessionaire, even though she had nothing to do with their making.

At the same time, it is important to recognize that the size and existence of rents can vary significantly over time; the Natural Dividend is incredibly dynamic. Today some of the largest rents can be found in the petroleum and mineral sectors, whereas other resource markets are unable to generate much rent at all. This situation can and will change as the demand for new exotic minerals, clean wind/solar energy, and even farmland grows. The point is to recognize the potential for rent capture, and to establish a management regime that will allow for this capture, once (or if) these rents become substantial.

Finally, these rents have little redeeming economic value, at least in terms of incentives. In this way, rents are very different from both wages and profits. Although wages and profits are understood to be just returns on individual efforts and initiative, their very existence incentivizes workers and investors to return to the market. By contrast, rents are an unearned prize for the concessionaire, who reaps the benefits by simply sitting on the most productive resources sites. If these rents are not taken away, they will appear as a subsidy to the concessionaire, and distort her incentives and actions accordingly. As none other than Adam Smith would note, "[T]he landlords, like all other men, love to reap where they never sowed and demand a rent [from the earth] even for its natural produce" (Smith 1976 [1776]: 56). Unlike profits, then, rents have nothing to do with entrepreneurship, innovation or investment; rather, they are a drain on productive activity. As we shall see in the closing section of this chapter, this makes them an especially attractive target for taxation.

Scarcity

The market value placed on nature is largely derived from its scarcity, when juxtaposed against the backdrop of significant demand. This scarcity is generated in two ways: the first is by nature (relative scarcity); the other is more political (induced scarcity). Labour and capital can be mixed with any natural resource to improve its efficient harvest, but the root source of the value being produced comes from the scarce natural resource.

Relative scarcity

As we saw in Figure 1.1, a relatively small share of the earth's surface area consists of habitable land and fresh water. Even the non-inhabitable areas of that surface area are fixed, while our demand for its resources continues to rise. As Mark Twain famously (and allegedly) noted, "Buy land; they're not making it anymore." For these reasons, it is likely that natural resources will become increasingly scarce in the future: as the world's population and its economy grows, they will continually press up against the inherent limits of nature.

This natural scarcity varies significantly across resource types. For some resources, scarcity is the result of declining stocks (consider, for example, the phenomenon of "peak oil"; Hubbert 1956), or because concerns about global warming will force us to keep these stocks untouched. For other resources (such as with exotic minerals), scarcity may be the result of their being difficult to locate/retrieve or because they are located far from an existing market or infra-structure. In still others, the physical size of the resource remains fixed (e.g. agricultural land and fresh water), but it can become scarcer – in effect – when harmed by over-exploitation and/or poor management practices, or in light of increased demand from demographic pressures.

In addition to the overall scarcity of natural resources, there is considerable variation in the productive quality of these resources, as spread out over ter-ritory. The most productive sites, even of abundant resources, will always be scarce. This means that each natural resource site can be ranked in terms of its productive capacity, and the most productive sites will always remain extremely scarce. After all, there are relatively few resource sites that are as productive as the Permian Basin (the world's most productive oil area), Sonora Mexico (the site of the world's largest lithium mine), Gansu China (home to the world's biggest wind farm) or the fjords of Norway (where the world's most productive salmon farms are found).

This variation in what Ricardo (1971 [1817]: 91) called "the original and indestructible powers of the earth" has long been recognized as the source of excess (unearned) value or rent. As Ricardo noted, some farmland will always be better and cheaper to develop than others (see, e.g., Box 4.2). As the popu-lation grows, and demand for food rises, farmers will be forced to expand out-ward into less and less productive sites. As they do, the market price of food will be set by the production conditions established by the least productive farms. The same dilemma, of random distribution of productive capacity, taints every natural resource market.

Note that this allocation of nature's productive capacity is completely random from a political perspective; countries, companies and people might fight to con-trol more productive land or resources, but they are in no way responsible for the underlying productivity of the resource. It is an accident of biology, geography, physics and time that make oil fields in Kuwait (for example) more productive than oil fields almost anywhere else. Consequently, those who are granted access to the most productive oil fields can enjoy an additional surplus, and this surplus is unearned: it comes from the random allocation of nature – not the actions of the landowner or concessionaire.

To illustrate how the Natural Dividend works at the global level, consider a simple comparative example, detailed in Table 3.1. This example comes from the market for petroleum resources – which we consider in more detail in Chapter 7 – but it is useful for understanding how rent is generated in other natural resource markets. The petroleum market is particularly interesting because of the phenomenal size of the Natural Dividend it can generate.

In 2014[8] the world's lowest operating costs for extracting oil were found in Kuwait, at $4.40/barrel.[9] The average market price for a barrel oil in that year was $89.44. In short, Kuwait was able to produce oil at $4.40 and sell it for $89.44 – a difference of $85.04 a barrel. Better yet, Kuwait produced, on average, 2.6 million barrels a day in 2014. If we then apply a fair rate of return on investment, say 4 per cent of the operating costs,[10] then the investors can expect to earn $457,600/day for their troubles. After the production costs and return on investment are deducted, the remaining Natural Dividend for the people of Kuwait remains a phenomenal $220,636,000 a day. This is largely a differential rent – and we examine its nature in more detail in the following chapter.

In Norway, by contrast, it is much more difficult to get to the oil; it lies deep in the ground, far offshore, covered by deep waters and whipped by terrible weather conditions. In 2014 the average operating cost for producing Norwegian oil was estimated to be $13.30 a barrel, and Norway was producing 1.5 million barrels a day. If we assume that the quality of Kuwaiti and Norwegian oil is the same,[11] then the Natural Dividend on Norwegian oil was significantly smaller than that

---

8. The year 2014 is when oil prices most recently peaked, before the war in Ukraine. We chose this year to underline the potential size of the Natural Dividend in petroleum markets. At the time of this writing, global oil prices are significantly higher because of war (even though variances in productive capacity will remain), so the overall Dividend for the most productive sites will be even greater than shown in this example. In the future the price of oil can fall, and the Natural Dividend from oil will fall along with it.

9. Operating costs (or operating expenses, often abbreviated as OPEX) usually include leasing, equipment and inventory costs, marketing, payroll, insurance and funds allocated for research and development.

10. We use the share of operating costs to facilitate an easy comparison, and to limit the amount of information required.

11. In practice, prices will differ based on the quality of the oil and on how complex the refinery process needs to be (e.g. content of sulphur or not). North Sea oil (Brent price) is considered high-quality oil, compensating to some degree for the higher production costs.

Table 3.1 Production, costs and rents in Kuwait and Norway, 2014

	[1] Daily production (mill. bbls)	[2] Production costs ($/bbl)	[3] World market price ($/bbl)	[4] Surplus value ($/bbl) [3–2]	[5] Est. profit per barrel (4% avg. [2])	[6] Est. rent per barrel [4 – 5]	[7] Daily gross, million $ [1 * 3]	[8] Daily rent, million $ [6 * 1]
Kuwait	2.6	$4.40	$89.44	$85.04	$0.18	$84.86	$232.5	$220.6
Norway	1.5	$13.30	$89.44	$76.14	$0.53	$75.61	$134.2	$113.4

Source: Calculations by authors; the underlying figures come from Knoema (2018).

of Kuwaiti oil, because of a simple accident of geography. Even so, the equivalent Norwegian Dividend per day, after subtracting out the operating costs and a fair return on investment (using the same method as described above), would be $113,415,000 a day. Not bad for a day's work. As in Kuwait, this Dividend was mostly generated by a differential rent, but it is smaller than Kuwait's, as the Norwegian site is less productive.

We recognize that it is possible to have differing opinions about what constitutes a "fair return" on investment. Some readers may think that a 4 per cent return, as suggested above, is too modest. But this is exactly our point. Depending on market conditions and the level of risk, a fair return might be 4 per cent, or 10 per cent or maybe even 35 per cent; but it is *not* 100 per cent, or 1,000 per cent. Anything above and beyond this fair return is the Natural Dividend. The size of this just return on investment will need to be negotiated between the sovereign authority and the concessionaire to ensure that returns are transparent and fair and that the Natural Dividend is not pocketed by the concessionaire.[12]

The reason that oil is such a lucrative industry is because oil is in high demand, is difficult to find and its production is limited by government licensing arrangements. The challenge for governments is to get this oil out of the ground efficiently, but in a way that secures the resulting Natural Dividend for its owners (the people). Too often governments agree to a management regime that allows private companies to walk off with this Natural Dividend (masquerading as company profits). Our task is to draw the reader's attention to the existence of the Natural Dividend in a range of natural resources and to show how it can and should be captured for public gain.

The same concern applies to the allocation of mines, land, forests, coastal waterways, wind corridors, hydroelectric sites, etc. The most productive sites will be remarkably scarce and randomly spread across political terrain. This scarcity allows the most productive sites to secure a differential rent – one important component to the Natural Dividend.

Induced scarcity

It should now be evident that markets for natural resources do not act like the ideal markets found in our economic textbooks and depicted in Figure 3.2: they are not, and cannot, be competitive. As we have just learned, this is partly

---

12. For example, a company may need to drill five wells before it finds one that is able to produce at sufficient quantity. That company will want to argue that the costs of all five wells should be included in deciding what is profit and what is a necessary cost. What is to be included as relevant production "costs" needs to be negotiated between the sovereign authority and the concessionaire. The importance of itemizing formal costs becomes more evident at the end of the chapter, when we describe how to tax this activity in a way that can secure the Natural Dividend.

because of the underlying scarcity of natural resources and partly the result of the varying productive capacity across sites, which are distributed in a relatively random manner (when seen from a political perspective, in terms of their access to markets). In both cases, sovereign political authority is obliged to manage these markets and regulate access to them. In doing so, political authority creates the conditions that generate two other types of rent: regulatory rent and locational rent.

The necessity of regulatory intervention is obvious when scarce resources need protection, but it has also proved necessary under conditions of apparent abundance (e.g. in the short term, or in particular places). Once discovered and exploited, this sort of abundance can have catastrophic consequences for the resource, the market and the surrounding community. For this reason, producers (or producing countries) often need to collaborate to restrict production so as to secure a stable price and/or the efficient exploitation of the resource. The Organization of Petroleum Exporting Countries (OPEC) oil cartel is the premier example of this sort of international collaboration, but we see it in other resource markets as well. As described in Box 3.1, this need for regulating the production of natural resources is even evident in the southern states of the United States – ones not usually associated with extensive regulatory traditions.

The need to regulate resource scarcity and abundance is not limited to the market for oil; we see it occurring time and time again under many varied contexts. We can see a sort of fever-driven response to many new resource markets, as is evident in coastal Chile's recent history, where one resource after the other became subjected to gold-rush-like behaviour: first whale hunting, then timber, then salmon, then mussels, and even the harvesting of peat (Bustos & Román 2019: 103). These rushes are often seen in the fisheries industry, where overfishing frequently results in falling prices and a collapsed resource.[13]

When political authorities decide to regulate access to natural resources they are redistributing the common wealth, as favoured groups are granted legal access to the scarce resource (and the resulting rents). The origins of this favouring may have been political (e.g. a royal decree or grant) or economic (e.g. to the highest bidder), even if this original allocation is often obscured by years

---

13. One revealing example is provided by Røed (2013: 118), who describes a rapid rise in the number of farmed Norwegian salmon on the market in the late 1980s. In response to confused signals from the Norwegian regulatory authorities, Norwegian salmon farmers were producing at maximum capacity and dumping their fish on the world market. This resulted in foreign dumping charges and the imposition of anti-dumping duties, and Norwegian fish were even excluded from the US market in 1991. In the end the market for Norwegian farmed fish was radically upset: many small producers went bankrupt, with banks and the largest industrial interests buying up the remnants – leading to the massive concentration that we see in the Norwegian farmed fish market today.

BOX 3.1 PRODUCING SCARCITY: THE REGULATION OF
THE US OIL MARKET

OPEC is a prime example of the need to control natural resource markets, but its inspiration can be traced back to the unregulated oil markets of east Texas in the early 1930s. At that time a huge new oil field – called the "Black Giant" – had been discovered, and it attracted a large number of small independent produ-cers. Within months of its discovery an army of small producers were spudding a new well every hour and producing over 1 million barrels a day. This rapid expansion of supply forced the price of oil, across the United States, to drop like a stone: in 1926 a barrel of Texas oil cost $1.85, but by the end of May 1931 it was being sold for as little as 2 cents.

Unregulated, the petroleum market became anarchic: when the price of oil fell below the cost of production, the nascent petroleum industry (and the pol-itical authorities whose ear it had) found it necessary to take action. The gov-ernor of Oklahoma moved first by declaring a state of emergency and martial law; he then deployed the state militia to shut down the major oil fields. Soon afterwards the governor of Texas followed suit, declaring a "state of insurrection" in east Texas and calling in the National Guard, along with the Texas Rangers, to forcibly shut down production. To stabilize these lower production levels (and higher prices), the Texas Railway Commission was drafted into action (while a "Commerce Commission" was established in neighbouring Oklahoma).

The state political authorities in Oklahoma and Texas had to regulate the oil market because of an apparent over-abundance. By restricting production and making the resource scarcer, the regulatory authorities were able to sta-bilize prices (and improve well efficiencies); in doing so, they created the value that eventually sustained the industry (now in a more concentrated form), and inspired the OPEC cartel decades later (see Yergin 2009 [1991]: 230–3).

---

of market exchange. Whatever the allocation mechanism, favoured interests are provided exclusive and legal access, while everybody else is excluded from accessing the nature (which they once enjoyed freely). In each case, political authority must first decide how to allocate access to the resource, and then decide whether to make access to the resource relatively scarce (i.e. a narrow distribution) or abundant (a wide distribution). Hence, in deciding how to allo-cate access to common resources, political authorities help to establish the value of that resource at market (as the market price is set by the quantity of supply at a given level of demand).

This relationship between political authority, natural scarcity and rents is as old as the enclosure process described in the previous chapter. In deciding how to enclose and allocate access to nature, political authority affects its relative scarcity. By making access to natural resources scarcer, political authorities create another type of rent: *a regulatory rent*, which we consider in more detail in Chapter 5. In such cases, rents are derived by licences or concessions granted for a limited period of time, to encourage efficient (but limited) production. It is this managed "monopoly" effect – created by the allocation process, in a context of high demand – that can create a substantial Natural Dividend.

In practice, political authorities decide who will get access to the most productive sites and/or to those sites that are closest to existing markets and infrastructure (or they will decide where subsequent infrastructure will be built, further enhancing the value of a resource site already allocated). In either case, the productive value of the site increases thanks to a locational advantage, which generates another form of rent: what we call a *locational rent*. This locational rent is the focus of Chapter 6.

Securing the Natural Dividend

Perhaps the easiest way to think about the Natural Dividend, and how it might be used, is to return to the anecdote from the introductory chapter: when a family has to decide whether it is better to secure the machinery and competence to drill for water themselves, or to pay a contractor to come and do the job for them. In doing so, the family needs to balance its current and future needs and costs. Political authorities face the same sort of calculation: they must decide whether to develop the resource themselves (e.g. by means of a state-owned company), to rely on a private contractor or to employ some combination of the two.

Because nature includes such a wide variety of resources (and resource markets), the nature of particular management regimes varies significantly. In the chapters that follow, we focus on particular resource markets associated with different forms of nature. On land, we consider the management of forests and agricultural farmland; in the water, we look to how authorities manage a growing aquaculture industry; in the air, we turn to the management of wind turbine and solar power installations; and, in the realm of subsurface nature, we look at the markets for minerals, gas and oil.

Each of these resource markets shares several characteristics that sets it apart from other (less fictitious) commodity markets. Most important of these is the fact that the original control and ownership of these natural assets lies with the commons (even if political authorities have decided to allocate access to individual interests, on behalf of the broader community). In addition, markets for natural resources tend to face several shared challenges, including:

- significant (heavy) sunk costs and long production (and payback) periods;
- pervasive uncertainty;
- volatile commodity prices;
- the exhaustibility of the underlying resource/licence.[14]

Despite these similarities, the potential for generating a Natural Dividend will vary significantly across resources and over time, but also within resource types (by site quality). Whether it is farmland, fishing grounds, oil reservoirs, wind sites or veins of ore, we can expect natural variation in productivity, processing needs, recoverability and market accessibility.

In recognizing this variance, political authorities need to employ a management regime that is sensitive to these unique characteristics of natural resource markets, but still capable of isolating and securing the Natural Dividend they produce. As we learned in the previous chapter, these management regimes determine the way in which we enclose and allocate access to natural resources; but they also include policy instruments that are used to incentivize the productive utilization and/or harvest of these resources.

In practice, the Natural Dividend can be realized in either political or economic terms (or both). In some instances, the authorities may want to exploit the resource themselves in order to create domestic competences that can sustain the community over generations. When this is the case, authorities prioritize local content policies (LCPs), even when these might prove to more expensive and less efficient (in the short run). In other cases, political authorities may choose to exploit the resource in the most efficient way possible, secure a large share of the commodified resource before it goes to market, or tax that efficient activity in such a way that can secure the Natural Dividend for the community. We look at these two different policy scenarios in the sections that follow.

Local content policies

Most countries hope to get more from their natural resources than a simple boost in national income. This is because natural resource wealth offers an

---

14. Of course, this last challenge can vary, in that some resources are more renewable than others. But, even in these cases, the licensing regime tends to limit access, and poor management regimes can exhaust what should have been renewable resources. At any rate, in markets for natural resources, as opposed to other commodity markets, extraction is often concerned with asset depletion rather than merely production.

opportunity to create even greater value – in the form of, say, domestic jobs, expertise, and increased economic activity. In this context, local content policies are designed to leverage natural resource abundance in ways that can build domestic industries, diversify local economies and extend productive capacity (and the resulting tax base) at home.[15]

Recognizing these potential spillovers, policy-makers and residents may be willing to forgo the (short-term) efficiency gains associated with hiring an experienced international contractor. Instead, they may aim to secure longer-term social and political objectives, such as encouraging and protecting domestic infant industries, balancing the market power between local and international companies and/or providing compensation for the many adverse impacts that natural resource exploitation can bring to local communities and vulnerable groups.

The nature of LCPs varies significantly across resource types. In some resource markets it is common to develop a national resource company, or NRC (e.g. national oil companies or national mining companies), in which local competences can be developed. In other markets it may be more common to require that a certain share of activity is reserved for domestic firms and/or domestic workers; that a certain share of innovation is secured in local universities and research institutions; that a certain share of purchasing needs must occur in local markets; etc. Some political authorities may want to maximize local employment creation; others may want to expand domestic ownership and entrepreneurial activity or encourage inward direct investment; still others may want to focus on building up a domestic supply industry, providing local skills and technical competence.

In recent decades many LCPs have been circumscribed by international agreements that limit the capacity of political authorities to protect and support local industrial initiatives. These constraints on sovereign authority have taken many forms and include limits on the use of subsidies, politically motivated procurement policies and/or the employment of tariffs and non-tariff barriers to trade. This international policy climate is beginning to change in the wake of the Covid-19 pandemic and a new war in Europe, as the international community is increasingly aware of the need to develop resilient home industries and supply chains. Whatever the international political climate, political authorities are always free to pursue concessions policies that secure a larger share of the commodified resource and/or a tax policy that can secure the Natural Dividend. We turn to these options now.

---

15. For a discussion of how LCPs are secured in the oil industry, see Moses and Letnes (2017a: ch. 8).

Resource rent taxes

In addition to (or in lieu of) LCPs, some communities may prefer a more direct and efficient means of securing the Natural Dividend. These communities favour cold hard cash on the barrelhead over the promise of future jobs and competences (and recognize that this income can be invested to secure long-term employment and local content objectives). These countries might simply claim the lion's share of the resource and secure the rents directly from the market (for example, by paying the contractor/entrepreneur a service fee in hard currency or as a small share of the resource produced). In the oil and mining sectors we can see this effort in the growth of service contracts and favourable production-sharing contracts (PSCs). We do not have the space here to elaborate on the variety of contract forms that can be used to secure a larger share of the resource, but see Moses and Letnes (2017a: ch. 5).

One convenient means of securing the fiscal form of the Natural Dividend is by way of a tailored resource rent tax. In introducing the thinking behind RRTs, we hope to avoid a detailed discussion about tax law and its administration. As we shall see, it is not always easy to decide what constitutes a fair return on capital and risk, or how to establish what counts as legitimate costs of production; there will be much bickering over when an RRT should be introduced, and how it should be calculated. Finally, we recognize that taxes are not a particularly exciting topic, and the language of tax accounting can be somewhat intimidating. For this we apologize in advance. Even so, this discussion is necessary if we are to deter the private taking of our Natural Dividend.

On land, we have long understood the need to design taxation regimes that can secure the Natural Dividend. It is not particularly difficult to separate the Natural Dividend from the just rewards to those who have invested their capital and labour in – and on the – land (e.g. building structures, fences, drainage systems, etc.). As we shall see in Chapter 4, land rent taxation schemes have been around since the nineteenth century, and have spread across Asia, the Americas, Europe and Oceania. Even today several local tax authorities (in the United States and elsewhere) apply a two-rate system of property taxes (one for property, the other for capital improvements), and capture the Natural Dividend by taxing the property value at a higher rate (Harrison 1994: 10–11). Still other communities are eyeing the potential of using RRTs to capture locational rents for expanding the public infrastructure – as the expansion of infrastructure will benefit some resource owners more than others (Connolly & Wall 2016).

At the turn to the twentieth century, with the development and spread of massive hydroelectric installations, there was widespread recognition of the need to keep the resulting Natural Dividend from landowners. We can find a glimpse of this interest in a passage by Marx:

> [A] waterfall cannot be created by capital out of itself. Therefore, the surplus-profit which arises from the employment of this waterfall is not due to capital, but to the utilization of a natural force which can be monopolised, and has been monopolised, by capital. Under these circumstances, the surplus-profit is transformed into ground rent, that is, it falls into possession of the owner of a waterfall.
>
> (Marx 1967 [1867], vol. 3: 646)

It was this desire to secure the Natural Dividend that prompted the Norwegian government to introduce a hydropower concession regime, inspired by the work of Henry George, and specifically designed to capture the Natural Dividend for local and national authorities (Vikse 1976; Thue 2003; Brigham & Moses 2021; see also Box 7.3). This concession regime was subsequently transferred to the management of Norway's petroleum resources later in the same century, as we shall see in Chapter 7.

At this earlier time, political authorities were preoccupied with securing local and democratic control over shared natural resources. In the early twentieth century political decisions were grounded in terms of both justice and efficiency, and policy-makers needed to assure the citizens of relatively young democratic states that wealthy individuals and interests would not be allowed to abscond with the Natural Dividends that these shared resources could produce. By the end of the twentieth century the political calculus had changed dramatically: the primary concern of policy-makers was now trained on the need to secure the efficient utilization of natural resources. Questions about justice and/or the just allocation of the Natural Dividend have largely fallen on deaf ears.

In the mid-1970s, however, we saw a new rise of interest in resource rents, in particular among tax specialists. This interest seems to have started with a 1975 article by Ross Garnaut and Anthony Clunies Ross, but was followed up by a flurry of subsequent reports and sources.[16] As a product of its time, this work was not so much concerned about the rightful ownership of the resource rent; its focus was on improving efficiencies (rather than on just rewards). In particular, this new literature argues that RRTs are attractive from the perspective

---

16. See, for example, Johnson (1981), Garnaut and Clunies Ross (1983), Boadway and Bruce (1984), McPherson and Palmer (1984), Goss (1986), Kumar (1991), Baunsgaard (2001), Sunley, Baunsgaard and Simard (2003), Otto *et al.* (2006), Lund (2009) and Land (2010).

of investors, and that they tend to be less distorting, more efficient and more flexible than alternative taxation regimes.

This literature begins by recognizing that most mainstream NRM regimes rely on regressive fiscal regimes based on low royalties and either flat or proportional income tax systems applied at rates that are negotiated in advance of investment. These are then combined with generous allowances (accelerated depreciation and investment uplifts). This happens because returns on natural resource investments are highly uncertain, and governments rely on these investors to gain information about the value of their own resources. Consequently, investors are often able to insist on mild tax regimes in cases when returns are expected to be low and they use their superior knowledge and experience to argue that this is more likely (Garnaut & Clunies Ross 1975: 284). In short, because of information asymmetries, high risks and uncertainties, and fiscal regimes that are negotiated in advance (and often are based on volume rather than profit), governments find it difficult to share in the benefits of any subsequent price escalations.

The literature then introduces a number of assumptions about how investors approach the market. For example, major investors are expected to evaluate any given project on the basis of its expected internal rate of return on the total cash flow. This is important, because natural resource projects tend to be characterized by very large investments, in contexts that are often very uncertain. Taxes on natural resources are often based on the size of the resource extraction (or the income generated by that extraction), irrespective of whether the extracting company can cover its costs and return a profit. Such taxes are "distortive", in that they induce a higher risk and can deter investors from both initial and ongoing investments to extract the resource. RRTs, on the other hand, resemble corporate taxes on general surpluses, as they do not kick in until all costs are covered: they are designed to soothe these investors' anxieties by providing an efficient means of taxing natural resource projects when there is significant uncertainty about future production costs and prices (Land 2010). At the same time, RRTs can prevent companies from exploiting the government's relative ignorance about costs and prices, because they are based on *revealed* profitability.

The starting point for any RRT is a recognition of two essential points. The first is that natural resources produce rents, and the RRT is designed to secure these for the political authorities. Although we see this as a moral issue, or a question of justice, the RRT literature sees it largely as a practical and legal matter: it is a way to find common ground between the states that own the resources and the contractors they choose to extract them. Second, RRT approaches recognize that investors are unwilling to walk away from a world-class natural resource so long as they can recover all their costs and earn a return sufficient to justify the investment (i.e. a minimum return). In recognizing these two essential points, RRTs are designed to tax only the rent, while leaving untouched the underlying return needed to propel the investment. As a result, RRTs do not distort investment decisions.

These investment decisions are not distorted because of the inherent immobility of natural resources and because both investors and host government can find advantage in a tax regime that shares information and minimizes risk. The introduction of a well-designed RRT will not provoke capital flight, for example, because investors realize that there are few available alternatives to a world-class natural resource. If an investor enjoys a concession to exploit a Norwegian fjord, which is recognized as one of the world's most productive areas for producing farmed salmon, why would she threaten to leave to a less productive production site? After all, they cannot farm these fish in Bangladesh. As the most productive resources in the world are inherently scarce, any investor's threat to leave is an idle one.

But a well-designed RRT is neutral (as opposed to distortionary) in the sense that the tax will not affect investment and business decisions or entail economic losses. When natural resource investors/producers are driven to maximize the value of their productive activities, a tax on that value will not affect the producers' (or investors') decisions. Quite simply, investment and operational decisions that are profitable *before* the tax will also be profitable *after* the RRT (only the profit will be redistributed). When the RRT also allows investors and producers to deduct all relevant costs against gross sales income (regardless of whether it employs an accrued profit-based or a cash flow tax), then the state becomes – in effect – a co-investor in these projects and ends up saddling much of the risk. In this way, RRTs reduce the risks that investors/producers face by promising a solid return before the RRT kicks in. By sharing information and ensuring that all the investors' costs (including a fair return) will be covered, both the government and the investor become better off. In substantially reducing the investor's risks, without distorting her investment and/or operational decisions, the investor can be satisfied with a much lower rate of return (see Norwegian government 2019a).

From a tax perspective, Natural Dividends can be understood as "the ex-post surplus of the total project lifetime value arising from the exploitation of a deposit, in present value terms, over the sum of all costs of exploitation, including the compensation to all factors of production" (Land 2010: 244). This definition, though framed in the convoluted language of tax lawyers, is similar to our own, from earlier in the chapter, whereby the costs cover all the inputs needed to bring the resource to market and exploit it until closure. This compensation includes a return on both labour (in the form of wages) and the capital invested (in the form of profit). It is different from our earlier definition in that the tax base is operationalized more narrowly: rather than thinking about the rent in terms of a resource, or country, the focus here is on a project, over the course of its lifetime (from exploration through exploitation to decommissioning).[17]

This need for "compensation to all factors of production" is fairly straightforward when applied to labour and fixed capital inputs (e.g. machines). The desire to provide a fair (compensatory) return on capital is somewhat more complicated in that it contains two component parts: (a) a basic return (equivalent to the rate of interest on risk-free long-term borrowing); and (b) an additional margin to compensate for the risks (technical, commercial, political) associated with the investment.

It is this explicit recognition of the need to compensate for risk that provides investors with the flexibility they desire. Conventional means of taxing natural resources (e.g. by way of royalties, fees or windfall/income taxes) apply rates that tend to be negotiated in advance of any investments. As these systems are price- (rather than profit-) based, they can raise taxes even in contexts in which profits are falling.[18] As a result of this shortcoming, conventional tax regimes leave investors sitting on a large and sunk investment, waiting on future returns, while all the time saddled with enormous risks. Conventional tax regimes are also unfavourable from the perspective of the political authorities, in that they tend to leave governments with an unnecessarily small share of the rent (Garnaut & Clunies Ross 1975: 284).

Adjustable RRTs are designed to let investors minimize this risk, by linking tax obligations directly to risk levels. As risk increases, investors can expect an increased return on investment; as risks decrease, they can expect a reduced return. This built-in flexibility, in turn, decreases the likelihood that governments will force a renegotiation of terms under different price environments (Land 2010: 246), or political climates. This type of obsolescing bargaining mechanism (OBM) is common in the more lucrative natural resource markets and is the source of much uncertainty – for governments and investors alike (Moses & Letnes 2017a: 64–6). Most significantly, by taxing the profit (rather than price) level, authorities are better able to capture the Natural Dividend, without undermining investors' appetite or incentives.

There are an incredible variety of ways to secure the Natural Dividend, and it would be fruitless to try and map this variety across countries, resources and time.[19] But the underlying principle of an RRT is very simple, as shown in the

---

17. This is done to avoid taxing so-called "quasi-rents", when rents are derived from a previous outlay of sunk costs. We return to the challenge of quasi-rents at the close of this chapter.

18. After all, prices might rise, but, if the underlying unit costs have also risen, the profits generated on a pre-tax basis will remain the same (or fall), even though the (price-based) tax will have increased.

19. A useful primer can be found in Norwegian government (2019b: 6–8). Here an expert committee assembled by the government distinguishes two types of profit-based RRT: an accrual type and a cash flow type. Under an accrual-based tax model, tax depreciation of operating assets that are

examples found in Box 3.2. In short, political authorities simply need to establish how much revenue is being generated from a resource, subtract the costs (including profits) of bringing that resource to market and then agree upon a "reasonable return" for risk, which should not be higher than the returns on risk that are required by investors on comparable investments in the host country. When these two costs (production and profits) are subtracted from revenue, what remains is the Natural Dividend.

In practice, then, an RRT tends to have three main component parts.

(1) The tax base is defined as an individual resource project (fully ring-fenced) with allowable deductions.
(2) An *explicit rate of return* is used on investment that would trigger the RRT (e.g. above 13 per cent for the example in Box 3.2), which is taxed at normal rates. This is to ensure that workers and investors get their fair return, before the Natural Dividend is taxed.
(3) *Explicit tax rates* are then imposed on the Natural Dividend, the net economic surplus above (2) – for example all returns above 13 per cent are taxed at a higher level.

Once the size of the Natural Dividend is established, it can be heavily taxed without affecting production or investment incentives. In theory, the rent can be taxed up to 100 per cent, although this is often unrealistic. In some areas, such as when regulating public utilities (such as water and power), the authorities may want to cap corporate returns with a 100 per cent RRT, to ensure that access to a natural monopoly is not used to generate scarcity rents on a public good. Indeed, in the case of hydroelectric power, the operating costs can approach zero, so the return on capital can be 100 per cent or more of the operating expenses. In other areas, however, an RRT that is seen as too high can incentivize tax avoidance (e.g. "gold-plating", when companies exaggerate their costs of production to minimize their tax burden), or undermine some of the incentives to seek out the most productive resource sites.

RRTs are not hocus pocus and they are not part of some larger socialist plot. They are proven, respected and popular mechanisms for securing the economic form of the Natural Dividend. As we shall see in subsequent chapters, RRTs are employed in a variety of different markets, under different names, at different times and for varying purposes. They can also be employed in new markets and

related to the resource activities liable to the RRT should be deductible in the relevant tax year. In a cash flow tax model, the incomes will be the same (as in the accrual-based RRT model), with the same costs being deductible. But the investment costs are directly deductible on an ongoing basis under a cash flow tax, whereas they are deductible through depreciation under an accrual-based RRT.

BOX 3.2 CALCULATING THE NATURAL DIVIDEND

The Natural Dividend can be measured precisely: it is what is left over after paying the labour and capital costs of production in a competitive market. In markets in which risk plays a large role, this risk premium needs to be included.

Consider a farm that grows parsnips. Assume the annual cost of producing parsnips is $10,000; this covers the wages paid and inputs (e.g. seed, fertilizer), interest on bank loans, *and profits* for the owner of the building and equipment used to plant, tend and harvest the parsnips. When the parsnips are sold, they generate a revenue of $15,000. The economic rent on the land is $5,000 ($15,000 minus $10,000).

The government can tax the underlying costs of production and profit ($10,000) at its regular rates using, for example, wage and income taxes (say at 35 per cent). But the Natural Dividend rests on top of this and can be taxed at a much higher rate (approaching 100 per cent) with no detrimental effects on production.

We can then complicate this example by adding risk. Imagine a patch of land, under which oil might (or might not) be lying. The petroleum contractor spends $100,000 a week on production costs (which include wages, input costs, interest on loans and profit for capital). These costs are complicated by the fact that several exploratory wells had to be drilled before striking oil, and these exploration costs need to be factored in. When brought to the market, a week's worth of oil sells for $900,000. To find the Natural Dividend, we subtract the exploration/production costs and profit levels from the overall revenues, and then estimate a fair return on risk. The latter can be estimated by using similar levels of risk found in nearby sectors (e.g. mining returns in the same country), and subtracting these.

Revenues = production costs (wages + inputs)
+ profits (compensatory, say 3%)
+ risk margin (say 10%)

Or:

Revenues	=	production costs (fixed)	+	normal profits (3%)	+	risk margin (10%)	+	Natural Dividend (remainder)
$900,000	=	$100,000	+	$3,000	+	$10,000	+	$787.000

In short, the Natural Dividend in this example would be:
$900,000 − ($100,000 + $3,000 + $10,000), or $787,000.

The $113,000 of normal economic activity is taxed at regular rates, and the workers and capitalists would all get a fair return for their contributions. The remaining Natural Dividend, in this example, is enormous. To ensure that it is returned to its just owners, political authorities can employ a much higher tax rate on the Natural Dividend (e.g. 80–100 per cent).

contexts, as political authorities become more aware of the existence of these Dividends. To do so, political authorities must first recognize the existence of the Natural Dividend, so it is not hidden as an unearned income for investors/ concessionaires. When this is done, a tailored RRT can be used to ensure that the Natural Dividend finds its way back to the public.

Caveats

Securing the Natural Dividend is not without difficulty, and it is important for us to note some of the challenges to the approach we are proposing. Here, too, we risk boring the reader with accounting details, but we believe this is necessary in order to convince experts of the viability of our approach. In doing so, we might also clear up a couple of common misperceptions.

The first of these is the argument that RRTs are too demanding of the tax authorities, especially in developing states. As an RRT can be secured only *after* the total costs and revenues for a project are known, governments and investors alike are forced to extend their tax horizons, and tie up their money, over a longer stretch of time. Although this allows the concessionaries to better manage their risks, the parking of this money can introduce challenges, especially for cash-strapped countries and companies. As a consequence, RRTs are almost always combined with other types of tax (e.g. royalty and/or corporate income tax: CIT), to spread out the government's revenue stream (and the company's tax obligations) over the lifetime of a project.

Although the need to collect costs, returns and revenue data can bring with it administrative challenges, they are not overwhelming for most political authorities. As Land (2010: 258) notes, "A tax office that is capable of imposing income tax on resource businesses consistently and effectively should, with a relatively modest augmentation of skills and personnel, be able to administer a resource rent tax." The real challenge is not found in the administrative realm but in the world of politics: it lies in recognizing the need to secure the Natural Dividend, in the name of its rightful owners.

A bigger problem lies in the threat that government efforts to secure the Natural Dividend will also result in the capture of quasi-rents (Marshall 1920 [1890], bk 5). A quasi-rent is an income earned from sunk costs; it is a return on a previous investment, but one that continues to deliver without the need for further investments. As we noted earlier, some investments in nature can improve nature's productive capacity, and these investments should be encouraged, not deterred, by the tax regime. In introducing an RRT, tax authorities need to ensure that such productive investments are not covered by the tax on Natural Dividends, so that any quasi-rents find their way back to their rightful owner (the investor).

Finally, the biggest problem lies in trusting the government with securing these rents for the public they represent. Although there is no convincing argument (moral or otherwise) for allowing private actors to abscond with this Natural Dividend, this does not mean that we should expect government officials to always do the right thing. This is a serious challenge, and one we return to in our concluding chapter.

For now, it should suffice to note that tracking the Natural Dividend is complicated by the fact that it involves two separate issues. First, how much of the Natural Dividend is returned to the state (or taken by private interests)? And, second, when/if the state manages to capture the Natural Dividend, does it share it with the people (or do corrupt public officials abscond with the rent)? To consider the different allocation possibilities, we have drawn a very simple decision tree, as shown in Figure 3.3.

When a Natural Dividend exists, it can end up in three different places (or some combination thereof): it can be taken by the private corporation (private taking); it can be taken by corrupt political authorities (corrupt public taking); or it can be secured by the political authorities and shared (just public taking). From the perspective of the general public, it matters little whether the rent is taken by private interests or by corrupt public officials; it matters only that it is not being returned to its rightful owners.

This means that we can expect at least three possibilities (or some combination thereof): (a) the state allows private interests to secure all the Natural Dividend; (b) the state uses a public contractor (e.g. an NRC) to secure all of the

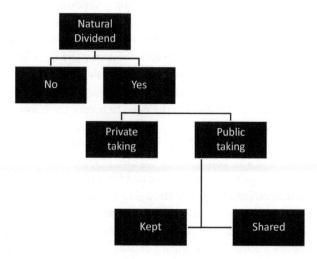

Figure 3.3 Natural Dividend decision tree
Source: Authors.

Natural Dividend, but none of it is returned to the people of that state; or (c) the state secures the Natural Dividend (by way of an NRC or RRT) for the people, regardless of whether it is secured by private or public contractors.

Behind all this calculation lies an awkward realization: if the authorities are unable or unwilling to capture the Natural Dividend, it will function like a subsidy for those who have been granted access. The effects of natural resource subsidies are well known (see, e.g., Porter 1996), and we can expect these effects to be found with those concessionaires who are allowed to pocket the Natural Dividend (i.e. the Natural Dividend will have the same effect as a subsidy). These effects distort the market and can have a detrimental impact on the underlying natural resource. Following Porter (1996: 6–7), the most common effects include the following.

- *An over-capitalization effect.* When private interests are allowed to pocket the Natural Dividend, it will draw more investment into that (natural resource) sector then would have otherwise been the case. This results in more money being thrown at natural resources, and an expanded scope of production (more land devoted to agriculture use; greater incentive to fish further out to sea; more and bigger processing plants; etc.).
- *A technology effect.* When private interests are allowed to pocket the Natural Dividend, investors will be incentivized to use technologies that can have a significant impact on the environment in a race to secure the resource. For example, farmers will have an incentive to increase their use of pesticides/fertilizers to increase their yields; fishermen will invest in larger and faster boats, with more efficient gear; etc.
- *A resource inefficiency effect.* By effectively subsidizing the exploitation of natural resources, political authorities remove the incentive for concessionaires to use/process these resources in the most efficient manner. After all, if wind is basically given away to the concessionaire, it cannot possibly reflect the actual value of the resource, and its use will probably be wasted (i.e. used inefficiently).
- *An overconsumption effect.* As with subsidies, an untaxed Natural Dividend will result in lower prices for the resource, which will lead to overconsumption, and the possible exhaustion of the underlying resource (or the political appetite to concede greater access).
- *A public resource deprivation effect.* By giving away access to natural resources, and allowing the concessionaire to pocket the Natural Dividend, political authorities are depriving themselves of the sort of financial resources that are needed to regulate and enforce the regulations that protect these natural resources and promote their sustainable management.

By taxing the Natural Dividend and returning it to the public (to whom it belongs), political authorities can deter these costly (and all too common) effects of poorly designed NRM regimes.

Conclusion

This chapter has shown how the Natural Dividend is created, and how polit-ical authority can secure it on behalf of the public. We argue that securing the Natural Dividend is both just and efficient, as it is created by a combination of nature and the political authorities that regulate access to that nature. It is only just that the Natural Dividend be returned to the authorities that own and create it; at the very least, it can be seen as payment for the cost of enclosing and regu-lating access to our shared resources. Securing the Natural Dividend is efficient, as an RRT can minimize the risks and volatility for the contracting party and deter the sorts of market distortion associated with subsidies.

The earliest literature on resource rents, following Smith, Ricardo, George and Marx, was aimed mostly at farmland; the more recent literature on RRTs is focused on the most lucrative resource markets (minerals, oil and gas). We argue that the Natural Dividend can exist in all types of natural resource markets, and the size of these Dividends will vary over time. More to the point, we hold that it is both possible and desirable to establish management regimes that are capable of isolating and capturing these Natural Dividends, in either political or economic forms.

In the chapters that follow, we provide illustrations of how several different resource markets are managed. Most of the current management regimes ignore the potential for a Natural Dividend and let the concessionaire abscond with it in the form of an unearned windfall, or what Obeng-Odoom (2021: 204) calls "rent theft". We then consider how these markets might be managed so as to isolate and secure these Natural Dividends, when and where they occur. In doing so, we can create a more sustainable approach to managing our natural resources – for the resources we currently exploit, as well as the new resource markets we will need to develop in the future.

In the next chapter we turn to the oldest and most developed market for nat-ural resources, as the concept of rent and the recognition for capturing rent is most developed in the market for land.

4

THE EARTH: THE MARKET FOR LAND

We begin by considering how to manage the markets for land, and its products. These markets are the most established and the most familiar, but probably also the most varied. There are several reasons why the market for land often serves as a point of departure for thinking about how other resource markets should be managed. One reason may be that we all have a relationship to how property in land is bought and sold in the place where we live. Another reason may be because land ownership has played such an important role in the way we think about managing nature, individual liberty and the role of government in the Western world. Yet another reason may be that most natural resources are located on, around or under the land – so controlling access to the land often means controlling access to valuable natural resources.

The total amount of available land on the earth (minus Antarctica) is roughly 33.7 billion acres (see Table 4.1). We use the acre here as our measure, as it offers a convenient mental measuring unit, covering roughly the size of a football pitch. We also know that the world population in 2019 was 7.7 billion. If equally divided, then, each person on the globe would enjoy a little more than 4.4 acres of land. Not all this land is equally productive, and much of it cannot be used for agricultural purposes. The World Bank (2021a) estimates that less than 12 billion acres ($c.$ 48 million km^2) could be counted as farmland in 2018 – that is, under a third of the total amount of land available.

In other words, farmland is relatively scarce, and global population growth will exacerbate that scarcity. From Figure 1.2 we learned that the world can expect 9.7 billion inhabitants in 2050. Every one of these individuals will need to find food, clothing and shelter from the land. Under optimal conditions, it might be possible to generate the caloric needs of 10 billion people on just 6 billion acres of land – but we also need land to feed animals, produce biofuels, sequester atmospheric carbon dioxide, grow timber, cotton and other clothing fibres, and

Table 4.1 World land area, with conversions

Land area/conversions	Acres 1	=	Hectares 0.404686	or	km² 0.004046856
World	37,203,566,988		15,055,762,710		150,557,494
Antarctica	3,508,896,417		1,420,001,255		14,200,000
World – Antarctica	33,694,670,571		13,635,761,455		136,357,494

Source: CIA (2020).

so on.[1] All the while, the soil may degrade, natural and climatic challenges may threaten production, and cities may continue to expand onto fertile territory.

Any realistic plan for the future must consider how we allocate access to our earth. In the face of the growing scarcity of land resources, relative to a growing population, we will need to increase the productive capacity of land, which usually translates into increased concentration of land holdings.[2] This pressure will push an even larger share of the world's population off the land that they need for survival (and into more precarious, market-based, relationships). Those who control the most productive resources can use that control to secure greater rents and acreage. This concentration will further exacerbate national and global inequality, both economically and politically.

This is the challenge facing land management in the future. We need a management system that can facilitate the efficient, fair and sustainable use of land resources, while minimizing the economic and political inequalities that can result. If we are unable or unwilling to manage the land properly, we risk creating land markets that are unable to provide us with the essential resources we need, and/or create a level of inequality that is politically unsustainable.

This chapter addresses the challenge of land management, in five parts. The first part introduces a historical backdrop wherein we can see how markets to land were developed, both in theory and in practice. The second part introduces contemporary markets for land and the varied management regimes that sustain them. Part three introduces the concept of a differential rent and the important role it plays in generating the Natural Dividend from land. Part four describes the current state of the resource, globally, and its potential to generate a Natural Dividend. Finally, in part five, we introduce several means of securing that Natural Dividend in land.

---

1. See Creutzig (2017).
2. This argument is trickier than it appears at first glance. The inverse relationship between farm size and productivity breaks down over time *if* the land is farmed too intensively. On the other hand, very large farms tend to use only part of their land productively, while the rest lies fallow. For an elaboration of this argument, see Brigham (2009: 115–21).

An historical backdrop

The market for land is remarkably diverse, as so many different natural resources are located on, beyond, below or above it. Subsequent chapters are dedicated to each of these tangential resource sites. This chapter examines how the world manages agricultural land, including forest land. In considering how to manage these resources, we focus on their three essential qualities: land resources are renewable; land is limited and increasingly scarce; and land ownership is tightly intertwined with political power. Our objective is to help the reader to understand how we have come to allocate access to these land resources, and how this access has important distributional consequences.

This is not a particularly easy task, as our history of managing land and our justification for doing so are two very different things. This history is relevant, because land began as a common resource, freely available to everyone, but we now find it in the hands of states, communities and individuals. How did that happen?

In most countries it is difficult to trace back the original owner/title of a particular slice of territory. In these contexts, it is common to accept a given allocation of land, until some sort of war or revolution forces a new allocation. In younger countries, settled or established in the eighteenth and nineteenth centuries (e.g. in the Americas, Oceania, and Africa), and in newly formed countries (e.g. Israel, post-Soviet Russia) it is easier to trace the lines of "original" ownership and how they were allocated. For this reason, we plan to begin with the sorts of hypothetical example that have become central to the way we legitimize ownership in land, and then contrast these with the ways that ownership in land has been allocated, in practice, in more recent times.

Land management in theory

Given the difficulty of tracing original title, there have been two main approaches to justifying the prevailing allocation of land. We have already met the first, in Chapter 2, when we introduced a number of traditional and religious approaches to land rights in which private ownership was not possible, as the land belonged to us all in common, or in the form of an omnipotent God.

The justification for allocating private access to land came later, and often in the form of hypothetical thought experiments used to conjure up some form of original enclosure. In these scenarios, we are asked to imagine a pre-political world, with an abundance of land, but with few people. In this context – as with the air today – there would be little need to consider private ownership in land: people were free to take what they needed, and they could do so without affecting others. Land was seen to be abundant and ubiquitous, and people used it freely without conflict (or the need for ownership).

As access to land became scarcer, for whatever reason, this free-access scenario became less viable. After all, when land is scarce, its access creates riches. Land scarcity also fuels conflict, desperation and suffering. By the seventeenth century it became increasingly obvious that access to abundant land could not continue indefinitely, and allowing it would increase conflict, create gold-rush-like conditions and reduce efficiencies (as in the tragedy of the commons). Something needed to be done.

The solution to the challenge of scarcity was to find a *just* means of allocating access to land. In the seventeenth century there were, basically, two competing approaches to justifying private land ownership: by means of common consent, or by way of a natural right. In the end, the notion of a natural right came to dominate, as advocated most famously by John Locke (1960 [1688]),[3] who used a thought experiment, in the form of a social contract, to consider how private ownership in land was established, and to argue that the first task of government was to protect those ownership rights.

Locke argued that, in the state of nature (before government), God had provided the earth and its products to all men[4] in common: we had an equal right to use the earth's resources to secure food, clothing and shelter, as they were necessary for our survival (Locke 1960 [1688], II, ch. 5). Locke's challenge was to explain how these once common resources became legitimate private property (allowing the exclusion of others from using or owning them). Before Locke, Grotius [1625] and von Pufendorf [1672] had argued that private ownership of nature was the result of consent granted under a state of nature.[5] Locke (realizing that consent, once given, could always be revoked) countered that private property was established by natural law, in the state of nature (not by the consent of mankind).

Locke did this by asserting that the value of land was established by the amount of human labour exerted upon it. By working the land, a person could claim rightful ownership over it: a natural right (Locke 1960 [1688], II, 329–30, §28). In this simple approach, there are physical and biological limits to land ownership – as a single person or family can work only a limited amount of land. But Locke

---

3. An earlier, but less famous, version of this argument can be found in a small 1629 pamphlet by the American settler, John Winthrop (1992 [1629]).

4. It should go without saying, but these are Locke's words, from the seventeenth century. A contemporary theorist would surely note that the earth and its products belong to all of humankind in common, or to the "benefit of [hu]mankind", as is the terminology used in UNCLOS (UN 1982).

5. For a discussion that contrasts Locke's view of original ownership with that of Grotius and von Pufendorf, see Seliger (1969: 180–8).

was able to extend the reach of individual ownership by arguing that the paid labour of others can be used to claim a larger plot of land (Locke 1960 [1688], II, 343–4, §48–50). In short, our family alone might clear and work 20 acres of land, and we might afford to buy the labour of another family and extend our land holdings to 40 acres. Even in this scenario, however, there are two famous provisos in Locke's argument.[6] The right to own private property was unlimited so long as (a) no one took more than [s]he could use without allowing any of his [her] property to spoil or go to waste; and (b) there were enough common resources of comparable quality remaining for anyone who wanted to create his [her] own property (Locke 1960 [1688], II, 328–9, 332, §27, §31).

Locke justified these claims to private ownership in two different ways. The first of these is the more familiar one to the modern reader: Locke asserted that the private ownership of land can increase its productivity, relative to land that is not cared for by any particular owner (Locke 1960 [1688], II, 335–7, §37). But this argument played second fiddle to a much more important argument (for Locke) about the need for a fair distribution. Locke believed it was important to secure a *just* allocation of access to land, or risk political turmoil.[7]

Even though the labour theory of value has fallen out of fashion, Locke's approach remains central to the way we justify private ownership in land and allow its owners to reap the value that land produces. More importantly, Locke argued that the sole task of government should be the protection of this private property, secured by natural right, and that people had a right to revoke the power of government when this simple protection was no longer provided. Hence, private land ownership and political power became intertwined as two strands in the same liberal rope.

Land management in practice

In practice, the actual allocation of land rights is far less just and has little to do with individual labour, initiative or efficiency. It is politics and power, more than just consideration, that have guided the original allocation of land. Today's distribution of property is largely a function of the needs of states, conducting the business of war. Throughout history states have sought to gain and defend land,

---

6. See also Roark (2012), Nozick (1974: 178–82) and Standing (2019: 66).
7. This was not idle speculation for Locke: he had worked as the secretary of the Lords Proprietors of Carolina, from 1669 to 1675, to deal with the correspondences and negotiations between the King's proprietors and the recalcitrant settlers of Carolina. The question they struggled over was this. Who could claim rightful ownership over these new lands: the proprietors, through a royal gift/grant, or the settlers, who actually worked, improved and defended the land? See, for example, Woolhouse (2007: 91f.).

and it is the capacity of a state to control and defend land that determines the (varying) nature of property rights regimes we see in the world today.

In practice, countries secure (and lose) territory, most often by force (or the threat of force). They then decide how to distribute this territory, in a highly political fashion, with very real winners and losers. The most famous of these include the English enclosures, Scottish clearances and colonial land grants, whereby powerful interests were able to claim private ownership over once common land – forcing others off their very source of livelihood. Although we like to think that this process of appropriation was completed in the sixteenth to eighteenth centuries, it repeats itself over and over again; we often see it in the wake of changes in political authority, and with every attempt to enclose and commodify new types of nature (as we shall see in subsequent chapters).

The political nature of land allocation was most transparent in the sixteenth century, when Queen Elizabeth I granted Sir Humfrey Gylberte permission to own "all the soyle of all such lands, countries, & territories so to be discovered … with full power to dispose thereof, & of every part thereof in fee simple or other-wise, according to the order of the laws of England" (Gylberte 1578). This pattern remained evident in the allocation of newly acquired colonial lands, and the pattern of land ownership varied significantly across colonial powers (British, French, Dutch, Spanish, etc.).[8] The same political processes can be seen in the United States' original determination to own outright any and all new lands it secured (whether by force, treaty or purchase), and to decide for itself how to allocate these new lands.[9]

We see the same political process and variation in outcomes with the creation of new states, or with new regimes in old states. For example, when the state of Israel was founded in 1948, nearly all of its territory was vested in the state and was available only for 49-year, or sabbatical-length, leases. A nearly opposite result can be found in the political rubble that was once the Soviet Union, when President Mikhail Gorbachev introduced a market economy: he reallocated much of the state property acquired under the Soviet Union, and this property became the seed corn for the growth of a new breed of Russian oligarchs. When seen from a larger historical perspective, land tenure regimes tend to ride the political currents.

In short, the market for land – in practice – is inherently political: control of land is secured by force, and then allocated by political favour. These political roots are often buried under decades and centuries of exchanges, which have subsequently transformed land into something that resembles a commodity.

---

8. See Linklater (2013) and Powelson (1988).

9. Witness the explicit terms of the Treaty of Paris (1783) or the terms settled in US Supreme Court (1823) *Johnson and Graham's Lessee v William M'Intosh*.

As a consequence, the management of land varies significantly across the globe – and only one continent (Antarctica) remains in a form of common ownership.[10] The rest of the planet's land resources are allocated by national political authorities, which set the parameters for national land markets: they decide how to allocate property and how much to keep on (and off) the market, and they decide whether to encourage large or small holdings. In doing so, political authorities determine the relative scarcity of land, and how widely it is distributed.

The market for land

This section aims to describe how land markets are currently managed, and it is divided into two parts. Land markets are different from other resource markets in that the enclosure process has largely been completed, and there is already widespread expectation that land can be traded as a commodity like any other (especially in the Global North). Even so, it is important to recognize the continued existence of many different forms of land allocation (including common, public and private). The first part of this section documents that variation. In the second part, we turn to see how value is created in agricultural markets, so that we can better trace the source of the Natural Dividend from land.

Management regimes

We begin by noting that much of the original enclosure and allocation of land has already been settled. More often than not, the political focus of land management is now aimed at restricting existing ownership rights (on the margin), rather than allocating access to raw nature. For this reason, perhaps, much land is already enclosed and allocated: private interests have been granted full and permanent access to these allocated parcels (and the products these parcels produce). Indeed, in much of the world, private land ownership is increasingly understood as the default position, championed for the efficiency gains that are associated with it.

It is common to refer to land management regimes in terms of "tenure", with the term being understood as meaning the terms and conditions under which land is held, used and transacted (see Box 4.1). In other words, a tenure system is a management regime that defines the terms of access to a parcel of land, its use and the conditions under which the parcel can be transferred or sold.

---

10. Even though seven sovereign states have made territorial claims on it: Argentina, Australia, Chile, France, New Zealand, Norway and the United Kingdom.

BOX 4.1 LAND TENURE DEFINED

Land tenure is the institutional (political, economic, social, and legal) structure that determines

(a) how individuals and groups secure access to land and manage land resources (e.g. trees, minerals, pasture, and water); and
(b) the terms and conditions of this access (i.e. for how long and under what conditions these individuals and groups are allowed access).

Hence, land tenure can include both spatial and temporal dimensions, and the form of tenure is usually defined by way of statutory and/or customary law (USAID 2013).

As we argued in Chapter 2, it is more accurate to consider this access in terms of a bundle of rights, which varies significantly (USAID 2006).

For our purposes, there are two critical components to land tenure regimes: lease periods and forms of concession (or ownership). This is not to ignore the many other limitations that can be placed on land rights, but to focus on those that are most relevant to securing the Natural Dividend. In general, and following the English tradition, it is usual to distinguish between freehold and leasehold titles (UK government 2002). A *freehold* title can be thought of as a permanent (but transferable) title to the land, while *leasehold* is a title to land that is limited in time (e.g. for a term of years). Leasehold arrangements can take many different forms, including concessions, whereby the relevant authority grants the right to access under very explicit terms and limits. In terms of concession/ownership forms, it is common to distinguish between four types, which we earlier traced back to Justinian law: open access, common property, public property and private property.

Some land remains in the form of *open access*, when there is no formal or recognized claim to ownership. Although this was the historical point of departure for all land, it is relatively rare today. Antarctica is the best example of this type of "unclaimed" land, and we look more closely at these types of special cases in Chapter 8. But pockets of open access land can also be found within existing sovereign states.

In some states – and for most of human history – *common property* of land is the norm. Today, sovereign states often grant common ownership in recognition of local or indigenous claims. It has been estimated that communities actually hold as much as 65 per cent of the world's land area through customary, community-based tenure systems (Alden Wily 2011), but formal or unencumbered ownership is often withheld by the sovereign authorities. In an innovative attempt to map land formally owned and controlled by indigenous and local communities, the Rights and Resources Initiative has mapped the scale of common ownership in 64 countries covering about 82 per cent of the global land mass (Rights and Resources Initiative 2015). The results suggest that 18 per cent of the earth's total land area is formally recognized as collectively owned.

Land that is held in common can be managed and distributed in any number of ways. In Botswana, for example, the African Development Bank (AfDB) estimates that 71 per cent of the total land area is classified as collective, or "tribal", land; 26 per cent of the land is deemed "state land"; and just 3 per cent of the land is held in private (freehold) form (AfDB 2016). These freehold arrangements take the form of a lease, which is normally limited to 99 years but is renewable. The common (tribal) lands are allocated for a wider array of uses (e.g. residential, commercial, industrial and agricultural uses), for which the holders of tribal land rights are

> given certificates that provide owners perpetual and exclusive tribal land rights, except in communal grazing areas where there are no defined property rights to grazing resources. Holders of these certificates can convert them into common law leases, which can then be registered at the deeds registry. Owners then obtain a title to their land. Tribal land belongs to the state and cannot be sold unless it has been developed, in which case *the sale is deemed to be a sale of improvements and not of the land.*   (AfDB 2016: 7, emphasis added)

Although common ownership was once the norm, the most widespread form of land ownership today seems to be *public property*, whereby the land remains in the hands of the state. This public ownership might be the result of a state's unwillingness to distribute all the land at its disposal (e.g. the United States), a significant historical/colonial legacy (e.g. the United Kingdom) or the result of a political effort to retrieve previously communal or private lands into public ownership (e.g. in the wake of the communist revolutions in China and Russia).

It is not easy to find reliable cross-national statistics on land tenure regimes, but the UN's Food and Agriculture Organization (FAO) does collect data on forest ownership types, across countries, world regions and the globe. Table 4.2 provides the tenure breakdown in 2015 and distinguishes between three tenure types: publicly owned, privately owned and "other", where "other" tends to be ownership that is disputed, or in transition (FAO 2020a: 9). Here we see that nearly three-quarters of all the world's forest lands remain in public hands.

There are no comparable statistics for agricultural land (or land in general), but we can assume that much of it is also falls under public ownership. This is

Table 4.2 Share of forest tenure types, by world region, 2015

	Public	Private	Other	Total
South America	60.4%	32.4%	7.2%	19.2%
Oceania	52.7%	46.6%	0.7%	4.5%
North and Central America	60.6%	35.2%	4.3%	18.9%
Europe	88.2%	9.1%	2.8%	25.5%
Asia	76.6%	21.8%	1.7%	15.2%
Africa	70.6%	5.5%	23.9%	16.5%
World	71.3%	21.6%	7.1%	100.0%

Source: FAO (2020b).

Table 4.3 Top ten countries in terms of total landmass

	Country	Area (km²)	Percentage of earth's landmass
1	Russia	16,377,742	10.9
2	China	9,326,410	6.2
3	United States	9,147,593	6.1
4	Canada	9,093,507	6.0
5	Brazil	8,358,140	5.6
6	Australia	7,682,300	5.1
7	India	2,973,193	2.0
8	Argentina	2,736,690	1.8
9	Kazakhstan	2,699,700	1.8
10	Algeria	2,381,740	1.6
	Sum	70,777,015	47.0

Note: The CIA World Factbook provides national figures for total water area, total land area and total area. The figures here are total land area. The earth's total landmass was estimated by adding all the national "land areas", totalling 150,557,494 km²; this includes Antarctica.

Source: CIA (2020).

evident from at least two observations. First, we know that the largest states in the world, in terms of landmass, hold a significant amount of territory in public hands. Most surprising of these may be the United States (the third largest state: see Table 4.3), where the largest single landowner has always been, and remains, the federal government. Recently the US Congressional Research Service (2020: 1) estimated that the federal government owned just under one-third of all land in the United States (or roughly 640 million acres). Access to these lands can be managed in a very restrictive manner (e.g. in the form of national parks, or border protection corridors) or in a very broad manner (e.g. through the US Bureau of Land Management [USBLM]), whereby grazing or drilling rights are leased or conceded to private interests.

Concessions on US federal lands tend to be for relatively short periods of time. For example, the USBLM leases lands for livestock grazing, according to specific terms and conditions (e.g. stipulating forage use and season of use) set forth in the issued permits and leases. These leases usually cover a ten-year renewable period (USBLM n.d.a). The leasing of lands for mineral and petroleum exploitation are for a similar (ten-year) period but include both competitive and non-competitive permits (USBLM n.d.b).

Public ownership is even more prominent in China and in Russia, although the formal figures are elusive. The largest country in the world, in terms of surface area, is the Russian Federation – and much of Russian land remains in public hands, even after the privatization efforts following the fall of the Soviet Union. In 2010, for example, Kevin Cahill estimated that the Russian state still owned almost 58 per cent of all land in Russia, or 2.4 billion acres (Cahill 2010: 351).

The second largest country in the world, in terms of land area, is China – and it provides the best example of extensive public ownership in land. According to the Chinese constitution, all land in China belongs to the people, so private ownership is not allowed (in theory). This means that there is no freehold of land, only different types of leasehold, whereby the state grants use rights to groups and individuals, under leases that typically last between 30 and 70 years (Nature Conservancy 2012: 69).[11]

In practice, China employs two main types of land ownership forms: state (public) and collective (common). In both types, the state or the collective (usually a village) allocates specific use rights to groups, individuals or other entities. The collectively owned land tends to be managed by villages, and peasants are allowed to contract land from the village collective. Hence, village membership confers an inalienable right to contract land from the collective, but the right to transfer the contracted lands is restricted and somewhat ambiguous (Cheng & Chung 2017: 2681).[12] As a result, rural residents are entitled to contract land from their villages, but urban residents are not. Instead, urban residents in China are entitled to various social services provided by their municipal governments, in lieu of land rights (this is the so-called *hukou* system; see Chan 2009, 2010).

Finally, we can see the continued prominence of "public" ownership in Table 4.4's list of the world's ten largest individual landowners in 2010. This list contains only monarchs, or heads of states, who owned their huge estates in the name of their

---

11. See also https://landportal.org/book/narratives/2020/china.
12. Individual households can further contract the land out into different sub-parcels, with varying rights of transfer – for example contract land (*chengbao tian*), ration land (*kouliang tian*), responsibility land (*zeren tian*), commodity land (*shangpin tian*), private plots (*ziliu di*), etc.

Table 4.4 Ten largest individual landowners on earth, 2010

	Individual	Country	Legal claim (km²)	Share of earth
1	Queen Elizabeth II	United Kingdom	27,106,437	19.9%
2	King Abdullah	Saudi Arabia	2,347,177	1.7%
3	Pope Benedict XVI	Vatican City	716,294	0.5%
4	King Bhumibol	Thailand	509,904	0.4%
5	King Mohammed VI	Morocco	445,154	0.3%
6	Sultan Qaboos	Oman	210,437	0.2%
7	King Gyanendra	Nepal	145,687	0.1%
8	King Abdullah	Jordan	97,125	0.07%
9	Sheikh Zaid	Abu Dhabi	67,319	0.05%
10	King Wangchuck	Bhutan	44,515	0.03%
Sum			31,690,049	23.2%

Note: We recognize that this table is dated, but we are unaware of any recent updates. The individual names may change, but there is no reason to expect the pattern of ownership to have changed since 2010. The UK queen's holdings include formal ownership of the Commonwealth, including Canada – the fourth largest country in the world. These landholdings were transferred to the new king, Charles III, on her death in 2022. Kevin Cahill (2010) works in acres, but we have converted to km² (see Table 4.1). Finally, Cahill ranks owners by land value; we have ranked them by acreage and ignored the value.

Source: Cahill (2010: 14).

people (de jure, not necessarily de facto, and often unfairly). At the top of the list was the queen of the United Kingdom, who enjoyed formal ownership over all Commonwealth land, including all of Canada's 2,467,264,640 acres.[13]

What remains, then, is *private property* – apparently the least common form of land ownership in the world, even if it dominates much of the political discussion. In practice, sovereign states have to decide how much land will be placed on the market (what is left over after public and common property is secured), divide it up into discrete parcels of real estate and then provide these with a legal title that can be borrowed against and sold to a third party, unhindered. Political authorities then distribute these discrete parcels of land – in the form of a gift or grant, in exchange for a fee, or in some form of auction – and these privatized parcels are subsequently traded on the market.

In practice, of course, this private title can still be constrained by temporal limits (e.g. a 99-year lease), user limits (by zoning laws), spatial limits (e.g. limited to surface rights), buyer restrictions (e.g. by citizenship or gender), and so on. But, as a result of this parcellation process, land – as real estate – appears as a

---

13. The United Kingdom is unique in that the monarch is the sole legal owner of all land. Everyone else has one of two forms of tenure arising from the 1925 Land Registration Act: freehold or leasehold. But both types of tenure are still explicitly granted as "fee simple", which is the medieval term for the sum paid to prove that the freehold was actually a tenancy; and that the monarch was the ultimate landowner.

commodity similar to others. Over time, we tend to forget about the original terms of enclosure/privatization.

Most nation states employ a mix of tenure regimes. The United States is a good example in this regard. In addition to the strong private property rights that we usually associate with that country, the federal government is the largest single owner of lands in the country. But a large portion of US land is also owned by collective entities: community property that was originally granted by the US federal government, such as tribal reservations, educational land grants, etc. Although private tenure arrangements in the United States tend to be in freehold form, collective and public tenure arrangements tend to take leasehold forms.

In this section we have focused on two important components of land management regimes: the form of concession/ownership and the type (or length) of tenure. In this brief summary we can see that three of the four forms of "ownership" rest directly on sovereign political authority: it is the state that allocates and defends the various titles to property. The fourth form, open access, remains mostly in those areas that are not yet claimed by sovereign authority. Thus, much of the earth's land area is owned by states, or in collective forms; private ownership in land is less common than many readers might think. Although the form of ownership varies significantly, at its core lies the force of political authority. Political authorities have the power to change current arrangements, but they can also determine the relative scarcity of land available on the market, and how it is allocated.

There is also significant variation in the lengths of tenure granted to land holdings. Freeholding is mostly associated with private ownership, whereas leaseholding is widespread on public lands (e.g. leasing grazing or timber rights), as well as on lands that are held in common. As the world's forests are predominantly in public hands, it is more common to see this land being leased to private individuals and companies using a wide range of concessionary arrangements (see FAO 2001). But states and communities also employ other arrangements for allocating private (or family) access to land, most often in the form of a leasehold, with varying lengths of time – for example when a tribe in Botswana, or a village in China, decides which of its community members will be granted access to which of its lands, for whatever period of time. The very fact that land tenure systems vary so much across territory and history provides evidence of the power and influence that sovereign political authorities have over land markets.

The source of the Natural Dividend

This section considers the source of the Natural Dividend from land, and how it can be captured. This is not easy, in that the land can be used in so many different ways. As we described in Chapter 3, the Natural Dividend is the value that remains after all the necessary input costs and returns on labour and capital investments are taken out. Hence, we need to consider the different ways that value is produced by the land and then determine who can rightfully claim this value. In doing so, we show the existence of a Natural Dividend that is produced by the underlying natural resource and/or its relationship to the community (and its political representatives).

In this chapter, we focus on the differential rent, as it was originally developed with reference to land resources. This is not to ignore the impact that regulatory and locational rents can also play in producing a Natural Dividend from land; we examine the unique aspects of these other sorts of rent in subsequent chapters. Whatever their source (differential, regulatory, locational), if these rents are not formally recognized, they are easily (and unfairly) captured by the landowner or concessionaire.

Differential rents

Our understanding of the differential rent grows straight out of the classical economic tradition described in Chapter 3, as represented in the work of the physiocrats, Adam Smith, David Ricardo, Karl Marx, Henry George, and others. This tradition begins by recognizing that land is naturally divided into more and less productive sites, and that the most productive sites will enjoy a windfall, or unearned gain, after all the necessary costs and fair (competitive) returns on labour and capital have been paid out.

The origins of the differential rent can be traced back to Ricardo, who described it as "that portion of the produce of the earth, which is paid to the landlord for the use of the original and indestructible powers of the soil. It is often, however, confounded with the interest and profits of capital, and, in popular language, the term is applied to whatever is annually paid by a farmer to his landlord" (Ricardo 1971 [1817]: 91). Ricardo described this productive advantage by using a number of hypothetical examples from farming (but also mining). Box 4.2 provides a similar example, inspired by Ricardo's writing. It is important to realize that the *difference* in productive capacity, which attracted Ricardo's attention, is not limited to farmland, but can be found in any natural resource: some wind farm sites are more productive than others; some mines are more productive than others; some aquaculture sites are more productive than others; etc. It is this difference that creates the unearned rent – hence *differential rent*.

Because of Ricardo, with some help from Marx and George, this (differential) form of rent may be familiar to modern readers. In light of this approach we can divide natural resources into more and less productive sites and recognize that these differences are the result of an accident of nature, not the effort, ingenuity or capital of the resource owner/holder. Those who secure the most productive sites

---

BOX 4.2 FRUITS OF THE VALLEY: A STORY ABOUT DIFFERENTIAL RENT

Imagine a pristine, unsettled mountain valley that contains productive and unproductive agricultural sites. These productivity differences are accidents of natural history. The first people who move into this valley would choose the most productive sites – most likely at the bottom of the valley, perhaps near a river. (As this is just a story, we can conveniently ignore the question of ownership rights and the role of government in recognizing and legitimizing the property claims.) Over time, these original settlers are able to produce and sell the products of their land, and the valley develops a reputation for its productivity. Rumours of the valley's productive potential spread, and new settlers arrive, hoping to cash in. As more and more settlers arrive, the best land is taken, and the latest settlers are forced to farm on land this is less productive: on the rocky soils high above the valley floor (and the river running through it). The latest settlers find the remaining farmland so unproductive that they can barely scratch out an existence. The first settler, on the most fertile property, is able to enjoy significant wealth; the last settler, on the least productive plot, is barely able to survive. Ricardo explains the difference between these two extremes with reference to differences in the underlying productivity of the earth, when harnessed by labour. This, in a story, is the differential rent.

Inspired by Ricardo (1971 [1817]: ch. 2, "On rent", esp. 93–8)

---

are able to harvest a windfall, or unearned gain, after all the necessary costs and returns on labour and capital have been paid out. This differential rent will vary from year to year – and some years it may be absent or even negative. But, over time, the most productive resource sites will accumulate significant rents, while the least productive resource sites can only break even, and are incapable of generating rent.

It is important to underline that the differential rent is derived from the natural productive capacity of the land. This is what economists often refer to as the "extensive margins", or what Marx called "differential rent 1", or DR1. When defined in this way, the rent does *not* include the capital improvements that the landowner might make on the land to increase its productive value (e.g. by adding irrigation, access roads, barns, fence lines, etc.).[14] Such capital improvements can have a significant effect on the land's productive capacity. Consequently, the effects of these investments must be recognized and rewarded – but they fall

---

14. This type of rent is often referred to as the "intensive margins", what Marx called "differential rent 2" (DR2), or which are today often referred to as "quasi-rents".

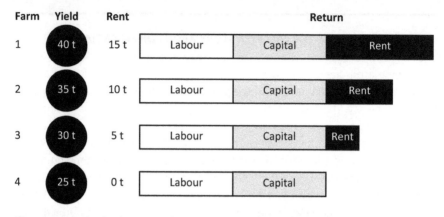

Figure 4.1 Differential rent: simple view

Notes: Each farm is equal in size, capital and labour inputs; in particular, each farm is one hectare in size, employs one full-time farmer and spends $1,000 in the course of a year. The variety in yield is completely attributable to natural factors (not capital/labour investments). t = tonnes.
Source: Authors.

outside what we mean by rent (and these legitimate rewards are paid out before the rent is calculated).

To help us conceptualize the differential rent, we can consider two related examples. The first is depicted in Figure 4.1, which provides a simple illustration of how holders of the most fertile land can reap an unearned rent. The underlying logic is simple: as labour and capital goods are mobile, and presumed to be uniform, we can expect (along with the classical economists, from whom this argument is derived) that their returns (wages and profits) should also be uniform. After all, in a truly competitive market, wages and profits should be constrained/equalized by the forces of competition (as we saw in the discussion around Figure 3.2). As land is not mobile, and varies in productive quality, the returns on land cannot equalize in the same way (as returns on labour and capital) and will vary along with its productivity.

In Figure 4.1, we limit the scope of productive land to four hay farms that vary only in terms of their productive capacity. Each farm is equally large (one hectare) and exposed to equal amounts of invested labour (one full-time farmer) and capital (say $1,000). Any difference in annual yield, then, must be attributed to the productive quality of the underlying farmland.[15] In this example, farm

---

15. This is a point of difference between Ricardo and Marx, concerning whether the rent is purely the result of the productive capacity of land or whether it also depends on prevailing socio-economic relations; see, for example, Ward and Aalbers (2016: 1765–6). For the purposes of our argument, these differences are irrelevant.

1 is the most fertile, producing 40 tonnes of hay on its one hectare (see the second column); farm 2 is a little less so, producing 35 tonnes; and farm 4 is on the margin of production: it can produce only 25 tonnes of hay with the same amount of labour and capital (as used in the other farms).

The price of hay in this imagined market would be set by the cost of production in farm 4 (on what is called the margins of productivity). This means that the more productive farms (1 to 3) would enjoy additional returns to their owners, as a result of their more productive land. In this example, the most productive farm, farm 1, enjoys a differential rent worth 15 tonnes of hay. This productive land is obviously scarcer than land with a more average yield, and more of this land cannot be produced to satiate higher demand.

The size of this differential rent will vary from year to year, depending on demand and the capacity of the market to meet it (e.g. weather conditions or war). Over time, the farmer who is granted access to farm 1 will accumulate rents. These rents are a windfall to the farmer – a result of having a monopoly hold on the best land.[16] This monopoly hold is provided by the political authorities (which recognize the landowner's legal tenure) that protect the farmer's right to keep the land (should others want to farm that same land).

This example can be depicted in another way. In Figure 4.2, we present what might be called a Heckscher–Salter[17] diagram, in which it is possible to denote the differential rent generated by each productive unit, and distinguish it from the unit costs of production (which includes profit). This figure is created by inversely ranking producers in a resource market by their unit costs (e.g. production price per kg production). We assume that these differences in productivity levels are site-dependent: that some sites are naturally more productive than others. This resource market might be for land, oil fields, mines, aquaculture sites, wind sites, etc.; and we might think of the producers as individual farms/wells/mines. For the purposes of discussion, we think of these individual producer units as "farms", like the farms in Figure 4.1. Hence, the most productive farm is number 1 (nearest the axis), and each additional farm is ranked in terms

---

16. When land is not freely available, exclusive ownership functions as a barrier against the investment of capital upon uncultivated soil. This is what distinguishes land from other commodities, for which there is always a ready supply of inputs available in the market. New land cannot be tilled until that barrier is removed by the payment of rent.

17. The apparent originators of this graph are Førsund and Hjalmarsson (1974), who combine Salter's (1960) diagram using sorted unit costs with Heckscher's (1918) market price line. Hence the supply curve is generated by smoothing out the distinct unit costs associated with individual producers, ranked by decreasing productivity. This figure has been used by Flaaten and Pham (2019) and Skonhoft (2020) to demonstrate the existence of what we call the regulatory rent and distinguish it from the differential rent. See the discussion on regulatory rents in the following chapter for further elaboration.

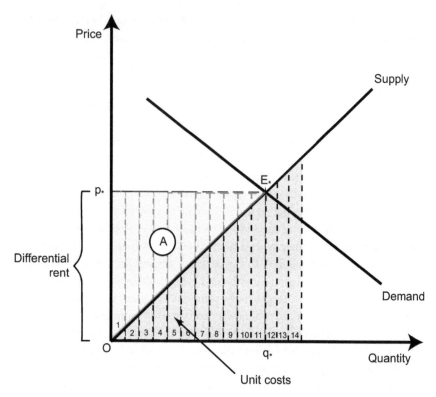

Figure 4.2 Differential rent: elaborate view
Note: See text for clarification.
Source: Authors.

of *decreasing* productive potential (higher unit costs), heading outward from the axis. In other words, farm 2 is less productive than farm 1, and farm 14 is the least productive farm, in Figure 4.2.

We can now use this ranking of productive farms to draw a (smoothed-out) supply curve, similar to the one found in Figure 3.2. We can then assume that the demand curve is also downward-facing, so that an equilibrium point, E., is determined in the same manner as in Figure 3.2. The productivity of each farm is measured along the horizontal axis, and the vertical axis measures the (running) average costs per unit produced.[18] That point, where supply meets

18. We recognize that there are some awkward elements in this graph, but they are not important. For example, the supply curve should not run through the origin, as this would mean zero operating costs per produced unit for the most efficient firm. In addition, we have made each farm column "thick", for purposes of illustration and interpretation, but this becomes a problem when smoothing them out to create the supply curve. We would like to thank Anders Skonhoft for drawing our attention to these challenges.

demand, generates a specific quantity of the resource commodity (q_*), at a specific price (p_*). This is the price that clears the market.

The advantage of this sort of figure is that it allows us to clearly see the effect of the differential rent – both at the individual level (farm by farm) and for the community as a whole. In Figure 4.2 we can see how the most productive farm (1) is able to produce land-based commodities at a much lower price than the market-clearing price (p_*). The result is a significant surplus for the individual farm owner (farm 1) that stretches as a vertical rectangle (1) above the supply line, from O to p_*. This surplus is not in any way related to the insight, investment or effort of the farmer; the difference is attributable to an accident of nature. Indeed, the first 11 farms in Figure 4.2 are able to produce commodities below the market price, and the first ten of these will enjoy a differential rent. The productivity level of farm 11 is just barely sufficient to clear the price threshold, and that farm will not secure a rent (but its owner still enjoys her requisite profit), while all the farms that are less productive than farm 11 (to the right of farm 11 – i.e. 12, 13 and 14) will be unable to survive in the market (in the absence of some form of subsidy).

In this figure, we assume that the unit cost estimates include a return on investment and risk. In deciding where to place their money, capitalists need to compare the returns on investment from different sectors, and then invest their money in projects that will generate the largest rewards, *ceteris paribus*. In a competitive market for capital, we can expect these returns on investment to equalize, as any super-profit would attract new entrants to the investment market, and erode the surplus, described in relation to Figure 3.2. Hence, we can assume that the returns on risk and capital are the same across the entire sector, and that the rate of return should be roughly equal to what we find in similar industries nearby.[19]

But land is not mobile or easily substituted. In the market for land, the return will vary across resource sites, depending on their level of natural productivity, relative to the farm that is just able to produce under the market-clearing price (p_*). These differences can be seen in the varying surplus going to each farm in Figure 4.2: the shrinking rectangles above the diagonal supply line to the equalization price line (p_*). Each farm, then, is able to secure a differential rent that varies with its natural productivity: a windfall that comes on top of all costs and profits paid.

Figure 4.2 also helps us locate the cumulative rents generated by nature, however, and these are significant. When we aggregate the differential rents accumulated by each farm, we can see that the natural resource produces a

---

19. This is not a controversial assumption to make and is a common one in most studies of resource rent and RRTs. See, for example, Greaker and Lindholt (2019) and Garnaut and Clunies Ross (1975, 1983).

surplus that is equal to the triangle OE.p., marked "A" in Figure 4.2. If political authorities do not tax the resource, in an effort to collect this cumulative differential rent, then farm owners are able to pocket this windfall, in the guise of profit.

In this section we have focused on the differential rent, but individual parcels of land can also generate regulatory and locational rents. We introduce these alternative forms of rent in the chapters that follow. For now, it is necessary to realize that these three types of resource rent share many qualities and aggregate as a Natural Dividend. First, these different types of rent are all independent of ownership form: Natural Dividends are produced in public, community- and privately owned property. But the distributional consequences of the ownership form can be significant. When land is publicly or collectively owned, the Natural Dividend can be distributed by providing equal access, by rotating access to the most productive or locationally advantaged sites and/or by limiting the tenure period, so that it cannot be monopolized by a particular interest. In this way, political and community authorities can ensure that the most productive and conveniently located sites are not monopolized by powerful interests. When land is held in private form, however, the Natural Dividend appears as a sort of windfall to the landowner. This has enormous political and economic consequences.

In addition, the Natural Dividend will vary over time, depending on a number of rather arbitrary factors (such as demand and varying conditions of production, including weather and consumer preferences). In recognizing this, it makes sense for political authorities to allocate access to land in a way that limits tenure over time – for example, by means of a concessionary agreement, or limited leasehold – which returns the land to the original (public) hands at the end of the agreed-upon period of time. It should go without saying that the length of tenure needs to be long enough to encourage productive investments and to provide sufficient time for the investor to recover her costs/rewards. But a limited period of tenure allows the authorities to change the terms of that tenure in ways that can reflect the changing nature of the Natural Dividend over longer periods of time.

Finally, Natural Dividends will accumulate and grow over time. If political authorities are unable to rotate access to these rent-producing sites, or to tax the Natural Dividend, it will pile up in private hands, exacerbating inequalities.

Value creation

We now need to consider how these different components of value are distributed. Land can be used in many different ways – for example as a field of hay, the site for an apartment building or as a forest. In deciding how to allocate value, we

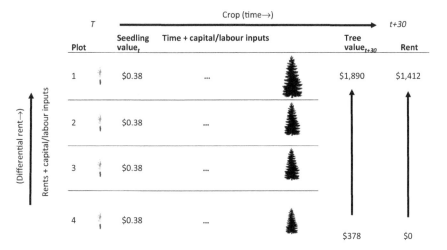

Figure 4.3 Land and crop values

Note: See text for clarification. Each plot is of equal size, but plot 1 is five times more productive than plot 4.

Source: Authors.

might have chosen any one of these crops (hay, apartment buildings, lumber, etc.) – as land generates two types of value: one that is associated with the land itself, and another one associated with the use of the land (i.e. the crop).[20] In this case, we can use a hypothetical plot of land to grow Douglas fir trees and consider how the value of the timber, and the value of the land, change over time.

The value of any crop changes over time. For an apartment, the value of the building diminishes over time; for a tree, it grows over time. To reap this increase in value, the owner of a concession on forest lands first prepares the land, plants a seedling, tends to it from year to year and then harvests that seedling (now a mature tree) after a long period of time, say 30 years. Figure 4.3 elaborates on this conceptual skeleton, by adding some market details. We might begin with a baseline calculation of an individual tree: in 2021 a Douglas fir seedling sells for $0.38, and a mature, knot-free sawlog that is 30 feet tall and 12 inches wide is worth $378.[21] We can then assume that this market price is set by a tree grown on the least productive plot (plot 4). The added value (the difference between the value of the cut log and the unplanted seedling) is determined by the returns

---

20. As we shall see in the following chapter, this situation is quite different from how we manage marine resources, where nobody is allowed to own the underlying "sea", and only the products of the sea are privatized.

21. These figures are from 2000, but are not unreasonable now. Our calculations come from Tree Plantation (2000).

to capital and labour and any additional capital inputs (e.g. tractor, chain saw) over the years.

But some land is more productive for tree farming than others, and some land is closer to the sawmill (or train tracks) than others. To simplify, we focus on productive capacity and the differential rent that results. To establish the value of this differential rent, we begin by recognizing that low-productive Douglas fir sites are about five times less productive than high-productive sites.[22]

This means that a forest planted on plot 1 will produce five times more lumber than a forest planted on plot 4. To convey this difference in productivity, across plots, we might image that a single tree in plot 1 will grow to be five times taller, or worth five times more, than a tree planted in plot 4 (i.e. it would be worth $1,890, compared to $378). As the returns on capital and labour, as well as the cost of capital inputs, should be the same across these four forest plots (in a competitive market), the concession holder on plot 1 is able to walk away with a significant added value, or differential rent, at each harvest. This surplus value is not earned in any way but is a function of the concessionaire having exclusive access to a scarce resource. It is a private taking of Nature's Dividend.

This differential rent will be accrued (and vary) at each harvest. If the use of the land does not reduce its productivity, then these rents will accrue to whoever has been granted access to the land. If the land is held by one family, indefinitely, then the value of the accumulated rents can be much larger than the value of the land itself (this is because the rent is dynamic; the sale of land is not). The value of the land might increase because of capital investments made by the concessionaire (e.g. the addition of irrigation or service roads) – and these investments should be rewarded – but the underlying productivity of the land is not a result of the concessionaire, and it is unfair for her to pocket the value that results.

State of the rent

Given the plethora of ways that land can produce value, it is impossible to map out the global distribution of our most productive lands. After all, each type of land usage will have its most productive plots: the most productive land for farming rice will be different from the most productive land for growing trees, and/or building a housing development. Even if there is a great deal of land in the world that can produce rice, the world's *most* productive plots for rice farming will always be scarce.

---

22. In particular, a low-productive site produces 100 ft³/acre year, or 4,400 ft³/acre in total, while a high-productive site can produce 400 ft³/acre a year; 22,000 ft³/acre in total. These figures come from University of California (n.d.).

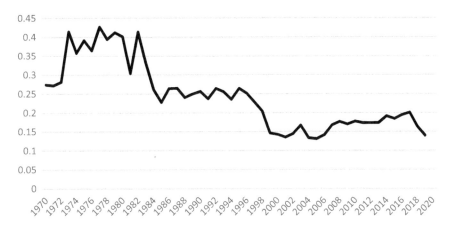

Figure 4.4 Global forest rents, percentage of GDP, 1970–2020

Note: The World Bank calculates forest rents by the roundwood harvest multiplied by the product of regional prices and a regional rental rate.

Source: World Bank (n.d.a).

This variety also makes it difficult to secure any comparative figures to demonstrate the existence and size of various land rents (and/or where they might lie).[23] The productive quality and locational advantages will vary within countries, but also across countries. After all, we cannot expect farmers in Norway (a country made mostly of rocks) to compete with those in Poland or the United States. Such is the fate of natural resource allocation: its distribution is random from a political perspective.

To generate a rough estimate of the potential Natural Dividends produced by the land, we can turn to the World Bank's measure of "natural resource rents", which includes a component indicator for "forest rents". The World Bank's "natural resource rents" indicator calculates the difference between the price of a commodity and the average cost of producing it, then multiplies the result with the physical quantities that are harvested/extracted, to determine the rents for each commodity as a share of GDP (see World Bank 2011a). In this way, the World Bank uses rent as a means to see whether countries are liquidating their capital stock (draining non-renewable resources, or overharvesting forests). The "forest rents" indicator uses the amount of roundwood harvested in a country, multiplied by the product of regional prices and a regional rental rate (World Bank n.d.a).

Figure 4.4 shows that the global rents from forest land are relatively small (e.g. contrast with Figure 7.4, on global oil rents). When we break the numbers down

---

23. There are private company estimates, but these data are proprietary, expensive and beyond our budget as public sector researchers.

Table 4.5 Country forest rents and areas, 2020

		Rents/GDP	Acres (2005)
Largest forest rent countries			
1	Solomon Islands	16.4%	5,367,125
2	Liberia	12.4%	7,793,698
3	Burundi	9.2%	375,600
4	Guinea-Bissau	8.6%	5,120,020
5	Central African Republic	8.3%	56,228,788
6	Congo, Democratic Republic	7.0%	330,157,258
7	Uganda	6.1%	8,962,506
8	Sierra Leone	6.0%	6,805,277
9	Mozambique	5.5%	47,597,404
10	Malawi	5.1%	8,406,519
Largest forest area countries			
1	Russian Federation	0.3%	1,998,562,147
2	Brazil	0.6%	1,180,416,598
3	Canada	0.1%	766,357,241
4	United States	0.0%	748,948,680
5	China	0.1%	487,513,849
6	Australia	0.2%	404,456,849
7	Congo, Democratic Republic	7.0%	330,157,258
8	Indonesia	0.4%	218,675,747
9	Peru	0.1%	169,865,057
10	India	0.2%	167,292,691

Notes: The rents/GDP data come from the World Bank (n.d.a) and the acres data from the FAO (2005), and the ranking of the largest forest area countries comes from the FAO (2020c: 10).

Sources: World Bank (n.d.a) and FAO (2005, 2020c).

into their country components, as we do in Table 4.5, we can see that the largest forest rents (as a percentage of GDP) are mostly found in states with relatively small forest holdings. With the exception of the Democratic Republic of the Congo, states with the largest forest areas tend to generate relatively low forest rents, as a percentage of GDP. This is probably an artefact of the country's size and level of wealth (large GDP).

Because forests tend to be state-owned (see Table 4.2), much of their harvesting is governed by concessionary agreements. In theory, this should facilitate the capture of rents; in practice, this does not appear to be happening. Evidence from a number of countries suggests that countries are unable (or unwilling) to secure their forest rents. In other words, most of the land's productive capacity is being given away freely to the concession holder. Even in forest-rich countries, governments are securing less than 30 per cent of the rent from timber (Heine, Batmanian & Hayde 2020: 15). Consider, for example, Canada, which is generally assumed to employ a fairly successful forest concession regime. Canada has been criticized for negotiating their concessions (rather than auctioning them off), and for agreeing to low stumpage[24] prices (see Gray 2003; Myers 2001).

Unfortunately, there is no consolidated global data on forest concessions (van Hensbergen 2018: 11), so it is difficult to compare the terms of different concessionary agreements. John Gray provides a useful overview of 23 different revenue mechanisms related to timber production (Gray 2002: 90ff., tab. A1), and he notes that one of these could be an RRT (revenue mechanism no. 12, 95–6) – but he tells us that it has *not yet been applied to the forest sector* (96). It appears that the most common revenue mechanism employed in timber concession is a requirement that the contractor pay for timber rights on a volume-extracted or area basis, or some combination of the two (van Hensbergen 2016: 1). These sorts of fee-based system are entirely incapable of capturing the Natural Dividend, as they do not collect data on the contractor's costs, revenues and returns.

As with agricultural land, more generally, countries tend to tax forest resources with an eye on stimulating production, rather than securing the Natural Dividend. With agricultural land there is often the added incentive to maintain or boost incomes for farmers (often an important political constituency), with significant effect on world agricultural markets. Indeed, it is broadly recognized that agriculture is the most distorted sector of the world economy (see, e.g., Panagariya 2005), in that production is heavily subsidized in the developed world. And the largest landowners tend to benefit the most from these types of distortion.[25]

Securing the Natural Dividend from land

We have endeavoured to show how the Natural Dividend is a result of nature and our regulating access to that nature. When political authorities grant exclusive access to the most productive land, they are also granting access to the Natural Dividend. In recognizing this, political authority may want to secure a larger share of that Dividend for their constituents. This section considers how this can be done.

To ensure that the Natural Dividend remains in public hands, the authorities can employ one of three options. First, land might be allocated in a more equal

---

24. Stumpage is the price paid for the right to harvest timber from a particular piece of property. Traditionally, the price was determined by the number of trees to be harvested (i.e. per stump); today it is more common to use a standardized measure, such as m^3, board feet or tonnes of timber to be harvested.

25. The enormity of subsidies granted to agriculture landowners in the developed world is already well documented. See, among others, OECD (2016, n.d.a, n.d.b), Food and Land Use Coalition (2019) and World Resources Institute (2019: 461, fig. 36-2).

fashion, with every resident assigned an equal slice of high-productivity sites. In considering this option, we recognize that the productivity of land will vary significantly with its proposed usage (e.g. land that is optimal for commercial development may not be optimal for farming rice) – but we will sideline that issue for the time being. Although it is egalitarian, this solution is problematic in two ways: (a) it would require an unfair taking and redistribution of land that is already allocated (or the liquidation of public lands, flooding land markets and lowering land values); and (b) it is likely to be inefficient, as the individual concession or landholding will be too small to secure economies of scale.

Second, political authorities can rotate access to the most productive lands, so that no single interest is allowed to accumulate rents. In this way, the Natural Dividend can be shared by more members of the community. This is already done in some places, where local community/political authorities can use the concession/lease terms to distribute the Natural Dividend in a fair and equitable manner, by ensuring equal (and limited) access to the most productive and best-positioned sites, or to draw up the concessionary arrangement in a way that secures the Natural Dividend.

This solution is not possible when land is held privately, in the form of freeholder arrangements. Under these conditions, political authorities can employ the third option: determine the size of the Natural Dividend being generated in each landholding, and tax it accordingly. This can be done simply by assessing the change of value in the underlying property differently from the change in value as a result of capital improvements and taxing the increased values at different rates. This option does not require a change in the ownership structure, or a public taking (and redistribution) of private lands. All that is required is that the political authority recognizes the existence of the Natural Dividend and introduce a fiscal mechanism that can secure it on behalf of the public.

This is neither a new nor a radical idea: the notion of taxing land rents has been around for centuries, and it has been practised in a number of very different political contexts. Neither is it rocket science: land tax systems are fairly straightforward and frequently introduced by local political authorities, with limited resources. A brief description of how this is done in practice can be found in Box 4.3.

More than anyone else, Henry George is most frequently associated with this approach to land management. Since George, there have been many attempts to demonstrate the utility and benefit from introducing an RRT on land. Indeed, there is very broad consensus among economists, across several centuries, about the attractiveness of such a tax, as it is seen to be both beneficial and economically efficient (Mirrlees *et al.* 2011; Corlett *et al.* 2018). This is because an RRT provides a broad, stable and identifiable tax base that is correlated with wealth;

BOX 4.3 TAXING THE NATURAL DIVIDEND FROM LAND IN PRACTICE

The first step is a conceptual one, whereby we think about the title to land as a usufructuary leasehold rather than fee-simple property.[1] This means that we recognize that natural resources belong to us in common, but we allow individual interests to lease them from us for a period of time.

The next steps are more practical. The political authorities need to assess the market value of the land and any improvements made to it (e.g. buildings). These two market values (land and capital improvements) are then taxed differently (see also Box 3.2).

Because the growth in value to the land portion is not the result of the landowners' efforts – but the result of community activity (such as new roads), and/or the difference in natural productivity levels – the land (site) value is taxed at a higher rate. In this way, the land's increased value is returned to the community. This value-based levy on unimproved land captures the rent and discourages speculation and/or the idle use of scarce (land) resources.

By holding land, but not utilizing it, the speculator takes productive land out of circulation, in hopes that its value will rise (without productive investment from the speculator). Meanwhile, this land cannot be used by others, and its market value is inflated by speculative trading. Large areas of land can be bought up by absent owners, who simply wait for its value to increase, while "buildings deteriorate, neighbourhoods lose their natural leaders and stabilizers, and communities disintegrate leaving slums and blight, crime and arson, public charges and vandalism … The sum of these factors makes for an inefficient market in land titles" (Gaffney 1994: 78).

By taxing the differential rent – an RRT on land, or a so-called land value tax (LVT) – political authorities provide a strong disincentive to speculate in land. Any exogenous increase in value is taxed, making it costly to "hold". In reducing its speculative value, this land is returned to the market, where it can be used more productively.

Capital improvements to the land are taxed at a lower rate (e.g. at the level used on other commercial incomes), so that, when a house, road or a fence is built, the resulting increase in value is due to the concessionaire. By taxing this added value at a lower level, political authorities can incentivize capital improvements and their upkeep.

By taxing the Natural Dividend on land, authorities can stimulate improvements to it, discourage land speculation, reduce its market price (by the present value of future taxes) and reduce the revenue that is required to be raised from other taxes (see HenryGeorge.org n.d.a).

---

1. There are some forbidding legal terms here. *Usufruct* is the legal right of using and enjoying the fruits (profit) of something belonging to another. A *leasehold* implies a temporary right to hold land, whereby the tenant (lessee) holds rights of real property from a landlord. These rights usually include the right to occupy land or a building for a given length of time. *Fee simple*, by contrast, is a form of freehold ownership, in which there are no temporal limits placed on the ownership but a recognition that this ownership is contingent on the permissions of a higher power (political authority).

---

it does not distort market behaviour in a negative way; it can promote the development of underutilized land; and it is immanently just, in that it taxes the unearned increment in the value of the land (Hughes *et al.* 2020: 1).

Economists sometimes use the term "land value tax" when referring to an RRT applied to land values. Support for LVTs can be found across a remarkably broad spectrum of leading economists and former Nobel laureates. As Mark Blaug reports:

> *Paul Samuelson* called LVT "the useful tax on measured land surplus." *Milton Friedman* agreed that "a pure land tax is one of the least bad taxes that is possible." *James Tobin* thought that it was "in principle ... a good idea to tax unimproved land, and particularly capital gains on it. Theory says that we should try to tax items with zero or low elasticity, and those include land sites." *James Buchanan* asserted that "the landowner who withdraws land from productive use to a purely private use should be required to pay higher, not lower, taxes." *Robert Solow* argued that "users of land should not be allowed to acquire rights of indefinite duration for single payments. For efficiency, for adequate revenue and for justice, every user of land should be required to make an annual payment to the local government equal to the current rental value of the land that he or she prevents others from using."
>
> (Blaug 2000: 283, emphasis added)

In an open letter to Mikhail Gorbachev in 1990, 30 prominent US economists urged him to introduce an LVT as part of the privatization strategy to be employed in the former Soviet Union. These economists noted:

> It is important that the rent of land be retained as a source of government revenue. While the governments of developed nations with market economies collect some of the rent of land in taxes, they do not

collect nearly as much as they could, and they therefore make unnecessarily great use of taxes that impede their economies – taxes on such things as incomes, sales and the value of capital.

Social collection of the rent of land and natural resources serves three purposes. First, it guarantees that no one dispossesses fellow citizens by obtaining a disproportionate share of what nature provides for humanity. Second, it provides revenue with which governments can pay for socially valuable activities without discouraging capital formation or work effort, or interfering in other ways with the efficient allocation of resources. Third, the resulting revenue permits utility and other services that have marked economies of scale or density to be priced at levels conducive to their efficient use.   (Tideman *et al.* 1990)

Clearly, an RRT on land finds broad support among professional economists. This does not mean that it can (or should) be seen as the only viable tax, or that it can replace all other taxes. Although this was the assertion of Henry George and many of his fellow travellers, it is unlikely that a single land RRT could secure enough funds to defray the expenses of modern government (see Blaug 2000: 278–9).[26] But it can still play a very important role in providing needed funds for political authority, discouraging the unproductive use of scarce resources and securing a more just distribution of the gifts of nature.

It is for this reason that RRTs on land have been employed in a remarkable array of political contexts over time: from pre-communist China (see, e.g., Silagi 1984, Peterson & Hsiao 2000, Chandler 1982 and Foldvary 2004: 175) to Australia, Canada, Estonia, Namibia, New Zealand and South Africa, and even in a number of different states and cities across the United States (see, e.g., Cord 1979; Chandler 1982; Andelson 2000; Hughes *et al.* 2020).[27]

Conclusion

This chapter covers a great deal of conceptual and empirical territory. We began with a brief history of land management regimes. Because the land market developed early, it has become a convenient baseline for thinking about how we should manage other national resource markets. For this reason alone, it is

---

26. All in all, it would seem that "[t]he totality of land rent and site rentals is much greater than generally recognized" (Foldvary 2004: 174), but Mason Gaffney (1970) estimates that site values are probably more than half of all real estate market value.

27. For surveys on the implementation of LVTs worldwide, see Andelson (2000) and HenryGeorge. org (n.d.b).

necessary to consider carefully the distributional consequence of previous land management regimes.

The focus of our attention has been trained on exploring how land resources can produce a Natural Dividend, and how that Dividend can be secured by political authorities. Although land also generates regulatory and locational rents, we have used this chapter to introduce differential rents and to demonstrate their importance in establishing the (market) value of the sundry products of the land.

Land markets tend to be the most developed markets for natural resources, and the literature and practice of taxing the Natural Dividend from land is among the most established. There is a broad consensus among economists about the utility and fairness of taxing the Natural Dividend on land, and this consensus has spanned at least two centuries.

Remarkably, this consensus has never been truly exploited (see, e.g., Blaug 2000: 28). Although LVT regimes have been introduced in a variety of different contexts, we share the surprise of Hughes *et al.* (2020: 1) that, "despite these seemly compelling economic arguments, land value taxation is not widely implemented". Worse, land markets in the Global North are famously bloated, as political authorities shower subsidies on landowners directly and indirectly (by allowing them to abscond with the Natural Dividend). These subsidies produce a number of costly effects, as noted at the end of Chapter 3, including overcapitalization and reliance on exotic technologies, increased resource inefficiencies, overconsumption and public resource deprivation – but these are accepted and swallowed for reasons that remain untested.

We can do better. Given sufficient political will, we can introduce land management regimes that can secure the Natural Dividend and distribute it more evenly across the community. Doing so would allow political authorities to increase efficiencies of production and the size of landholdings without an increase in economic and political inequality. Introducing an RRT on land could provide better utilization of scarce land resources and discourage speculation in those resources. Finally, political authority could use this type of RRT as a new and significant source of government revenues.

The market for land is the most familiar of our natural resource markets. It is also the most politicized, in that we have long recognized how power is closely aligned with property ownership and control. As James Harrington noted, as early as 1656, power clearly follows property (Harrington (1992 [1656]). It may be for this reason that our approach to managing access to land has received so much attention and yet varies so significantly across time and countries.

By contrast, our approach to managing marine resources – in the sea that surrounds sovereign territory – receives remarkably little attention. The next chapter directs our attention to this lacuna and considers how we might better manage our water resources.

5

THE SEA: THE MARKET FOR SALMON

In this book, land is placed squarely in the middle of a three-dimensional study. We do this because the world has a great deal of experience in managing land resources, and this experience is bound to influence our approach to the management of other natural resources. In subsequent chapters we consider the management of resources that exist above and below the land. In this chapter we move laterally: from land to the water that surrounds it. In doing so, we move from the solid to the soft, in more ways than one.

To paraphrase Arthur C. Clarke, ours is a watery planet, yet we call it "earth". As we noted in the introduction, seven-tenths of the earth's surface is covered by water. Because the sea is so vast, and because it runs so deep, something like 95 per cent of the habitable space on our planet is found under water. And yet the management of these vast marine resources receives remarkably little public or academic attention.[1]

Like the resources found on land, water is also essential to our survival – in both its fresh and salty variants. This is both clear and obvious with respect to fresh water, which Vaclav Smil (2022: 173) describes as "a perfect example of an almost universally mismanaged resource, with the added complication of highly uneven access".[2] Indeed, on 28 July 2010 the UN General Assembly explicitly recognized the human right to clean drinking water and sanitation with UN Resolution 64/292 (UN 2010). But our reliance on water stretches beyond this important UN resolution. In addition to our need to consume water, we need water to irrigate our crops and to provide habitats for additional human food sources, and water – in the form of hydroelectric power – is an important source of energy. These are the many aspects of water management that we wish we could address; each has its own list of challenges, and each has the potential to generate a Natural Dividend. But our focus in this chapter is on fish; in particular, on the farming of fish.

---

1. A recent exception can be found in Armstrong (2022).
2. For a recent survey on the global water supply, see Biswas, Tortajada and Rohner (2018).

There is no market for "sea"

Our traditional approach to managing the sea could not be more different from our approach to managing the land. On land, we have gone to great lengths to draw boundaries, creating discrete territorial parcels with distinct concessionaires or owners (be they nations, communities or individuals). This has created a market for land, in addition to the markets for products of the land. In the previous chapter we learned how the nature and scope of these tenure regimes varies significantly across time and space, but the utility of parcellation is seldom questioned. In the name of both justice and efficiency, we have embraced the notion that land should be enclosed into distinct parcels. In addition, many would argue that the privatization of these parcels is necessary to secure their efficient utilization.

Unlike land, there is no market for "sea". On the hard (*terra firma*), we commodify land and allow land "owners" to reap the fruits of its bounty. At sea, we have not been able, or willing, to enclose the resource in the same way. Instead, we license access to particular products of the ocean: we allow individuals to take (catch) products from our common resource and claim ownership upon capture. For this reason, the focus of this chapter – unlike the chapter on land – is trained on the products of our ocean, rather than the ocean itself.

The difference in how we approach land and sea tenure has important consequences for how we approach the management of marine (versus land) resources. Since (at least) the 1608 publication of Hugo Grotius' *Mare Liberum* [*The Freedom of the Seas*],[3] international law has treated the oceans and their resources as common property, or *res communis*. But the scope of this common property has been receding in recent decades, as territorial states have managed to claim more and more sovereignty over the seas that surround them.

This reduced scope is clearly evident in the 1982 United Nations Convention on the Law of the Sea,[4] which holds that "[t]he sovereignty of a coastal State extends, beyond its land territory and internal waters [to an area] described as the *territorial sea*" (UN 1982: art. 2, §1, emphasis added). This sovereign control covers the water, the seabed and the airspace above the territorial sea and is subject to certain conditions (such as the right of innocent passage for maritime transit: see UN 1982: art. 2, §§2–3). As can be seen in Figure 5.1, this territorial

---

3. Grotius argued that property rights could extend only as far as was possible for the holder to defend from others. This meant that countries or individuals could not claim property beyond a narrow band of seas along their coastlines, which could be occupied and defended.

4. This 1982 treaty replaced the four Geneva conventions of 1958, which covered the territorial sea; the contiguous zone; the continental shelf; and the high seas.

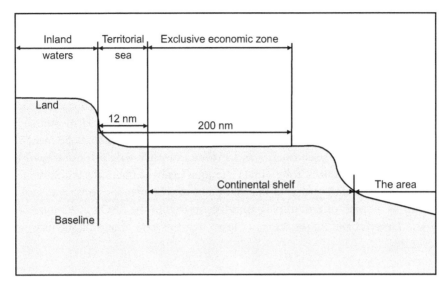

Figure 5.1 The sovereign sea
Source: Authors.

sea extends 12 nautical miles (nm) off the coast (UN 1982: art. 3),[5] where it meets an exclusive economic zone (EEZ), which extends another 200 nm off the coast-line (formally, from the "baseline").

The EEZ provides coastal states with "sovereign rights for the purpose of exploring and exploiting, conserving and managing the natural resources, whether living or non-living, of the waters suprajacent to the seabed and of the seabed and its subsoil, and with regard to other activities for the economic exploitation and exploration of the zone, such as the production of energy from the water, currents and winds" (UN 1982: art. 56, §1a). In short, territorial states are able to maintain sovereign control over their territorial seas and EEZ, so long as they do not interfere with their other international obligations (e.g. with respect to allowing for free navigation).

In theory, then, sovereign states *could* divide their marine territory up into parcels, in the same way that they do their land territory, and they *could* introduce different tenure regimes for these parcels. But they *do not*. In practice, national maritime laws tend to treat coastal waters as inherently public, or the

---

5. In addition, there is a so-called "contiguous zone", where the coastal state may exercise the sort of control necessary to "prevent infringement of its customs, fiscal, immigration or sanitary laws and regulations within its territory or territorial sea (UN 1982: art. 33, §1a). This continuous zone extends for another 12 nm, or a total of 24 nm from the coastline; but this is less relevant for our purposes.

common property of the nation – such as in the form of a public trust. In fact, the allocation of exclusive use rights to marine resources/territory is remarkably rare and is mostly limited to semi-enclosed near-shore environments.[6]

In terms of resource management regimes, the global community has accepted, and continues to accept, open access to the world's fishery as its foundational legal principle; fish are classified as wild animals (*ferae naturae*), as distinct from domestic animals (*domitae naturae*). Although domesticated farm animals can be owned and controlled over their entire lifespan, wild fish can be owned only after they have been caught, and anyone can catch wild fish using lawful methods. In other words, fish swim in a unique legal and political environment.

This traditional approach to managing marine resources is under pressure, mostly as a result of diminishing wild fish stocks. In the FAO's 2020 *State of World Fisheries and Aquaculture*, we learn that the state of our marine fishery resource

> has continued to decline. The proportion of fish stocks that are within biologically sustainable levels decreased from 90 per cent in 1974 to 65.8 per cent in 2017 (a 1.1 per cent decrease since 2015), with 59.6 per cent classified as being maximally sustainably fished stocks and 6.2 per cent underfished stocks. The maximally sustainably fished stocks decreased from 1974 to 1989, and then increased to 59.6 per cent in 2017, partly reflecting improved implementation of management measures. In contrast, the percentage of stocks fished at biologically unsustainable levels increased from 10 per cent in 1974 to 34.2 per cent in 2017. In terms of landings, it is estimated that 78.7 per cent of current marine fish landings come from biologically sustainable stocks.   (FAO 2020d: 7)

In response to these declining wild (and sustainable) fish stocks, the world is turning to sea farming, or aquaculture. In 2019 almost a half (47.3 per cent) of the nearly 177 million tonnes of total global seafood "catch" came from aquaculture (FAO n.d.). The growing importance of aquaculture can also be seen when we compare values (not just tonnage) and the provision of seafood for human consumption. In 2018 the *value* of global fish production was estimated to be $401 billion, 62 per cent of which came from global aquaculture production; in terms of *human consumption*, 52 per cent of the fish we eat today is produced by aquaculture (FAO 2020d: 2).

Our growing reliance on aquaculture is shown in Figure 5.2, where we can see that the global catch of marine and inland fisheries plateaued in the mid-1980s,

---

6. See, for example, Osherenko (2006) and Tecklin (2016: 287); but also Steinberg (2001).

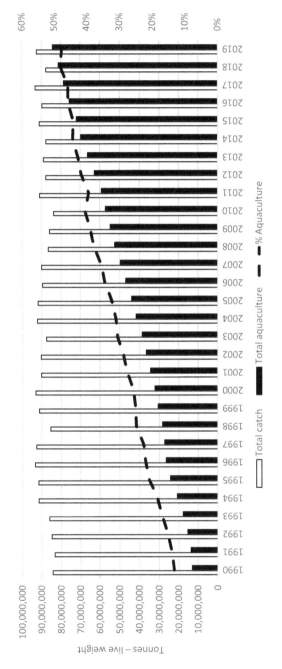

Figure 5.2 Global shares of seafood catch, 1990–2019
Sources: FAO (2020d: 24) and (n.d.).

and the growth in total global fish production since then has been fuelled by inland and marine aquaculture (or mariculture).[7]

In this figure, we can see the rise of a new approach to managing our marine resources, one that borrows heavily from land-based management approaches. In aquaculture we find a new market developing, in which individuals and firms are granted access to our common resources, and they use this access to produce commodities for sale. Fish farmers – like their land-based brethren – can maintain ownership and control over the entire production (and life) cycle of their fish. In short, we are witnessing an important transition in the way we manage our marine resources – but it is a revolution that has largely gone unnoticed. As David Tecklin (2016: 284) notes: "Given the long-standing recognition of the importance of property regimes for terrestrial ecosystems and wildlife, it is striking that even as the aquaculture revolution unfolds, the design and impact of sea tenure has received so little analysis and debate."

The market for salmon

We can better understand the distributional costs of sea tenure by focusing attention on one of the most profitable, efficient and lucrative forms of aquaculture: the farming of Atlantic salmon. In taking a closer look at the way we farm salmon, we have few illusions about the environmental sustainably of an industry that has managed to avoid much critical public attention (but see Lien 2015 and Feedback & Changing Markets 2020). We set these environmental concerns aside, however, and focus our attention on how our approach to managing these resources can create a Natural Dividend.

Salmon is one of the leading species in modern industrialized aquaculture. Although salmon farmers are not the leading producers of seafood, measured in live tonnage, salmon are highly valued, making them among the most traded (and lucrative) of the commodities produced by our marine resources (see Box 5.1).[8] The remarkable success of the salmon-farming industry offers a glimpse

---

7. Of course, aquaculture is about more than fish (and, for that matter, human consumption): aquaculture grows algae (kelp/seaweed), molluscs and crustaceans, in addition to finfish. If you break down the global aquaculture figures, you will find that the largest share is produced by inland aquaculture, with a heavy predominance of white fish (grass carp, silver carp, Nile tilapia, common carp, bighead carp, catla, *Carassius spp.*, and fresh water fishes not elsewhere included). For a useful overview of the challenges of regulating aquaculture commons, in general, see Partelow *et al.* (2022).

8. Although farmed salmonids account for just 4 per cent of the globe's total aquaculture production, they account for roughly 13 per cent of its production value in 2010 (Asche & Bjørndal 2011: 1).

BOX 5.1 SALMON

Salmon, along with trout, are part of the *Salmonidae* family of fish. Salmon are generally of two types, as determined by their natural habitat (Pacific salmon and Atlantic salmon), but both are anadromous. This means that wild salmon eggs are spawned and hatched in fresh water and the resulting fry remain in fresh water for varying lengths of time. Eventually these fry undertake a complex physical change, known as smoltification, whereby they adapt to life in a saltwater environment. The smolt then migrate to the sea, where they can spend from two to eight years (depending on the species), before they return to the native fresh water source to spawn. After spawning, Pacific salmon always die, whereas Atlantic salmon can live to spawn again.

There are six commercially important salmon species, all of which are native to the Northern Hemisphere. It is still possible to find wild stocks of all six types of salmon, although their strength varies significantly (wild Atlantic salmon, in particular, seem to be under heavy threat; see, e.g., International Council for the Exploration of the Sea 2021), but only three of these species are commercially farmed: Atlantic, chinook and coho (these are shaded in the top three rows of the table below). Something like 69 per cent of the world's salmon harvest is farmed (Mowi 2020: 7), and most farmed salmon are Atlantic salmon. But many of the Pacific species are supported by extensive hatcheries projects, involving the release of fingerlings (salmon parr) into the wild, to boost the wild harvest.

Common name	aka	Scientific name	Native to
Atlantic salmon		*Salmo salar*	Atlantic
Chinook	King	*Oncorhynchus tshawytscha*	Pacific
Coho	Silver	*Oncorhynchus kisutch*	Pacific
Sockeye	Red	*Oncorhynchus nerka*	Pacific
Pink	Humpy	*Oncorhynchus gorbuscha*	Pacific
Chum	Dog or keta	*Oncorhynchus keta*	Pacific

---

into future developments: its management regimes have leveraged private control over common resources in ways that promise greater efficiencies and value creation. In short, the industry has found a way to enclose, commodify and profit from our shared marine resources. For all these reasons, salmon farming should attract our attention.

Instead of parcellation, political authorities have relied upon two, competing, management regimes for our marine resources: one for wild fish and another for farmed fish. These responses have been applied to a number of different marine products (e.g. algae, shellfish, finfish, marine mammals, etc.). When managing wild salmon, political authorities aim to limit the overall harvest (in an effort to protect the salmon population). With this limit (or quota) in place, they then manage the harvesting rights, by controlling access to the area, the species or the type of fishing.[9]

Our management approach to farmed salmon is quite different, and more similar to what we find on land. Some of the details of these management regimes are described in the section that follows, but for now we need only point to the fact that political authorities allocate access to particular sites (for fish farms), and then regulate the scope of production that is allowed at these sites (to protect the fish and surrounding environs). These two management regimes (one for wild fisheries, the other for aquaculture) end up producing three different types of salmon: uncommodified; partly commodified; and fully commodified, as depicted in Figure 5.3.

Wild salmon

Wild salmon exist on their own, for reasons that are not particularly obvious to the economist. They cannot be owned and are free to roam. Salmon are born from eggs, swim downstream as tiny fry and enter the ocean as smolt. Here they can migrate over significant distances (e.g. over 3,000 miles, or about 4,800 km), with some species averaging about 18 miles/day, or 29 km/day (US Fish and Wildlife Service n.d.). After years on the run, these salmon mature and return to their native fresh water habitat to spawn (and die), as shown in Figure 5.3a. When they survive (remain uncaught), wild salmon have no market value, and they will reproduce and die for reasons that are entirely unrelated to market demand. For these reasons, we can say wild salmon are uncommodified.

Caught salmon

Wild salmon that are caught suffer a radically different end to their life cycle. These fish live most of their life in uncommodified form, indistinguishable from the life

---

9. We do not have space to elaborate any further on the myriad of management regimes used in the wild fishery, but see, for example, Gordon (1954), Scott (1955) and Munro (1982) for influential approaches. For a more general introduction to access, harvesting and use rights in fishing, see Charles (2002).

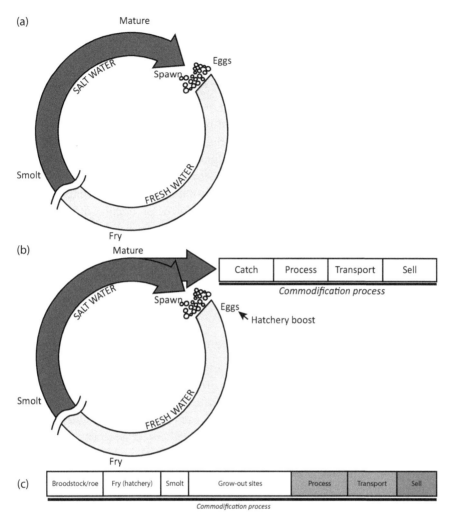

Figure 5.3 Three types of salmon (a) Wild salmon (uncommodified); (b) Caught salmon (partly commodified); (c) Farmed salmon (fully commodified)
Source: Authors.

of a wild salmon: they are free to roam and belong to no one. Even hatchery-grown fish have no proprietary status: once released into the ocean, they become *ferae naturae*, just like their wild brethren. As these salmon reach maturity, however, and return to their native spawning grounds, their fate deviates significantly from that of the wild salmon (see Figure 5.3b). At this point, a licensed fishing industry positions itself to catch wild salmon and can claim ownership over any salmon caught. Once caught, the fish become a commodity: they are gutted, sometimes processed and sent to market.

The wild salmon industry effectively free-rides on nature, which provides all the inputs and feed: the salmon grow to maturity, completely unaided by market actors.[10] The salmon are returning to their home rivers to spawn and die, having effectively fed and cared for themselves over the entirety of their lifetime. Because these fish are caught, they are unable to finish their life cycle and return to spawn; hence the need for hatchery support.

Consequently, producers/fishers have remarkably little control over their product. Their first challenge is to find the fish. Once the fish are located and targeted, producers often end up with a significant (undesired) by-catch. Worse still, the fishing season is determined by the location and life cycle of the fish, not by market demand. All these challenges make it difficult to design efficient logistics and production systems (as are common in the production of land-based commodities). In short, the wild salmon industry invests little in the actual production of the commodity produced (this is done mostly by nature, on its own), but concentrates its efforts and capital on accessing the catch (i.e. securing a part of the quota), and the necessary boats/equipment.

Farmed salmon

A farmed salmon is a very different creature, the result of private ownership and control from conception to market.[11] The production of farmed fish is modelled on the life cycle of wild salmon, but significantly modified to ensure greater control and productivity. More to the point, each phase in the production process can be owned, valued and transferred to others. In contrast to the two-phase production process found with wild salmon (caught/sold), farmed salmon undergo an additional four phases of production, as seen in Figure 5.3c: (a) the production of broodstock and roe; (b) the production of fry (in hatcheries); (c) the production of smolt; and (d) the production of fish proper, in so-called grow-out sites (or pens/nets). The end of the farmed fish is like that of a caught fish: it is slaughtered, processed and then sold.

---

10. There is one important exception, as seen in Figure 5.3b. Political authorities can use hatcheries to complement the wild stock. These hatcheries are usually run by public or community-oriented, non-profit organizations. Once hatchery fish are released, however, they are no longer owned by any particular interest; they become part of the wild stock (although they can still be identified by special markings).

11. Indeed, the aquaculture industry is challenging the very meaning or definition of what constitutes a salmon. How can an Atlantic salmon be both a wild, iconic image of wilderness and a farmed industrial product of a multinational corporation? See, for example, Law and Lien (2012) and Lien and Law (2011).

These fish are private property for their entire life (unless they should escape from their pens and join the wild salmon beyond); they are entirely commodified. Their life cycle is determined more by the demands of the market and the needs of investors than by nature. In contrast to the wild fishing industry, the fish farmer can assume total control of the production process, determining all the inputs, feed, heat, light, control of predators, disease, time of harvest, growth rate, size, location and even the genetic make-up of the fish being farmed. In this way, fish farms are able to control the habitat (e.g. lights and temperature) to ensure a year-round supply of fish, no longer dictated by the seasons. Although most of the inputs and juvenile fish can be owned, controlled and sold by private interests, the most important input in this production process – the marine resource – is on loan from the community.

Each of these three types of salmon faces a different life cycle, which varies in terms of the degree of commodification and scope of control. This, in turn, has resulted in two competing markets for salmon: one for wild caught fish;[12] the other for the farmed fish.

These competing markets highlight the different ways these salmon have been commodified. For example, wild salmon are a seasonal delicacy (late summer/ autumn, when the salmon return home to spawn), whereas farmed salmon are available all year round; wild salmon are available in a variety of species, and there are even specialized markets within each species, but farmed salmon are sold as a standardized commodity;[13] the shelf life of wild salmon tends to be shorter than that of farmed salmon; and the health benefits seem to be more evident (higher risks associated with increased chemicals/antibiotics with farmed fish), although this is often disputed by the aquaculture industry (see, e.g., Trilling 2017). Farmed fish have a higher fat content, whereas wild salmon have fewer calories and more protein.

Perhaps the most noticeable difference between the two types of salmon is their cost: wild salmon tend to cost significantly more than farmed salmon. As a rule of thumb, wild fish tend to sell for more than twice the amount of farmed fish.

---

12. This is a convenient simplification, as the market for wild salmon varies by salmon type, and even by spawning destination. The Pacific wild salmon fishery is trying hard to segregate the market by spawning river (e.g. Yukon River [king] versus Copper River [sockeye and coho]), as the resulting fish vary in fat, muscle and colour content – a consequence of very different migratory challenges.

13. Farmed salmon are graded into three categories: superior, ordinary, and production (see Industry Standards for Fish 1999). This standardization allows these salmon to be traded like other commodities, with a going spot price (see Box 6.2 for a definition of the spot price). For more information about commodified salmon markets, see, for example, Fish Pool ASA – a stock exchange for trading financial salmon contracts, forwards, futures and options (www.fishpool.eu/spot) or the NASDAQ salmon index (https://salmonprice.nasdaqomxtrader.com/public/report;jsessio nid=697B60B8AE80421021ED9FF24B089C89?0).

Comparing prices is complicated by the fact that many wild salmon fishmongers are unwilling to include farmed salmon in their inventory. Box 5.2 provides a simple snapshot of the price of salmon in the wholesale and retail markets.

BOX 5.2 SALMON PRICES

The price of fresh fish varies significantly, in response to market conditions. Accordingly, any price comparison will reflect market conditions on the day the salmon is brought to market. The table below provides only a very rough indicator of the price of different types of salmon, using published landing and spot prices, as well as more accessible retail outlets. We have calculated the rough cost of smolt released from hatcheries, to signal how much of the increased value in a wild caught salmon can be credited to nature (i.e. from 0 to $5.85/lb when completely wild, or from $1.80 to $5.86/lb from a hatchery smolt). We have also compared wild/farmed salmon prices for three types of salmon on 10 November 2021: king, Atlantic farmed and wild sockeye. This is because king salmon are relatively rare compared to other types of salmon: in 2019 the forecast catch for pink salmon was 138 million; for sockeye it was 42 million; and for king it was just 250,000 (Quality Seafood Delivery 2021). See the detailed notes for more information, or contact the authors for more details about how these calculations were made.

	Wholesale	Retail
Smolt[a]	$1.80/lb	
Farmed king (Ora King)[b]		$25–30/lb
Wild Alaskan king[b]		$35–75/lb
Farmed Atlantic[c]	$2.6/lb	$7.15/lb
Wild Alaskan sockeye[c]		$13.58/lb
Wild Alaskan chinook[d]	$5.86/lb	

Notes

1 lb = 0.45 kg.

a. Hatcheries in the state of Alaska released 1.7 billion smolt in 2017. The total cost of this production can be estimated by taking the total budget ($63.3 million) divided by the number of smolt (1.7 billion), or $0.04/fish. If we assume the average weight of a chinook smolt on release is 10 g or 0.02204623 pounds, then the average cost of chinook smolt at release is $1.80/lb. www.adfg.alaska.gov/FedAidPDFs/FDS15-29.pdf.

b. Quote from Quality Seafood Delivery (2021) on 10 November 2021.

c. Quote from Walmart.com (Sacramento Supercenter), meal-sized portion figures, on 10 November 2021.

d. Quote is for a caught and processed (headed and gutted, Western cut) chinook, delivered fresh to Bristol Bay in 2020. www.adfg.alaska.gov/index.cfm?adfg=commercialbyfisherysalmon.salmoncatch_wholesale.

Management regimes

Salmon farming is a global industry, with production on all continents, save Africa. Even so, most of the global production is concentrated in a few regions, and there are very good reasons for this. There are only a handful of locations in the world that enjoy the optimal mix of biological, environmental and infrastructure conditions that are essential to success, and four countries dominate the global production of farmed salmon: Norway, Chile, the United Kingdom and Canada together provide 90 per cent of total production (Asche & Bjørndal 2011: 17; see also Figure 5.6).

This cannot be emphasized enough; salmon cannot be farmed just anywhere. Successful farms require deep-sheltered sites, with favourable hydrographic conditions (stable temperatures, salinities and biological parameters). Among the most important conditions is that of temperature, as salmon can survive only in temperatures ranging from 0 to 20°C, but the optimal temperature for salmon aquaculture is between 8 and 14°C (MOWI 2020: 27). Another necessary condition is access to a steady flow of water; the current cannot be too strong (as the fish need to be able to move freely around the sites) or too weak (as this would not provide enough nutrients and flush). These conditions are most typically found in protected inland waters (archipelagos, sounds, fjords), and these demanding requirements rule out many potential sites. Even when these natural conditions can be found, they are often located in relatively isolated areas, where the lack of a sufficient transportation and social infrastructure makes it costly to set up production. In a word, the requisite resources for productive salmon farming are remarkably scarce.

This scarcity creates a number of challenges. The first has to do with overcrowding. As salmon aquaculture has proved to be extremely lucrative, there is much interest in securing access to these scarce sites. It is the job of political authorities to regulate access to these scarce resources; they decide how many of these sites should be exploited, and who should be granted access. For these reasons, the salmon farm industry is regulated wherever it is found (although the stringency of these regulations varies significantly across political contexts). Accessing public waters and setting up shop require some form of licence or permit, and this permit provides the holder with a very lucrative benefit: the opportunity to run an exclusive operation on public waters.

In granting access to these resources, however, political authorities expose these pristine sites to any number of undesirable ecosystem effects, including habitat destruction both on land and in open waters, coastal eutrophication though increased nutrient loading from land, and organic enrichment of sediments and loss of benthic biodiversity. Although the industry markets itself as a provider of sustainably produced healthy food, its production systems are under constant review by regulators, who are concerned about the ecological burden of its feeding sources, the environmental damage caused by escaped fish and lice infestations, the ethical issues connected to high mortality rates and antibiotic use and a number of other environmental and moral concerns.

Generally, political authorities have two main approaches to regulation. The first governs access to the resource; the second governs the environmental consequences of this access. Both regulatory efforts increase the relative scarcity of the resource. The focus of this regulation tends to be aimed at the grow-out sites, but there can be significant environmental regulations placed on the input sectors as well (broodstock farms, hatcheries and smolt producers). As the grow-out sites are the focus of regulatory action, and what we usually imagine when we think of a salmon farm, we can focus our attention on these.

The first regulatory effort is aimed at limiting access to the resource. This is necessary for three reasons. First, fish farms are located on public waterways. Second, fish farms can impede the alternative use of these public waterways. Finally, fish farms can have a negative environmental impact on the surrounding waters. In these contexts, political authorities need to protect the environment and consider the optimal use of these coastal waters (for the entire community). In doing so, they act as gatekeepers to the industry, deciding how many actors will be allowed (and who they will be). This is usually done by means of a concession or licensing system, the nature of which varies significantly across political contexts. Potential fish farmers need to seek permission from political authorities to set up a fish farm; in exchange for this permission, the industry accepts significant regulatory constraints.

The details, obviously, will vary from country to country (and over time). Box 5.3 provides a snapshot of three prominent management examples. The general pattern is as follows. A private interest wishes to secure access to coastal waters that are especially attractive for salmon aquaculture. As this potential production site is part of the commons, the private interest needs to secure permission (concession/licence/lease) to gain access. This can be done in any number of ways, but the effect is limited access and increased value of the underlying resource (and its products). The applicant usually has to pay a one-time fee for the licence, sometimes in the form of an auction; but some political authorities (e.g. in Scotland) impose an annual rent for leasing the underlying resource. The length of time for which access is granted also varies: in some contexts the lease/licence may be for a specified time (e.g. 25 years); in others it can even be indefinite. Once secured, this licence can usually be bought, sold and borrowed against.

Once access is granted, it usually requires an obligation to comply with all relevant regulations, including a number of environmental regulations. These are aimed to ensure the production activity does not overwhelm the local

BOX 5.3 THREE PROMINENT AQUACULTURE REGIMES

Norway

Norway has the oldest and most established salmon management regime. The Norwegian authorities currently employ a two-stage process, whereby applicants are first deemed qualified, and then qualified applicants compete for a limited number of licences. Licences can be bought and sold, and they are awarded in perpetuity. The ceiling on licences is set with an eye on both market and environmental needs. In practice, the government decides how many licences should be allocated, and sets a maximum capacity associated with each licence. Formally, the regional offices of the Director of Fisheries decide how these licences should be distributed around the country (but with information and advice provided by local political officials). In the past, these licences were provided free of charge, but they are currently allocated by means of an auction; the resulting income is then directed into a fund (Havbruksfondet). Even so, about 80 per cent of the aquaculture licences have been awarded free of charge (Norwegian government 2019b: 3). Beyond this auction price, fish farms pay an ordinary rate of corporate income tax, a property tax (where relevant) and a number of lesser fees. Upon receiving a licence, producers face a number of stringent regulations on production, the most important of which is a regulation that limits the maximum capacity per licence, measured in terms of a maximum allowable biomass, or MAB (see Hersoug 2021). There are also a number of additional regulations aimed at reducing the threat of sea lice and escapes. In 2015 a new "traffic light" system was used to assess and monitor the regional carrying capacity of 13 coastal regions. For more information on the Norwegian management regime, see Hersoug, Mikkelsen and Karlsen (2019), Aarset and Jakobsen (2009) and FAO (2021a).

Chile

The government in Chile has actively promoted the growth of the salmon aquaculture industry as part of its development strategy (UNCTAD 2006), and so the regulations in this country are more liberal than elsewhere. As in Norway, the government defines the coastal waters as public assets for public use, but then allocates concessions for private use (see Tecklin 2016: 290). Originally (also as in Norway) the licences were granted for an indefinite period of time, but they are now limited to 25 years. Licences can be bought/sold and traded, and there is only a modest (but annual) fee charged for the licenses. Chile also employs a two-staged regulatory process. In the first phase, concessions are distributed by the Maritime Authority, but these are dependent on the Ministry of Defence conferring the right to use and benefit from state property. In the second phase, a formal authorization of aquaculture is granted by the undersecretaries of fisheries and aquaculture. This authorization grants permission to use the national sea area at a particular site and includes an explicit plan of complying with all environmental and other applicable regulations. For more information on Chile's management regime, see MOWI (2020), Hishamunda, Ridler and Martone (2014) and FAO (2021b).

Scotland

In the United Kingdom, the Crown Estate formally owns and manages most of the seabed (out to 12 nm), so potential salmon farmers must apply for a lease from the Crown Estate and pay a rent to install and operate a farm on the Crown's seabed (see Crown Estate Scotland 2021). These leases contain no regulatory obligations or statutory function in relation to the industry. This regulatory system is somewhat different from that found in Norway and Chile, in that there is no formal licensing regime, but applicants must apply for permission from four organizations: planning permission from the local Planning Authority; a marine licence from Marine Scotland; an environmental licence from the Scottish Environment Protection Agency (SEPA); and an aquaculture production business authorization, also from Marine Scotland. As in Norway, Scotland sets MAB limits on individual production sites, and additional regulatory restrictions were added in 2019 by SEPA. The aquaculture industry pays an annual fee for the environmental licence and a minor fee for the planning application, and a standing rent is levied by the Crown on the basis of production levels – currently set at £27.50 per tonne of salmon (Crown Estate Scotland 2021). For more information on Scotland's management regime, see MOWI (2020), FAO (2021c), Kenyon & Davies (2018) and Scottish government (n.d.).

---

environment, by placing limits on the number of pens, the size of pens, the number of fish, the amount of live biomass and even the amount of feed that is allowed for each production site. In addition, political authorities can introduce specific requirements that ensure farms are not located too near one another, that they minimize the threat of escapes and the spread of lice and/or limit the use of chemicals and medicines employed.

The source of the Natural Dividend

As with the other natural resources considered in this book, our marine resources are capable of producing a significant Natural Dividend, the result of three component rents: a differential rent; a regulatory rent; and a locational rent. This chapter focuses on the production of regulatory rents, as they are especially evident in our approach to managing marine resources (in general) and aquaculture (in particular). Access to our common marine resources is highly regulated by political authority, and this regulation produces a value that belongs to that political authority, and the community it represents.

This is not to suggest that the other two types of rent are unimportant. The natural productive capacity of aquaculture sites varies in the same way (and for the same reason) as the productive potential of farm or forest lands – and this difference in productive potential generates a differential rent. Thus, the lessons learned about differential rents in the preceding chapter can be applied to the management of aquaculture sites as well. We can easily rank aquaculture sites in terms of their productive potential (as we did in Figure 4.2), to demonstrate their varying capacity to generate a differential rent. As we have already covered this territory in Chapter 4, we do not retrace these steps, but simply point to the fact that our most productive marine resources also produce a differential rent.

Aquaculture sites can also benefit from being located near a publicly funded infrastructure (to facilitate the transport of inputs and outputs from/ to surrounding markets). Those sites that are located nearest the market, or are near to an efficient infrastructure that facilitates access to that market, are more valuable, *ceteris paribus*, than aquaculture sites that lie far off the beaten path. As we shall see in the chapter that follows, this difference in locational advantage generates another part of the Natural Dividend – what we call a locational rent.

But the most evident component of the Natural Dividend from managing our marine resources is the existence of a regulatory rent, and this rent can be significant. This is because productive aquaculture sites are remarkably scarce (globally); access to these scarce productive resources is strictly regulated by political authority; and the scope of this regulation has a significant impact on the potential supply of these resources to global markets.

There are at least two reasons why regulation plays such an important role in how we manage our marine resources. The more important reason is the absence of a market for the underlying resource: there is no market for "sea", and private tenure over marine resources is remarkably rare. This means that political authorities play a more active and evident role in deciding who can gain access to our common resource. In the market for land, this political allocation is often hidden by market forces and forgotten with time. In allocating aquaculture sites, this regulatory role is plain for everyone to see.

In addition, regulation is needed to protect the resource and the surrounding environment and communities. Indeed, the need for regulation will only grow over time, as we come to rely more heavily upon these resources, and they become increasingly scarce. After all, aquaculture production can have a significant negative impact on the surrounding environment, and political authorities need to ensure that fish farms do not overwhelm the local environment, disrupt the activities of others who rely on these public waterways or facilitate the spread of illness across farms.[14] Although the nature of regulation will vary across time and countries, their effect is to constrain the overall level of production – to ensure that not everybody who wants to start a fish farm is allowed to do so. This regulatory activity generates a rent by further limiting access to already scarce resources.

Regulatory rent

We should begin by noting that political authorities regulate access to all natural resources – even farmland and domestic housing lots – as they decide how much of the resource should be placed on the market, how it should be taxed and the limits that should be placed on its use. In accessing many natural resources – such as underground petroleum and minerals, wind and solar energy sites and coastal sites for aquaculture – political authorities play a large role in determining how easy it will be to secure access to the resource (determining its relative scarcity), and who, exactly, will be granted access to that resource (determining its distribution). It is not an act of God, or some invisible hand, but a distinct political authority that grants legal access to the most productive coastal waters, mining sites and wind corridors.

Access is usually regulated by means of a concessions/licensing regime. In the case of aquaculture sites, these concessions are used to protect the resources from overexploitation; to avoid a rush on scarce resources (farm sites); to ensure that coastal areas can still be used for other purposes (e.g. inland traffic and wild fisheries); and to limit farm density, in an effort to minimize biological and environmental risks. For these reasons, political authorities need to decide how many fish farms should be allowed, where they should be located and who should get access to these locations. These are the sort of "nuts and bolts" regulations that we use to manage our natural resources – and they leave a significant impact on the supply of these resources that can make it to market (i.e. they make them scarcer).

---

14. In the absence of adequate regulation, there can be enormous consequences for the fish, the local environment and the industry, as witnessed by Chile's recent disease crisis. In 2009 Chile's aquaculture output plunged (from 403,000 MTs in 2008 to 130,000 MTs in 2010) as a result of an outbreak of infectious salmon anaemia, a viral disease with a very high mortality rate. See Asche *et al.* (2009); Tecklin (2016); Barton and Fløysand (2010); and Asche, Cojocaru and Sikveland (2018).

By limiting access to already scarce resources, regulation generates a rent of its own: a *regulatory rent*. The roots of this rent can be traced back to Adam Smith's (1976 [1776]: 162) early recognition that rent is a monopoly price, and Karl Marx's (1967 [1867]) subsequent elaboration of two types of monopoly rents.[15] Many other economists, both then and now, have been aware of the rents that are derived from monopolizing access to land and other resources.[16] Among them is Henry George, who noted that "[t]he value of land ... is the price of monopoly" (George 1992 [1879]: 343).[17]

But it was Marx who explicitly recognized two types of monopoly rent that were related to, but different from, the differential rent. In particular, Marx recognized the existence of "natural monopolies" in land, because highly productive land is relatively scarce and made scarcer by allowing private ownership/control. The existence of such natural monopolies means that the price for natural resources will be determined by effective demand, as the natural monopoly makes it impossible for new suppliers to enter the market. These natural constraints create what Marx called a "monopoly rent". In addition to these natural monopolies, social and political barriers can be used to further restrict competition, and these political/social barriers produce another type of rent, which Marx called an "absolute rent." These absolute rents are generated by the regulatory impositions made by the class of rentiers themselves, and were said to be particularly evident in the extractive industries (Marx 1967 [1867], vol. 3: 772).

By pointing to the existence of regulatory rents, we are focusing on the way that legitimate political authority restricts access to natural resources, further increasing their scarcity.[18] Such regulations are ubiquitous and can come about for any number of reasons. It is not necessary for these regulations to be made in the name of any particular class (as Marx asserted); they might be wielded in the name of protecting the resource or the environment and/or community that surrounds the resource. But it is also possible that restrictions are imposed

---

15. Marx discussed four types of rents: two types of differential rents, monopoly rent and absolute rent. See Ward and Aalbers (2016: 1764) for a clear presentation of each in tabular form. See also Harvey (1984: 349–58) for elaboration.

16. The mainstream economics and business literatures also recognize the existence of this monopoly power. The whole point of a patent is to create a temporary monopoly, so that the innovator is able to recover her sunk investment costs and secure a return on these. In this light, the monopoly rent is usually framed in terms of an "entrepreneurial" or "Schumpeterian" rent (see, e.g., Teece 1986, 1998, 2003 and Pisano 1991).

17. In his "The condition of labor", George (2019 [1891]) specifically mentioned the role played by land monopoly in introducing a "monopoly rent".

18. A similar argument is made in the literature on the monopoly rents associated with intellectual property rights and the knowledge economy. See, for example, Zeller (2008), Birch and Tyfield (2013) and Cooper and Waldby (2014).

to protect the interests of existing resource holders, workers or other particular interests. Whatever the motivation, by limiting access to a scarce resource, political authorities shift the market equilibrium by reducing the quantity of commodities and the number of suppliers released on the market, thereby increasing their price.

> Thus the rent is a result of a systematic shortage of supply created by the property monopoly of the supplier of a key product, which encounters no direct competition from substitution goods. The amount of the monopoly [regulatory] rent depends on the concrete demand and supply conditions. The more inelastic the demand reacts to price increases, the larger the rent. If substitution goods exist, the demand is more elastic and thus the monopoly [regulatory] rent smaller.   (Zeller 2008: 98)

To demonstrate the existence of this regulatory rent, consider Figure 5.4. This is an elaboration on Figure 4.2, which the reader will recall was used to introduce the differential rent in Chapter 4. But here we rank *fish farms* in terms of their productive potential, with the most productive site (nearest the origin) able to secure the largest differential rent. In Figure 5.4, we show how regulations can impose a limit on the number of licensed (producing) fish farms. In limiting the number of producers, political authorities can expect less fish to reach the market ($q_\bullet \rightarrow q_1$), and the price of the commodity (here fish) will increase (from $p_\bullet \rightarrow p_1$).

As in Figure 4.2, we can still see different producers (1 to 11), with their varying unit costs, ranked by decreasing productivity (increasing unit costs). These unit costs include a standardized profit, in return for the capital lent and the risks taken, and we can still find a substantial remainder associated with each individual farm in the form of a differential rent (especially in the most productive farms). So far, the story told by Figure 5.4 is the same as the one told by Figure 4.2. When political authority begins to regulate (limit) access to these resources, however, it impacts the scope of production, such that the market equilibrium now moves from $E_\bullet$ to E_1, creating a new market outcome, with corresponding losses and gains. Figure 5.4 allows us to see how these new gains and losses affect individual farmers, and the resource market in total.

The imposition of regulations limits the supply of fish produced in the market (from $q_\bullet$ to q_1). This results in a higher equilibrium price: p_1. These new conditions hurt any producer with unit costs that are higher than those found in farm 9, and these regulations effectively force these producers out of the market. But the regulations also increase the surplus for the remaining nine farms. As with Figure 4.2, the largest gains are found in the most productive farm (1), which now enjoys an unearned surplus that stretches from O to p_1. The increase in farm 1's

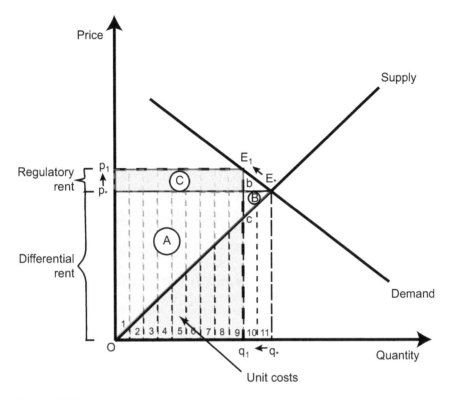

Figure 5.4 The regulatory rent
Source: Authors.

surplus, relative to what we saw in Figure 4.2 (i.e. the increase from p_* to p_1), is the result of the regulation. This is the regulatory rent. When accumulated across the market, these regulatory rents are captured by the rectangle labelled "C" in Figure 5.4 – i.e. $p_*p_1E_1b$.[19]

In employing this diagram, we can clearly see how restricting the number of actors affects the surplus generated (and how it is distributed). As a result of the higher prices and smaller quantity produced, a significant surplus is placed on top of the profits and differential rents that we found in the unregulated context (Figure 4.2). As with the differential rent, these regulatory rents belong with the political authorities that created them. But, if the resource is not taxed correctly by the responsible political authority, these unearned gains will be pocked by

---

19. When considering the cumulative benefits from regulation, we should note that the regulations reduced the differential rents found in Figure 4.2 by the size of the triangle marked "B" in Figure 5.4 (i.e., bE_*c). Hence, the overall gains from regulation to the community are the gains from rectangle "C" minus the losses from triangle "B".

the licence holders, who will (unfairly) claim them as profit. Obviously, capturing this rent will require some political will, and the political authorities can expect resistance (from concessionaires) when deciding how to calculate costs and normal/standard profit rates. When this rent is not taxed, however, the owner of fish farm 1 can abscond with both her earned profits (already included as part of the operating costs), along with the differential rent (p. − O) and the regulatory rent (p. − p_1). These gains are not the result of anything that the fish farmer did; she is able to pocket them because the political authorities have not claimed them.

This book is aimed to draw attention to these unclaimed rents so that political authorities, and the communities they represent, can secure them for the public good. In focusing on the regulatory rent, we do not mean to suggest that the other component rents (differential and locational) are absent in the market for marine resources. Nor do we mean to suggest that other natural resources (land, wind, solar, subsurface petroleum and minerals) are not capable of producing regulatory rents. Rather, we have used the example of salmon aquaculture to demonstrate the existence of regulatory rents, because they are most evident in this market.

Value creation

In order to calculate the size of the Natural Dividend from salmon-producing sites, we need to estimate the total revenues generated by the natural resource, and then subtract from these revenues all the costs of production. These costs must include a fair return for the capital invested and the risks taken. This section considers these costs to ensure that they are neither downplayed nor ignored in any attempt to tax the resource and secure the Natural Dividend (when and should it arise).

Compared to the wild salmon fishery, the costs associated with salmon aquaculture are considerable. Although the wild fishery can free-ride on much of nature's bounty (see Figure 5.3b), the aquaculture industry has to pay for most of its input costs – and these costs can be substantial. Not only are the industry's costs significantly higher but the resulting product is worth only half as much (as we saw in Box 5.2). Figure 5.5 presents an overview of the significant capital outlays in Norwegian salmon aquaculture, and how they are distributed.

In contrast to the wild fishery, salmon farms have to buy their smolt and feed them until they reach maturity, so, consequently, they have substantial full-time outlays in terms of both labour and capital. Unlike their wild brethren, farmed fish require constant supervision, and this supervision is costly.

In return, the aquaculture industry is able to avoid many of the risks associated with the wild salmon fishery. The capital outlays provide significant control over the entire production process, so producers no longer need to hunt down the fish, or wait for the appropriate season or worry about the logistics of getting wild fish processed and transported to market. By controlling the entire life cycle of the fish (from eggs to the mature salmon), the industry is able to minimize many of the risks associated with the wild fishery and deliver a standardized commodity, on demand, to world markets. When we try to establish a fair return on capital and risk in the aquaculture industry, it is important to recognize the significant capital investments required, especially when compared to their competitors in the wild fishery. At the same time, however, the risks associated with these investments are much lower than in the wild fishery, as these investments provide much more control (and less uncertainty/risk) over the production process.

If you look more closely at the cost breakdown of farmed fish in Figure 5.5, you will notice that something is missing. The industry spends most of its

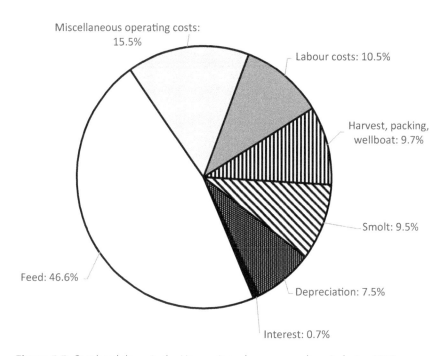

Figure 5.5 Cost breakdown in the Norwegian salmon aquaculture industry, 2019
Note: A "wellboat" is a fishing vessel with a well or tank for the storage and transport of live fish.
Source: MOWI (2020: 60).

money on feeding these fish, and it makes significant investments in labour, fish stocks (smolt), automized technology (with a high rate of depreciation) and the costs associated with transporting, slaughtering, processing and packing the fish. But there is no explicit account for the cost of the most essential input in this entire production process: the cost of using our common (and scarce) natural resource.[20] In almost every case, the political authorities simply gift these resources to the concessionaire in hopes that the gift will produce jobs and tax income for the surrounding community. This gifting may make sense when political authorities want to encourage the development of a new industry, but, as surpluses begin to mount, the responsible political authorities should recognize that a Natural Dividend is being produced and aim to capture it.

This sort of gifting is so commonplace that it is seldom noted or commented upon, by either the industry or its regulators. When we recognize that this gifting includes access to the Natural Dividend, however, communities should become concerned. These farms could not exist without access to the underlying marine resource, and they could not succeed without access to our most productive sites. When fish farm owners threaten to relocate in the face of rising tax/regulatory demands, political authority should simply ignore the threat: the industry needs access to our scarce marine resources, and it is willing and able to pay for that access, if need be.[21]

State of the rent

It is impossible to know the full productive potential of our marine resources. Unlike many of the other natural resources considered in this book, there are no published estimates of the total productive potential of the world's marine resources, or the location of the most productive sites for different marine products (such as salmon). With regard to specialized salmon aquaculture sites, we might assume that the most productive sites have already been claimed, but that new technologies will increase the productive potential, allowing less productive sites to become profitable (and increasing the rent generated by the most productive sties). This is, after all, what we have seen in the market for land and the products of the land.

---

20. The category "Miscellaneous operating costs" does not explicitly note the costs of accessing the resource. These costs are defined as "[o]ther costs include direct and indirect costs, administration, insurance, biological costs (excluding mortality), etc." (MOWI 2020: 60).
21. This may change in the near future, as new salmon aquaculture opportunities are being developed on land (see, e.g., Watson *et al.* 2022) as well as far offshore (see, e.g., Kramer 2015).

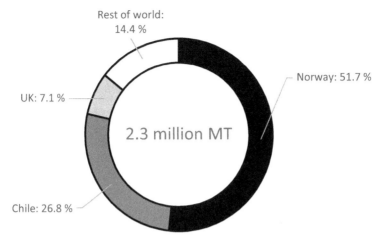

Figure 5.6 Global salmon aquaculture production, 2019
Source: Derived from MOWI (2020: 25).

Nevertheless, it is clear that the most productive marine resources are scarce, in that there are only a few places in the world where salmon farming has been successfully and profitably developed. This scarcity reveals itself in one of the most concentrated natural resource markets covered in this book. In 2019 the total production of farmed salmon in the world was said to be over 2.3 million metric tons. As can be seen in Figure 5.6, more than a half of this salmon was produced in a single country: Norway. Two countries alone (Norway and Chile) combined to capture almost 80 per cent of the global market! The third most productive salmon farming sites were found in the United Kingdom (mostly Scotland), which accounts for about 7 per cent of global production. In total, then, the top three producing countries produce over 85 per cent of the world's total production of farmed salmon (see also Asche & Bjørndal 2011: 17).

This Norwegian dominance is also evident when we look at who is harvesting most of the world's farmed salmon. In 2019 it was estimated that the world's 20 largest salmon farms harvested a total of 1,867,000 tonnes of fish. The top four companies on this list were all Norwegian: Mowi – the largest – was over twice the size of the other top four producing firms (Lerøy, Cermaq[22] and Salmar). Together, these four Norwegian firms harvested almost as much fish as all the other 16 companies combined, as shown in Figure 5.7.

---

22. Although Cermaq is now Japanese-owned (by Mitsubishi), the company still has its headquarters in Norway.

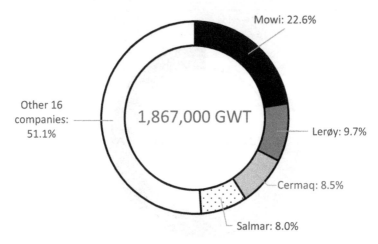

Figure 5.7 Top 20 farmed salmon companies, 2019
Note: GWT = gross weight tonnage.
Source: Derived from Berge (2020).

The remarkably high level of concentration in the salmon aquaculture industry is evidence of the scarcity in the underlying resource, and its capture by a handful of private interests. This scarcity is partly a function of nature and partly a function of the regulation that political authorities have placed on accessing the most productive sites. In granting access to these sites, political authorities have granted private interests monopoly access to the most productive aquaculture sites in the world. What is remarkable is that these interests do not pay for the privilege of using these scarce and productive sites. As we have seen, the industry may pay licence fees, and income tax, and they may even pay a rent or auction price for accessing the site – but the sea resources that are essential to their production (and profits) are, in effect, provided for free. The political authorities in these countries are gifting powerful private interests our Natural Dividend.

Securing the Natural Dividend in salmon aquaculture

It is clear that these marine resources are able to produce a substantial Natural Dividend. The largest differential rents will be found in the most productive sites in Norway and Chile, and access to these sites has been strictly regulated. As we have seen, this regulation produces a regulatory rent, which will also be considerable. Finally, some of these farms can produce locational rents because they are lucky enough to be located next to an infrastructure (provided by political authority and the surrounding community) that facilitates easy access to markets. These different rents accumulate into a significant surplus: the Natural Dividend. To date, this Dividend is being pocketed by a salmon farming industry that is remarkably lucrative, and highly concentrated.

If political authorities are interested in securing this Natural Dividend for the public, then they might consider four options. The first option is to encourage a more equal allocation of access to these scarce resources. As in the early years of Norwegian aquaculture, the authorities can encourage small, local land farms to take up salmon farming. This strategy was used to stimulate rural economic growth, and limits were placed on the size of each farm so that they would not be attractive to international investors (see, e.g., Aarset & Jakobsen 2009). Such a strategy would allow more people along these coastlines to harvest and share the Natural Dividend. This management strategy is likely to be less effi-cient, however, because smaller farms would find it more difficult to access the technology and capital needed to boost efficiencies, and be unable to secure economies of scale. In short, more people would be able to access the Natural Dividend, but it would probably be smaller (in aggregate) when compared to the highly concentrated and capital-intensive strategy pursued today. In some pol-itical contexts, this trade-off may be worthwhile – even if it appears inefficient.

A second strategy would be to introduce a natural resource company, employed in the same way that countries employ national mining or oil com-panies. As in the petroleum sector, this company could be encouraged to develop operational competences by pairing it with more international aqua-culture firms in joint ventures (to secure the transfer of the knowledge and skills necessary to become internationally competitive), or the NRC might be set up as a financial holding company that holds a share of each licence that the pol-itical authorities grant. In this way, political authorities could secure a share of the Natural Dividend in a more political form, using it to access competences and to build local content and jobs, or to secure the Dividend by means of a joint ownership in allocated licences.

A third strategy would be to rotate access to the most productive sites. Rather than granting private interests a perpetual licence to our common resources, political authorities might limit the concession to a shorter period of time, and then ensure that different interests are granted access over time. We find this type of concession strategy in other sectors (e.g. in the concession for hydro-electric installations and with subsurface minerals and petroleum resources; see Chapter 7), where it is has proved to be very successful. Political authorities can choose a concession period that is long enough to ensure that investors are able to secure a return on their investments, but short enough to allow access to be rotated (hence creating greater access opportunities for others). In addition, this strategy allows the authorities to reset the terms of the concession, under varying market conditions. For example, in times when the Natural Dividend is small, the terms of the concession can be more generous; as the Natural Dividend grows, though, the authorities would be able to introduce more appropriate terms (and demands) at each new concession round.

Finally, political authorities can continue their present effort to encourage concentration and maximize efficiencies, but simply tax the industry in a way that allows us to secure the Natural Dividend. This can be done by establishing a resource rent tax, as discussed in the preceding chapters. Such a tax would allow reasonable returns on investments, but tax the windfall at a higher rate. In short, an RRT could provide a broad, stable and identifiable tax base that is linked to surplus wealth but does not negatively distort market behaviour (i.e. it is neutral).

Remarkably, there are currently no political authorities willing (or able) to secure the Natural Dividend being produced by salmon aquaculture. Whereas some states charge a number of fees for diverse licences and permissions, or to lease public lands, none of the three largest producing countries tax the salmon aquaculture producers any differently from other economic actors: the industry is subject to the same corporate income tax as every other type of commodity producer.[23]

As we saw in the cost breakdown of Norwegian fish farms, there are no costs associated with accessing the world's most productive salmon farming sites (at least, they are not significant enough to be noted) – sites that are now generating enormous wealth for a handful of private companies. Indeed, salmon farming is proving to be *extremely* lucrative: the wealth of some of Norway's richest families was secured from rents produced by Norwegian coastal waters (and their regulation). In each of the most prominent producing countries, political authorities simply give away access to the world's most productive salmon aquaculture resources, sometimes for indefinite periods of time!

To be fair, the political authorities in these countries emphasize the need to attract investments and ensure that their producers can compete internationally. Citizens are told that the gains can be secured in the form of increased local employment and business taxes. Hence, when the Scottish government justifies the allocation of public resources to private aquaculture interests, the explicit and direct "benefits to Scotland of aquaculture" are limited to the tax revenues generated by the added value of salaries and profits and the increase in jobs – both directly, and indirectly, through the local supply chains (see, e.g., Crown Estates Scotland 2021; Marine Scotland 2014; Bridge Economics 2020). These estimates of the job/tax benefits vary widely (see, e.g., Bridge Economics 2020: 7–9, tab. 1.1) and have been criticized for ignoring the negative, and/or

---

23. This may be changing in Norway. At the time of writing, a new Norwegian government has announced its intent to introduce an RRT on aquaculture in 2024. See Box 9.2.

net, effects of the industry. At any rate, the focus is myopically set on regular tax revenue and job creation, not on securing the Natural Dividend.

The Norwegian authorities have employed a similar approach, although there has been growing political and academic pressure in the country to introduce a tax system that can claw back the Natural Dividend that is clearly being produced. In 2018 the Norwegian Ministry of Finance (Finansdepartementet) created an expert committee to consider an RRT on the industry. This committee compared the rents being generated in the aquaculture industry with those that are produced (and taxed accordingly) in the Norwegian petroleum and hydro-electric sectors (see Norwegian government 2019a).

The work of this committee produced a Norwegian public report (Norges offentlige utredninger, or NOU) that confirmed the existence of a resource rent, or what we call the Natural Dividend, and then a more specialized report was commissioned that documented the scope of this rent, and its variability over time (Norwegian government 2019b: 2; Greaker & Lindholt 2019). Although the Natural Dividend from salmon farming in Norway varies a great deal over time, as seen in Figure 5.8, it was estimated to have been in excess of 20 billion kroner (kr) annually (roughly $2.3 billion) over the period from 2016 to 2018 (Greaker & Lindholt 2019).

These rents are not currently taxed by the Norwegian authorities, and this allows private interests to pocket them and to secure phenomenally high returns on investment. Recognizing this, the majority of committee members proposed that an RRT be imposed on the Norwegian aquaculture industry.[24] They explicitly recognized that the current auction model might capture a share of the present value of future resource rents, but is unsuited for capturing the resource rent – especially from licences that had already been awarded (sites already allocated).[25] Instead, the committee's majority recommended the use of a profit-based RRT, to ensure that investments that were profitable before tax were also profitable after the resource rent tax (Norwegian government 2019b: 11).

Despite the broad consensus among economists, and significant pressure from the public and a majority of the committee members, the Norwegian government at the time discarded the committee's proposal to introduce a 40 per cent RRT and decided to continue with only a minor production fee (MOWI 2020: 81; see also Åm 2021). Remarkably (and rather uncommonly, in the

---

24. The minority also agreed on the need to distribute the income from natural resources, but wanted the major part of this payment to go to the local communities (rather than to the national government).

25. In 2022 the aquaculture industry in Norway paid only the ordinary corporate income tax plus a small market and research duty (*markedsavgift* and *forskningsavgift*) on the fish that are exported. Some farms may also pay a local property tax, when applicable.

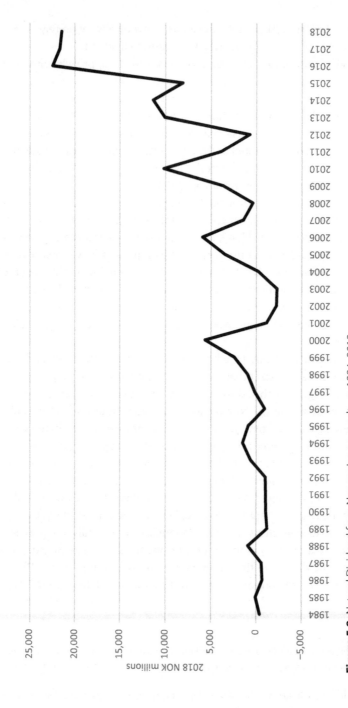

Figure 5.8 Natural Dividend from Norwegian aquaculture, 1984–2018

Source: Greaker and Lindholt (2019: 26, tab. A3).

Note: Greaker and Lindholt refer to the "resource rent" rather than to a Natural Dividend. At the end of 2018 one Norwegian krone was worth about 11 US cents ($0.11), so the US dollar total of the 2018 Natural Dividend was roughly $2.5 billion.

Norwegian context), the parties making up Norway's coalition government used their party congresses to oppose any attempt to introduce an RRT on aquaculture. This opposition was set, before the export committee report was published; the committee's work was, effectively, squandered and ignored.

Conclusion

As demand for scarce natural resources grows, political authorities will be tempted to grant private interests monopoly control over once common resources to impede the tragedy of the commons, increase efficiencies and establish new markets. We have written this book because we think this new enclosure movement will develop along several resource frontiers, in response to the challenges produced by climate change and the limits to growth.

This type of new enclosure is clearly evident in the near-lying sea, where a nascent aquaculture industry has managed to wrest control over once common resources and use that control to secure enormous (private) riches. We are witnessing the birth of a new market for "sea", and its development is following a familiar path. This new market has already begun to generate significant inequities – like its older sibling, the market for land – because policy-makers have been unwilling or unable to safeguard the Natural Dividend that is being produced.

As with land management, there are strong moral and economic reasons to tax the Natural Dividend produced by our shared marine resources. This Natural Dividend is a gift of nature (which belongs to us all), and this gift can grow by our need for prudent regulation. By taxing the underlying rents, we can ensure that private interests do not pocket the Natural Dividend when it is produced. By employing an RRT, we can secure the Natural Dividend in a way that is less distorting, more efficient and more flexible than other forms of taxation. As we saw in the previous chapter, this kind of tax has a long history, shared across many different political contexts. As we shall see in Chapter 7, RRTs have been employed in a highly effective manner for taxing subsurface mineral and petroleum resources. When it is not taxed, the Natural Dividend created by our marine resources is left as a windfall for concessionaires who are not in any way responsible for its creation. Worse, the windfall acts like a subsidy, with a number of costly consequences (as listed in the conclusion to Chapter 3).

This argument is not particularly radical. It is only different, because we have broadened our focus to include issues of justice (in addition to efficiency). As we have endeavoured to show, there is a broad consensus among economists on the utility of taxing these component rents to the Natural Dividend. In addition, a strong moral argument can be made that the Natural Dividend should be returned to the community, from which it is derived. Indeed, the Norwegian expert committee that was assigned to study the matter agreed as much: "The aquaculture industry exploits sea resources which belong to the public. Aquaculture licences are issued by the central government and confer a perpetual protected right to conduct business operations. It is therefore reasonable that the public obtains a share of the supernormal profit [Natural Dividend] generated by exploiting this resource" (Norwegian government 2019b: 3).

Although this chapter has focused attention on the creation of a regulatory rent, it is important to emphasize (yet again) that the Natural Dividend from marine resources also draws from the two other forms of rent (differential and locational). In practice, it is not possible to distinguish among these three rents; they blend to create a Natural Dividend. But the Natural Divided, itself, is easy to trace and capture, given the requisite political will. This Natural Dividend varies over time, and it can be substantial in the future, as our natural resources become even more scarce, and our reliance on them grows. But now is the time to create the regulatory framework that secures our access to this Dividend; if we wait too long, it will be difficult to contain powerful private interests, whose influence grows along with any Natural Dividend they are able to capture (unfairly).

Nowhere is the potential for future rents larger than in the market for renewable resources, to which we turn in the chapter that follows.

6

THE SKY ABOVE: THE MARKET FOR RENEWABLE ENERGY

One of the most exciting and rapidly developing resource markets is the one for renewable energy (RE). This market is remarkably varied and broad, as it draws from a number of competing natural resources and technologies – many of which lie at the heart of the phenomenal transformations taking place across the global energy system. For this reason, the market for RE attracts a great deal of attention from policy-makers, academics and entrepreneurs. The enthusiasm and interest are exciting, but it is also important to place these developments in a larger context: RE still accounts for a remarkably small share of the world's primary energy consumption.

Because these markets are in transition, we can expect our current regulatory focus to change as the resources and technologies mature and become more competitive. Today, most regulatory attention has been aimed at supporting infant technologies and markets, so that they can better compete with more traditional (dirty and non-renewable) forms of energy.

The contemporary market for RE is dominated by three natural resources (water, wind and solar) and several underlying technologies (e.g. turbines, photovoltaic [PV] devices, concentrated solar power [CSP] furnaces, etc.). Globally, RE resources were able to generate an impressive 2,537 gigawatts (GW) in 2020 (International Renewable Energy Agency [IRENA] 2020: 1). As shown in Figure 6.1, hydropower (at 1,190 GW) makes up almost half the existing RE capacity in the world today, while the other half – roughly – comes from wind and solar energy.

Here we focus on the energy produced by the wind and the sun.[1] There are three reasons for this particular focus. First, and foremost: wind and solar energy

---

1. It would be fruitful and informative to include a study of how the hydroelectric power sector is (and has been) managed with an eye at securing rent. As this technology is almost 150 years old, we have decades of experience in building and managing hydroelectric installations for the public good. One proven example of this is described in Chapter 7 (see Box 7.3); the Norwegian

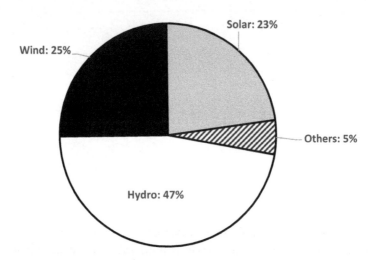

Figure 6.1 Global RE generation capacity, by energy source, 2019
Note: End-2019 figures, with total global capacity of 2,537 GW. These figures exclude pure pumped storage; including pumped storage would add an additional 121 GW.
Source: IRENA (2020: 1).

are remarkably special and attractive. These unique traits are elaborated upon in the section that follows, but for now we can note that these resources are ubiquitous, apparently free for the taking, clean (pollution-free) and renewable. For all these reasons, there has been a significant effort by political authorities to stimulate the production of wind and solar energy – i.e. to shift consumption from non-renewable to renewable sources of energy.

This effort has been propelled by a number of national and international initiatives.[2] Indeed, by the end of 2020 nearly every single country in the world had some form of renewable energy support policy, albeit at varying level of ambition and effectiveness (REN21 2021: 18). As a result of these efforts, global wind and solar PV capacity is expected to surpass that of natural gas in 2023 and coal in 2024, with 60 per cent of the renewable capacity coming from solar PV, and 30 per cent from wind (International Energy Agency [IEA] 2020: 12).

The second reason to focus on these two resource types is that they both derive their energy (ultimately) from the same shared source: the sun. It is estimated that the earth is bathed in solar radiation that provides the equivalent of 1.7 x 10^{14} kilowatts (kW) of power (Mathew 2006: 46). This radiation

---

regulatory regime for hydropower was developed early in the twentieth century, and was strongly influenced by the work of Henry George and other classical economists.

2. Such as the UN's "Sustainable Energy for All!" (SE4ALL) project. See, for example, https://sustainabledevelopment.un.org/sdinaction/se4all and www.seforall.org.

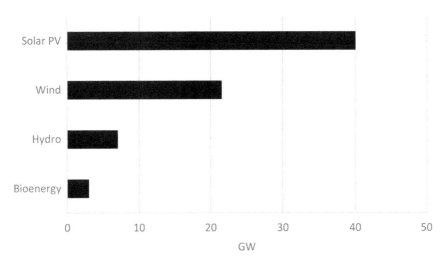

Figure 6.2 Growth in global RE capacity, by technology, 2020
Source: IEA (2020: 17, fig. 1.2).

heats up the atmospheric air, but does so unevenly; it is most intense when the sun is directly overhead, around the equator, and less intense at the poles. As the hotter air around the equator rises into the atmosphere and dissipates, the air pressure in these areas falls, attracting colder air from the polar regions. It is these pressure gradients – the result of an uneven heating of the earth's surface – that creates wind. Basically, then, wind energy is an indirect form of solar energy.

Finally (and consequently), these are the fastest-growing and most promising RE resource markets. As seen in Figure 6.2, our global capacity to tap into solar PV and wind resources is growing more rapidly than in any of the other renewable sources. In 2020 the greatest growth in capacity – by far – occurred in the solar PV sector, followed by wind-generated power.[3]

For all these reasons, the management dynamic surrounding these resources is quite different from what we see in the management of more mature and self-sufficient resources (such as with land, petroleum and minerals). In these more mature markets, the enclosure and commodification processes have long been established, and producers no longer depend on the heavy support that they received in their infancy. Today, the management regimes for mature resource markets focus on securing sustainable (mostly economic, but also environmental) development; the harvesting of these resources is assumed to be cost-effective and profitable.

---

3. For a deeper dive into renewable capacity additions; see IEA (2020).

The RE industry remains in its infancy, however, and it benefits greatly from a number of regulatory supports and protections. In RE markets, political authorities encourage expanded production so that renewable sources can replace the energy produced by oil, gas and coal. Consequently, regulatory discussions regarding wind/solar are usually concerned with *subsidizing* production, with political authorities often catering to the needs of the industry.[4]

We recognize that there are good and legitimate reasons to encourage the growth of these natural resource markets, and to steer our energy reliance in the direction of more renewable resources. Temporary subsidies and supports can facilitate the necessary transition to a more competitive and sustainable RE sector. But we also recognize that there are long-term costs to a regime that provides financial support and guarantees to private interests exploiting common resources. Over time, as our reliance on renewable resources grows, and the energy produced by them becomes more competitive, we will find these resources producing substantial Natural Dividends. This chapter helps us prepare for that eventuality.

The market for renewable energy

The market for wind and solar energy is unique. Like other natural resource markets, the market for wind and solar power is different from the markets that sell genuine (non-fictitious) commodities. But this market is also different from the other natural resource markets considered in this book. Consequently, political authority plays a more prominent and instrumental role in the RE market – as a regulator, but also as a major consumer/purchaser of the energy produced.

In this section, we point to five unique characteristics of the RE market for wind and solar power. These unique qualities complicate the underlying ownership structures and commodification pathways to RE markets (compared to what we find in other natural resource markets). As we shall see, this complexity often gets in the way of discussions about the need to capture the rents generated in these markets, whether they are now or in the not too distant future. Box 6.1 introduces some of the most commonly used terms and acronyms to facilitate discussion.

---

4. The length to which political authorities are willing to carry water for this infant industry is evident in a 2016 interview with a Wyoming wind entrepreneur (cited in Yardley 2016), who believed that any attempt to tax his activity would constitute an unjust burden: "Just about every legislator we've met asks us, 'You tell us how much we can tax you before we put you out of business,' said Bill Miller, chief executive of the Power Co. of Wyoming, which is planning the wind farm. 'I just shake my head and say, "Zero."'"

BOX 6.1 RE TERMS AND METRICS

Photovoltaic (PV) materials and devices convert sunlight into electrical energy. A single PV device is known as a cell; cells are usually small and thin – typically thinner than four human hairs and producing only 1 or 2 watts of power. These cells are made of various semiconductor materials and are sandwiched between protective materials in a combination of glass and/or plastics.

Concentrated solar power (CSP) technologies use mirrors to reflect and concentrate sunlight onto a receiver. The energy from the concentrated sunlight heats a high-temperature fluid in the receiver. This thermal energy can then be used to spin a turbine or power an engine to generate electricity.

The energy transfer of electrical power is measured in watts, named after James Watt, the eighteenth-century Scottish inventor. One **watt (W)** is the equivalent of 1 joule per second. In discussions about RE, watts are often aggregated up to **kilowatt (kW)**, or 1,000 (10^3) watts; **megawatt (MW)**, or 1 million watts (10^6); and **gigawatt (GW)**, or 1 billion (10^9) watts.

When sold, energy is often packaged in terms of a **kilowatt-hour (kWh)**, which is the equivalent of one kilowatt of power used continually for one hour; or a **megawatt-hour (MWh)** – i.e. one megawatt of power used over one hour. The amount of energy within a system (or panel) also has a peak value, which is the rate at which the system generates energy at peak performance (e.g. on a sunny afternoon). This peak is often measured in terms of a **kilowatt peak (kWp)**.

The most unusual aspect of RE markets, from the perspective of capturing rent, is that these resources (wind and sunlight) float above the earth's surface in a part of nature that is legally ambiguous. As we learned in Chapter 2: no one owns the sun. With all due respect to Accursius (or, for that matter, Lord Coke), ownership of the air has not, cannot and should not be seen as a simple legal extension of land ownership rights.[5] (If it was, someone should tell the airline industry.) The energy inherent to the wind and the sun are found in a layer of nature (the lower atmosphere) that remains firmly in the commons. In principle, this should make it easier to secure the resulting Natural Dividend for the public/common benefit.

---

5. The maxim *Cuius est solum ejus est usque ad coelum et ad inferos* [For whoever owns the soil, it is theirs up to heaven and down to hell] is usually attributed to Lord Coke, but it can be traced back to the thirteenth-century jurist Accursius; see Law (2015).

The second unique characteristic is that the market for (electrical) energy draws from several different sources and technologies, including other renewable (e.g. hydro and bioenergy) as well as non-renewable (such as coal, gas and oil) and nuclear resources. This means that the price for electricity in any given market is set by the marginal producer in *several* resource markets – not just by the producers of wind, water or solar power. Given this source elasticity, wind and solar power are forced to compete in price with power produced by other sources, such as coal. Hence, any potential rent will be the result of the different productive capacities across several natural resources.

Third, the commodity sold on this market, "electrical energy", is somewhat perishable (or, at least, costly to store). This means that producers are sometimes forced to "spill" their excess production.[6] Consequently, energy markets need to be organized or coordinated in such a way as to ensure that the most perishable forms of energy are used first, while more storable forms can be placed in reserve. This need for coordination makes energy markets less competitive (than other commodity markets), as consumers, regulators and producers are forced to both monitor and coordinate their behaviour in the market. The RE market is not some sort of faceless market, filled with countless price takers, as depicted in Figure 3.2; it is a restricted market, with limited players engaged in highly coordinated activities.

Fourth, the energy sold in these markets is not just perishable and interchangeable; it is necessarily local. This is because each energy market is confined to a distribution grid consisting of a closed network of power lines, limited in size/range. Because of this, the price of energy on one grid will differ from the price of energy on another, until a high-voltage cable can link the two grids together. Even then, there is significant energy loss associated with long-distance electrical power transmission. Indeed, the energy price variance across the European "common" market is phenomenally large, as shown in Figure 6.3, where the price of electricity in pre-war Ukraine at (€0.04/kWh) was roughly a tenth of the price of electricity in Germany (€0.30/kWh) in the second half of 2020.

Consequently, RE producers do not enjoy a world market for their products (as is the case for producers of oil, rice, fish or copper). RE producers must sell to local markets, at a local "spot price" for a particular place and time (see Box 6.2). Unlike other spot prices in the global economy, however, the spot price in one energy grid will differ from the spot market in another network, with little

---

6. This was apparently a significant problem in China's early wind markets, as wind capacity far exceeded the amount of energy being transmitted; see Moe (2017: 361–3). Storage is obviously less of a problem with regard to hydroelectric power, as the power can be stored as water, in reservoirs, to be used at a later date. But wind and solar energy do not enjoy these benefits and need to be used upon production (or stored in costly battery facilities).

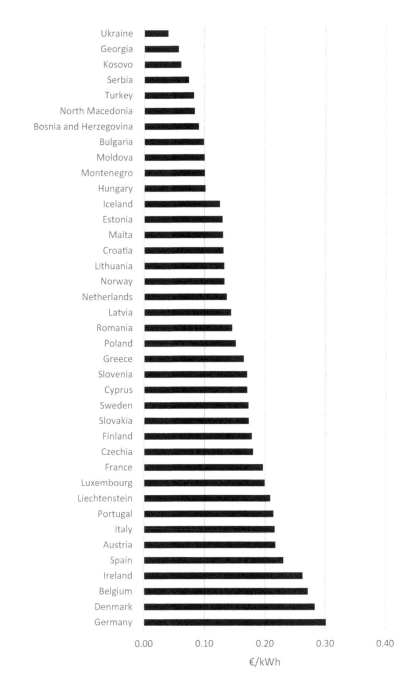

Figure 6.3 European electricity prices (including taxes) for household consumers, 2020
Note: Data are for the second half of 2020 only.
Source: Eurostat (n.d.).

BOX 6.2 SPOT PRICE

"The spot price is the current price in the marketplace at which a given asset – such as a security, commodity, or currency – can be bought or sold for immediate delivery. While spot prices are specific to both time and place, in a global economy the spot price of most securities or commodities tends to be fairly uniform worldwide when accounting for exchange rates."

(Chen 2021)

---

possibility of direct arbitrage. This may change in the future, as local/national/international grids are extended and intertwined, and as battery technologies improve. For now, though, the markets for electricity are remarkably parochial.

Finally, like most of the resource markets considered in this book, the energy market provides communities with an essential commodity. Electrical energy is used to warm/cool houses, keep foodstuffs from perishing, run life-saving equipment, etc. Significant regulation – and often support – is needed to secure power at a just price (sometimes in places that are not particularly cost-effective). Traditionally, electricity markets have often been organized as public utilities, subject to significant public control and regulation. This is because the transportation of power can be considered a natural monopoly, which grants an advantage that is easily abused when it falls into private hands. Even though much of the energy market has been liberalized in recent decades, the underlying infrastructure used to distribute that energy remains concentrated, and mostly under public control.

All these unique qualities complicate the regulation of RE markets. This is a market that includes many actors competing to access the Natural Dividend (landowners, entrepreneurs, local political authorities), and the size of the Natural Dividend will be determined by local variations in productive capacity, over a broad range of competing resources and technologies. Not only is the territorial size of these markets limited to the reach of the grid, but the reach of these grids is determined by political, more than economic, logics. Finally, the overwhelming desire to replace carbon-based sources of electrical power (coal, oil, gas) with cleaner and renewable energy sources (wind and solar) has meant that these local energy markets are skewed by massive subsidies and support systems. These supports have been channelled through a number of different mechanisms to provide RE suppliers with a leg-up on competitors that draw from non-renewable (and dirtier) sources. When gathered together, these unique characteristics create a market with remarkably complex ownership frameworks and regulatory pathways. The next two sections look at each of these challenges.

Ownership frameworks

Unlike many of the natural resources we consider in this book, there is a general consensus that the wind and the sun remain in common ownership. After all, there are few people willing (or able) to claim ownership of the air and sun above us. Even though these two RE resources are located in the upper atmosphere (beyond private ownership), most wind and solar energy production facilities are located on land, and these land-based facilities are regulated and managed in a variety of different ways, in accordance with local legal and political traditions. This means that the landowner (whether private, public or communal) functions as a sort of intermediary between the resource (owned in common) and the energy entrepreneur (who seeks access to the resource).

As the landowner functions as an intermediary, the nature of the underlying land tenure regime will influence the way that political authorities can manage and regulate the solar and wind industries under their jurisdictions. As we saw in Chapter 4, some countries allow for individual ownership in property (with a broad spectrum of tangential rights), while other countries keep land resources in public and/or community hands. Although the actual form of ownership is not relevant to securing the Natural Dividend produced by these resources, it will affect the kind of tools/incentives needed.

To help us navigate these tricky regulatory waters, we can consider how the regulatory regime will vary according to the resource type and where it is landed. Figure 6.4 does just that by creating a 2 × 2 matrix, in which the rows are used to distinguish between wind and solar resources, and the columns distinguish between location sites – i.e. whether the capture of these resources happens onshore or offshore (but still within sovereign territory).[7]

Most offshore territory falls under the control of public officials (whether local, state or federal), as there has been little need or interest in allocating private property rights to offshore property (this may be changing, however, as we saw in the case of fish farming, along with an increased focus on farming offshore or on land).[8] For now, though, we can assume that offshore territory is usually controlled/owned by the state (not private interests), and permission to access offshore wind and solar resources will come from political authorities, by way of some form of concession.

---

7. This distribution is currently more relevant for wind (than solar), but there is no reason to think that offshore solar sites cannot become more viable/common in the future. For the time being we set aside the challenge of managing offshore production plants that might be located in international waters, beyond sovereign territory.

8. There is also considerable disagreement about what, exactly, constitutes "offshore" activity in these sectors. For a discussion regarding wind, see Haggett (2008).

	Onshore		Offshore
Wind	Private	Public/common	Public/common
Solar	Private	Public/common	Public/common

Figure 6.4 Ownership frameworks for RE
Source: Authors.

Onshore production of wind/solar energy is further complicated by the variance in land tenure regimes (as we saw in Chapter 4), as the scope of land ownership can vary significantly from country to country (and over time). Thus, and in contrast to the offshore context, we find both private and public/communal landowners controlling access to onshore wind and solar resources in Figure 6.4.

The result is a cacophony of ownership interests vying for control. At first glance, then, the ownership of RE resources is not complicated, as there has been little effort (to date) to try and enclose or privatize these resources. Ownership of both the wind and the sun remain firmly with the commons. In practice, however, accessing these resources requires the permission of site owners, who hope to secure a share of the Natural Dividend when allocating access to their site. The variance in ownership frameworks, as laid out in Figure 6.4, is only one challenge to managing RE markets. Another significant challenge lies in the extraordinarily complex regulatory pathways. These are the subject of the section that follows.

Regulatory pathways

As with ownership issues, the RE market path, from nature to commodity, is less than straightforward. After all, producing solar and wind power from nature requires a great deal of refinement/transformation. In these markets, the path from nature to finished commodity is long and complex, and the entrepreneur plays a central role in turning natural resources into saleable commodities. To do this, the RE entrepreneur (REE) needs the help of landowners and political authorities alike.

This more involved production process offers significant opportunities for entrepreneurs and investors, but it can also (like the complex ownership structure describe above) obscure the scope of the resulting Natural Dividend. To see how these resources transition from nature (free for the taking) to valuable commodities (such as electrical energy), we can distinguish between four distinct phases, as sketched out in Figure 6.5. In traversing these four phases, nature

Phase	1	2		3		4
Stages	Nature	Enclosure and allocation		Value creation		Commodification
Actions	Wind/sun	Harnessed and licensed		Energy produced		Sold
Relevant actors/owners	Commons	Landowner, entrepreneur, local regulatory officials	→	Entrepreneur	→	Buyers/sellers on local network; network regulator
Value	Free for the taking	Potential value is monopolized		Value is created, but not secured		Returns and rent determined by supply/demand forces

Figure 6.5 The regulatory pathway to commodifying RE resources

Source: Authors.

(in the form of the wind and the sun) is harnessed and enclosed, used to produce energy and then sold on a local energy market (i.e. commodified). In this schematic depiction, we can see a number of different actors involved in each of the four phases.

In the first of the phases in Figure 6.5 (column 1), the wind and the sun are left in their natural state: they are free for the taking, ubiquitous and accessible to all. In this phase, the wind and the sun remain as classic examples of common resources.

The transformation from nature to commodity form starts in the second phase. To better understand this transformation, it might be useful to consider this transformation from the perspective of an REE. Any REE hoping to produce and sell renewable energy must first secure access to a "land" site near the resource in question (i.e. wind or sun). As we have already learned, the more productive the resource, the more attractive the site. This is done in phase 2 of Figure 6.5. In particular, an REE starts by looking for the most productive resource sites – the windiest mountain tops or stretches of sea, and/or the most sun-drenched desert floors – and then tries to secure access. As we have already learned in Chapter 3, these sites are those where the largest rents will be produced, and the entrepreneur is hoping to secure access to these rent-producing sites.[9]

All this is rather odd, in that it is not the land/property itself that is producing the energy (and subsequent rent). Rather, the property is being used as a landing site, through which this energy can be brought to market. As we shall soon see, this access produces a locational rent. Although there may be some who continue to hold that a landowner has a right to the Natural Dividend produced on her land (we do not), it is difficult to extend this argument to the capture of rents from resources that are *not owned* by the landowner (or anyone else, for that matter). It is for this reason that we used the first section to clarify and map out the various ownership frameworks. In the end, the most productive sites will be scattered across both publicly, communally and privately owned land resources, depending on the national regulatory context and land tenure regime in place.

Once a productive site is located, the REE will need to negotiate with the property owner to secure access to the desired resource. The end result of these negotiations will look something like a concessions agreement, whereby the property owner grants access to the entrepreneur to build a production facility,

---

9. We do not mean to imply that the REE is searching for a site with an eye on stealing the Natural Dividend. The entrepreneur probably does not recognize the existence of the Natural Dividend and is simply searching for the most productive site in an effort to increase her returns on investment. The REE can then justify any extraordinary return with reference to an unearned windfall/ luck. This is a convenient and common view, albeit a skewed one – and it is a view we hope to correct with our work.

for a limited period of time, in exchange for some form of payment. Sometimes this access is auctioned off to the highest bidder; sometimes it is the result of private (secret) negotiations, with the surrounding community kept in the dark about the terms of the exchange. Note, however, that the entrepreneur is not paying for the wind/sun (and the landowner does not enjoy any form of tenure/ownership over these resources, so she cannot legally transfer them). In effect, the wind or solar energy is being given away, free of charge – by a landowner who does not have the legal authority to do so. The form of this agreement, and the nature of the negotiations, will vary significantly between private and public landowners (even if the effect on the surrounding nature/community will be the same).

The result of this agreement is worthless, however, unless the REE is granted permission from political authorities (who may, or may not, own the underlying site) to build a production facility at that particular site. Depending on the nature of the regulatory regime, the entrepreneur may need to secure planning, land use and building permits, as well as some form of environmental and social impact assessment. In these ways, the regulatory process is not unlike what we saw with fish farms in Chapter 5. After all, there can be substantial local resistance to the creation of a large-scale wind farm or solar array/furnace, and political authorities regulate land use to mitigate this resistance. On top of this level of regulatory complexity lies yet another, in that the allocation of formal regulatory power can also vary significantly across national, regional and local decision-makers. In some countries, local authorities are granted substantial regulatory discretion; in others, it may be the strategic needs of the nation that are determinant, and these are allowed to over-ride local preferences.

By the end of this long and complicated second phase, the resource has become – in effect – enclosed and allocated. The entrepreneur has received formal recognition by the relevant political authority of a right to produce power, from a common natural resource, at a particular site, for a limited (or sometimes unlimited) period of time.

Although the natural resources may be enclosed during phase 2, the entrepreneur is still not producing any energy. All the effort extended thus far has simply secured a sort of legal and regulatory foundation, upon which the entrepreneur hopes to build an energy production facility. The actual production of energy occurs during phase 3 in Figure 6.5. Here the entrepreneur builds a production facility that captures the natural resource and turns it into electrical energy, using any number of relevant technologies (turbines, PV cells, furnaces, etc.).

It is in phase 3 that we see the economic attraction of RE production. Once the initial investments have been made, there are few running costs associated with producing RE – as the main inputs (wind/sun) are provided free of charge.

In other words, once the initial investments are covered (e.g. building the wind turbine or solar furnace, and hooking it up), and a small amount is deducted for regular maintenance needs, investors are able to harvest money with each new windy (or sunny) day.

Even now, though, at the end of phase 3, the REE is not out of the woods: the power produced is worthless because it has not yet found its way to market (and potential buyers) – i.e. it has not yet been commodified. In the absence of some direct consumer (e.g. a nearby industry), or an enormous battery, the energy produced will have to be spilled. It is, effectively, worthless.

The source of the Natural Dividend

This brings to the fourth and final phase in Figure 6.5: the commodification phase. Even if a tenacious entrepreneur is able to secure access to a productive site, and receives all the necessary permissions and licences to build a production facility, and then builds the facility to the highest standards, she will be unable to cash in on those efforts/investments without access to a nearby energy grid. To do this, the PEE needs some form of permission or licence to access the grid (which is usually owned by a public entity), along with a requisite remuneration scheme. This permission generates a locational rent.

Locational rent

As we have frequently noted, the Natural Dividend is made up of three component rents: the first two – differential and regulatory – have been introduced in the preceding two chapters. Here we turn to the third component rent: the locational rent.

The first recognition of a locational rent can be traced to Johann Heinrich von Thünen (1966 [1826]), who extended Ricardo's argument by demonstrating how transportation costs generated a rent of their own in important agricultural markets, which varied with distance to market (see Clark 1967; Blaug 1985: 295). In other words, farmland that was located close to the market was valued more than farmland located at a distance. Henry George, in turn, emphasized how this infrastructure is usually the result of public investment, not private initiative. Thus, nearness to a city generates a rent: property values nearest the city tend to be much higher than the property value on lots that are furthest from the city. The benefits to landowners of being near civic services and public works (or even cities in themselves) can be capitalized into higher land values. As with differential and regulatory rents, the added value is not the result of the acumen, initiative, labour or risk of the concessionaire; it is created by the community.

Locational rents are especially important in the market for renewable energy – as electrical energy is difficult to sell when it is not connected to a grid. But we begin with a couple of examples that employ land, rather than renewable energy, as it is with land resources that locational rents were first recognized.

There are several examples of land values increasing significantly as the result of new public works projects (and of landowners lobbying strongly for their construction). In 1958 Gilbert M. Tucker estimated that the construction of the George Washington Bridge across the Hudson River increased New Jersey site values by some $300,000,000, or by six times the cost of the bridge (Tucker 1958: 11).[10] Several recent studies have been conducted on the rent-creating effects of extending London's public infrastructure. For example, it was estimated that the Jubilee Line extension of the London Underground increased local land values by about 52 per cent; and extending the Docklands Light Railway generated a 23 per cent land value uplift. In addition, the City of London estimated that a sample of eight prospective Transport for London (TfL) projects, which were projected to cost around £36 billion, could produce land value uplifts estimated at £87 billion (TfL 2017: 7). In short, public investment in infrastructure can create massive rents; in many cases these rents are large enough to pay for the infrastructure projects.

To bring this discussion a little closer to the ground, we can report the findings of Nationwide's (2014) study of the effects of an extended infrastructure on expected property values, as illustrated in Figure 6.6. Nationwide examined how nearness to a tube or railway station affected property prices in Greater London, while controlling for other relevant property characteristics (e.g. size, neighbourhood type, type of property, etc.). The building society found that a property located 500 metres from a station could secure a 10.5 per cent higher price, relative to an otherwise similar property located 1,500 m from the station. The further away from the station, the smaller the price increase: at 750 m it was 7.6 per cent; at 1,000 m it was 4.9 per cent; etc.

In this example, the property located 1,500 m from a station is akin to the least productive farm in Figure 4.1: this offers the baseline market price, against which the other property prices are compared. The closer one gets to the station, the higher the market value, *ceteris paribus*. The different prices reveal the locational rent: nearness to an underground station increases the value of the property, independent of any improvements made to the property by the owner.

---

10. Similarly, Harrison (2008: 115) tells an amusing story about how the Russian mafia collects rents from kiosks that vary along with their distance from nearby metro stations.

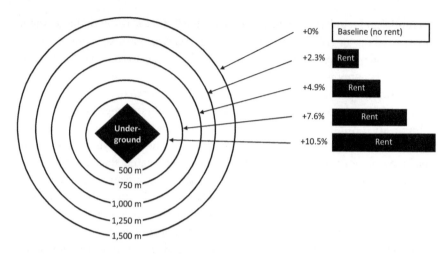

Figure 6.6 Locational rent
Source: Nationwide (2014).

As with land (and sea) resources, wind and solar resources have the potential to produce a Natural Dividend thanks to their advantageous location: resources that lie closest to the market, or to existing infrastructure, enjoy a rent that is not found in more remote resource locations; housing lots that are located near established public infrastructure (e.g. a city bustling with jobs, a train line, or a water/sewer system) are worth more than those that are not; gas fields that lie near an existing pipeline infrastructure are more valuable than those that are not. In RE markets, the most productive resources are often located far from demand and existing distribution networks. When this is the case, it matters little if the most productive solar resources are in Namibia, when the purchaser of that energy lies in Europe: excess energy produced in Namibia will need to be spilled. As with differential and regulatory rents, the additional value that is created by location in these examples was in no way the result of the concessionaire's efforts, ingenuity or willingness to take risks: it is a product of the society around her.

Remuneration schemes

To better understand the market for RE, we need to see how REEs tend to be reimbursed by political authorities. As can be seen in Box 6.3, political authorities draw from a number of different remuneration schemes,[11] including feed-in tariffs

---

11. For an overview of different policy instruments for fostering these projects, see Enzensberger, Wietschel and Rentz (2002), Aparicio *et al.* (2012) and IRENA, IEA and REN21 (2018).

BOX 6.3 MAIN TYPES OF REIMBURSEMENT SCHEMES IN THE RE SECTOR

Price regulation schemes include *feed-in tariffs* (FITs) or *feed-in premiums* (FIPs), which regulate/control the price paid for energy – i.e. they fix the price for power that is licensed to enter the grid. This is the dominant approach used in China, but it has also been used in a number of other markets. The popularity of these schemes rests on their simplicity and their capacity to offer REEs a certain (and stable) long-term revenue stream. In effect, these schemes shield project developers from energy price volatility by guaranteeing a fixed payment for each MWh of renewable energy produced.

Quantity regulation schemes include quota systems, tradable certificates, *renewable purchase obligations* (RPOs) and *renewable portfolio standards* (RPSs). Although these systems were popular in the early days of RE, and they remain fairly prominent in the United States, they appear to be on their way out. They start at the other end of the price/quantity continuum, where political authorities require that energy suppliers (grid managers) include a minimum amount of renewable energy sources in their supply (for example, authorities requiring that X per cent of the total supply in a given grid needs to be from RE sources, before a given date). This scheme helps the REE by promising a guaranteed purchaser for a given quantity of power (even though the price of that energy can fluctuate significantly).

A **power purchase agreement** (PPA) is an arrangement in which third-party developers install, own and operate an energy system on a customer's property (e.g. the site of an industrial production facility). The customer then purchases the system's electric output for a predetermined period of time. This purchase can be arranged as a competitive auction. PPA schemes allow a customer to receive a stable and often low-cost supply of electricity with no upfront costs, while enabling the REE to take advantage of tax credits and long-term revenue certainty.

Tenders and auctions refer to a procurement process that relies on some form of competitive bidding. This procurement process is then limited to electricity generated from renewable energy or when renewable energy technologies are eligible. These schemes are growing in popularity, especially in Europe, and in the first half of 2020 13 countries awarded nearly 50 GW in new capacity, breaking a record for auction capacity. Tendered processes tend to attract and encourage large developers, which can benefit from economies of scale and use these to achieve lower bids (IEA 2020: 40).

(FITs), quota systems (e.g. tradable certificates) and renewable purchase obligations (RPOs), power purchase agreements (PPAs) and competitive auction systems. These schemes are often supplemented with a number of other sticks and carrots, such as government-mandated (renewable energy) targets and/or tax reductions. Although these remuneration schemes can change over time, each enjoys a strong footing in one of the three large RE markets: China, Europe and the United States.

Although auction regimes predominate in Europe, they remain relatively uncommon in China (around 10 per cent), where FITs still dominate. In the United States, by contrast, most new facilities are generated under corporate PPAs (a little more than 40 per cent) combined with other incentives, such as tax credits and renewable portfolio standards (RPSs), along with additional revenue sources (e.g. green certificates) (IEA 2020: 79, fig. 4.3). These regional patterns seem to be changing, as the International Energy Agency has noted how many countries are moving away from support schemes that rely on administratively set tariffs to competitive auctions for long-term power purchase agreements. The agency's *Renewables 2019* expected that more than two-thirds of all new utility-scale renewable capacity over the next five years would be set competitively (IEA 2019: 154).

Figure 6.7 provides an overview of the most common remuneration schemes in the RE sector, for the near future (up to 2025). The IEA (2020) estimates that roughly a third of these schemes will be in the form of administratively set tariffs (35 per cent), 35 per cent will be in the form of competitive auctions and another 26 per cent of the arrangements will rely on a potpourri of different schemes (7 per cent in the form of PPAs, 6 per cent unsolicited,[12] while another 13 per cent will be spread across green certificates, merchant plants and mixed regimes). Only 4 per cent of these future agreements are expected to rely on government utility investments.

Although the remuneration schemes vary significantly, they all follow a similar logic, whereby the commodity price of the energy produced is either given (regulated) or is established in competition with other resource providers, with a resulting spot price. Given the localized nature of these markets, each spot price will be set by the least productive resource/technology in that local market – while the most productive resources will be generating the largest rents. Consequently, the resulting Natural Dividends will vary significantly across local markets, but be limited by the size of the market/grid.

As part of an infant industry, RE producers required substantial support in order to outcompete the non-renewable (and dirtier) energy resources. To date, our regulatory emphasis has been on subsidizing RE producers rather than measuring or securing the Natural Dividend. Today's RE management regimes are not aimed at demonstrating a link between resource ownership and value

---

12. An unsolicited contract is a bilateral contract between a power producer and the utility.

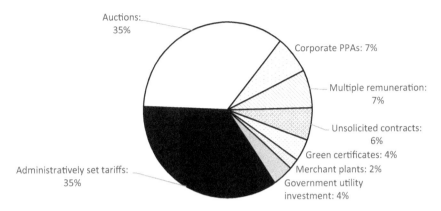

Figure 6.7 Variance in RE remuneration schemes, 2020–2025
Source: IEA (2020).

creation. Indeed, there is remarkably little mention of the fact that our underlying resources are simply given away, free of charge, in hopes that the REE
can reduce the threat of climate change, and perhaps deliver some jobs and tax
revenues to local communities.

As these RE markets mature, however, we expect them to become more productive, more concentrated and more capable of generating a significant Natural
Dividend. The problem is that we have not yet developed a regulatory regime
that can capture those Dividends when they arise.

State of the rent

In mapping the state of global wind and solar rents, it is important to distinguish
between the availability of the resources (their natural potential) and their capture in, and delivery to, markets around the world. These two things are very
different. As with every other type of natural resource, there is no political logic
to the distribution of RE resources; from a political perspective, the most productive sites are, in fact, misplaced. As we shall see, the strongest RE resources,
in terms of natural productive potential, are found at a great distance from the
most powerful states and their large markets.

Resource potential

We can begin by mapping the natural distribution of these resources. Figure 6.8
presents data from the World Bank on the most promising spots on the globe for
producing photovoltaic power. Their indicator for theoretical solar PV potential is determined by a number of factors, including latitude, terrain and air

Figure 6.8 The world's best PV power potential sites

Notes: This map employs the World Bank's estimate of "solar-photovoltaic (PV) power generation", which is measured in terms of kWh and kWp (kilowatt peak). The marked areas on the map are those areas of the world that have the greatest solar PV power potential, scoring on average above 5kWh per day, or 1,825 kWp per year. See the original source for model information that explains how these estimates are generated.

Source: Global solar atlas; https://globalsolaratlas.info/map?c=11.609193,8.349609,3.

temperature (see World Bank 2020b: viii). When mapped onto political space, we see that the (potentially) most productive PV sites are remarkable scarce. The site with the highest average practical potential is located in Namibia and the lowest practical potential is found in Ireland. More to the point, only about 20 per cent of the global population lives in those countries that can boast excellent conditions for PV, where long-term daily expected PV output averages exceed 4.5 kWh/kWp (World Bank 2020b: ix).

In this map, we can clearly find the greatest PV potential in the middle (between 30 degrees north and south) and southern latitudes. The strongest potential seems to be bunched into four areas: the Middle East and north Africa (MENA) region; sub-Saharan Africa; the western hip of South America (at the nexus of Chile, Bolivia and Peru); and in Australia. Although the south-western regions of the United States and China also have formidable PV resources, most of these countries – and almost all of Europe – are poorly endowed in long-term PV power potential.

An even more pronounced pattern can be found in the global wind power potential map shown in Figure 6.9. Here we find the best resources sites located at the extreme latitudes (north and south) and at the most exposed capes and land protrusions (Cape Horn, Tasmania and New Zealand) and narrow channels (the Davis Strait separating Greenland and Canada; the Denmark Straight between Greenland and Iceland; the Norwegian and Barents Seas surrounding Norway; and the waters surrounding the Korean peninsula – e.g. Sea of Japan, Yellow Sea and Korea Bay). As with solar PV resources, the most productive wind resources tend to be located far away from the largest and most powerful states (e.g. United States, Russia, China).

In short, the most productive RE resources lie at a great distance from the markets that will need them. As demand for RE grows, the world's richest and most powerful states will seek access to these resources, and the most productive sites in a global market can expect to generate significant future rents. In theory, the states that control these resources should be able to attract REEs and secure the Natural Dividend for their citizens. This is the same pattern we have seen in other natural resource markets, such as the markets for minerals, oil and salmon. The difference, of course, is that these RE markets are not yet global. This means that energy produced at the most productive sites cannot yet make it to the markets with the greatest demand.[13] When and if these markets are unified into a global market, the resulting rents could be astonishingly large.

---

13. This situation is similar to what we saw in the early years of the natural gas industry, when gas resources were often spilled/flared at the site, in the absence of market delivery mechanisms. Eventually, producers constructed pipelines, connecting to distant markets, as well as developing new technologies (e.g. liquefying), which allowed gas to be transported over long distances to meet demand in an increasingly global market for gas.

Figure 6.9 The world's best wind power density potential sites

Notes: This map employs the World Bank's estimate of "mean wind power density" at 100 m above the surface level. This indicator varies from 0 to over 1,200 W/m^2 (watts per square metre). The marked areas on the map are those areas of the world that have the greatest wind power potential, scoring above 900 W/m^2. See the original source for model information that explains how these estimates are generated.

Source: World Bank, "Wind resource map"; https://s3-eu-west-1.amazonaws.com/globalwindatlas3/HR_posters/pd_World.pdf.

Resource capacity

The productive potential of RE differs significantly from its productive capacity. This is partly because of the localized nature of RE markets. The drivers of RE capacity are not found in the hottest spots in the MENA region or on the wind-swept polar areas. The world's largest and most powerful states are now competing with one another to establish technical dominance in RE technologies, even if their own resource pools are relatively shallow.

To date, we see RE markets developing most quickly in some of the wealthiest and most powerful states. It is here that the race for the Natural Dividend is unfolding, as powerful states support domestic champions in hopes of capturing global markets (and rents). Figure 6.10 provides an overview of global solar energy capacity in 2020, and it is divided into three component figures. In the top panel of Figure 6.10, we see the total amount of solar capacity available in 2020, which totalled 716,152 MW (IRENA 2021: 40). This total capacity was made up almost completely (99 per cent) by energy produced by solar PV, as only 6,378 MW was generated in concentration facilities.

In this top (total) figure, we find that global capacity of solar energy is dominated by the top three producing states, which together generated over 55 per cent of this capacity. China dominated the global solar market, generating 35.5 per cent, followed by the United States (10.6 per cent) and India (9.6 per cent).

The bottom two panels in Figure 6.10 break down this solar market into its component parts. The global capacity generated by PV in 2020 was 709,674 MW. As PV represents the lion's share of global solar capacity, it is not surprising to see that this market is also highly concentrated, with the top three PV producers capturing over 55 per cent of global capacity, and China dominating these statistics as well. More surprising, perhaps, is that Japan is among the three dominant producers of PV energy, producing 9.7 per cent of global PV capacity. Finally, the concentrated solar energy market is remarkably small, and less concentrated politically, with the top three producers capturing just 44 per cent of global concentrated capacity. The United States has managed to capture a little more than a quarter of this capacity, followed by Morocco and China.

The global capacity for wind energy is similarly concentrated. In 2020 total wind energy capacity, globally, was estimated at 732,410 MW – just slightly more than the global solar capacity. As with solar energy, this global market for wind energy can be further subdivided into its two main sources: the energy produced onshore (95 per cent) and the remaining (and much smaller) share that was produced offshore. Figure 6.11 illustrates this breakdown in a way that is similar to Figure 6.10.

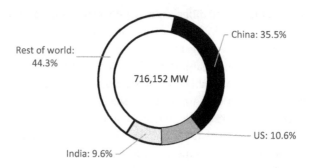

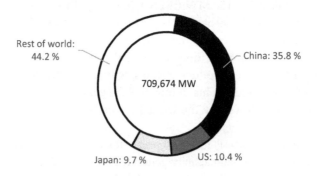

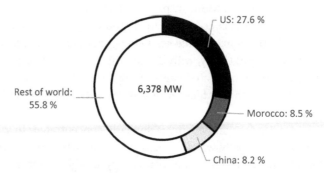

Figure 6.10 Global solar capacity, 2020
Source: IRENA (2021: 39–53).

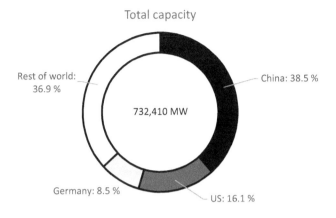

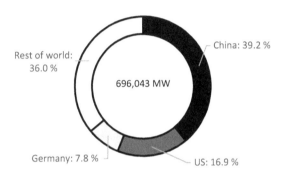

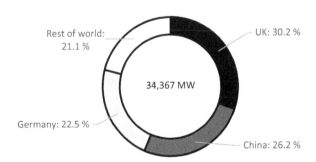

Figure 6.11 Global wind energy capacity, 2020
Source: IRENA (2021: 26–38).

In Figure 6.11, we see that global wind capacity is even more concentrated politically than we found with global solar capacity: about 63 per cent of the worlds' total wind energy capacity is estimated to have been generated by the three largest producer states in 2020. Once again, China dominated global capacity (38.5 per cent), followed by the United States and Germany.[14] When we break this capacity up into its component parts, we see that most of this capacity is generated onshore (696,043 MW), where the major producing states are the same as we see in the overall figures (with China dominating, followed by the United States and Germany). By contrast, the offshore capacity remained rather limited (34,367 MW), but highly concentrated, with nearly 80 per cent of all offshore capacity being produced by the three top producing states: the United Kingdom (30.2 per cent), China and Germany.

In both types of RE market, we see a stark division between the location of the most productive potential and the location of the world's most productive capacity. In the markets for solar energy, Morocco is the only state that has managed to leverage its gift of nature into a significant capacity to produce concentrated solar power energy. The same pattern is evident in global wind markets, where the United Kingdom is the only state that is exposed to significant wind power density potential (see Figure 6.9).

The most prominent capacity-producing states in the world are not those with the most productive potential: the most prominent states in Figures 6.8 and 6.9 differ markedly from those in Figure 6.10 and 6.11. Rather, capacity is concentrated in the largest markets and strongest states. This is clearly a function of aggregation and demand (large states are able to record larger capacity), but it is striking to see how little overlap we find between potential and capacity. In these larger markets, we are already seeing the sort of concentration that drives efficiency gains. It is here we see the race for market dominance.

Over time, these large markets will need to expand their supply by tapping into the world's most productive wind and solar sites, as shown in Figures 6.8 and 6.9. This expansion is bound to look like the early (and phenomenal) growth of international oil companies – for example Shell, Standard Oil (now Chevron, ExxonMobil) and British Petroleum – as they scoured the globe in search of new petroleum resources and created a global market in their wake. This will require new technologies and expanded networks, but it is not unreasonable to expect both in the near future. The result of these changes will be a more global market for RE resources. These global markets will facilitate economies of scale, allowing greater concentration, efficiencies and the capture of significant Natural Dividends.

---

14. When European states aggregate their capacity at the EU level, then the scope of political concentration is even greater.

Securing the Natural Dividend in renewable energy markets

There is remarkably little interest in trying to measure, secure and/or tax the Natural Dividend generated in local RE markets.[15] As in the agricultural sector, the political focus has been trained on providing subsidies to support domestic producers. In the early years this support was necessary to help shift our energy reliance away from non-renewable carbon-based resources to more renewable resource forms. As these markets become more competitive, they will begin to generate rents, and political authorities should want to capture the resulting Natural Dividend.

This effort to capture the Natural Dividend is especially challenging in the RE market, given the complex ownership frameworks and regulatory pathways outlined earlier in this chapter. These uniquely complex features obfuscate the Natural Dividend and provide access to many competing interests, all of which hope to capture a slice of the rents. But even in this complex setting it is possible to secure the Natural Dividend. What is needed, first and foremost, is the political will to do so.

From Chapter 3, readers will recall that the Natural Dividend is simply the difference between a producer's overall revenues (here the amount of energy sold on the local market at the spot price – or the guaranteed price from an FIT) and all the costs of producing that energy, *including* a fair return on labour, capital (and risk). For the political authorities to secure the Natural Dividend, they need to do two things.

The first task is a simple matter of justice. Political authorities need to justify their role in securing the Natural Dividend for the public. This is not difficult, in that much of the (market) value of RE is generated by nature and the regulation of access to that nature (in terms of a concession, but also access to the surrounding infrastructure). When energy markets become volatile, say because of poor weather conditions or war, then the Natural Dividend can be used to help buffer consumers from volatile prices, as described in Box 6.4.

The second task is a simple matter of accounting. As with the market for farmed salmon, political authorities will need to negotiate with the concessionaires to determine relevant costs and normal profit levels so that they can agree on when, exactly, the Natural Dividend is becoming large enough to retrieve. They then need to collect basic revenue/cost information from energy producers and

---

15. One important exception is the work done by Greaker and Lindholt (2019), for the Norwegian statistical bureau. They estimate the rent on the Norwegian power sector but combine wind and water resources. Although the rents generated in this sector (about 35 billion kroner in 2018, or roughly $4.3 billion) are less than in the Norwegian petroleum sector, they are impressive, and will surely grow in the future. See also Brigham and Moses (2021).

BOX 6.4 USING THE NATURAL DIVIDEND TO TAME VOLATILE ENERGY MARKETS

In 2022 the price of electricity in Europe skyrocketed. These high prices were partly the result of a push to replace carbon-based energy (coal and oil) with cleaner wind and solar power. This has made the European energy market extremely susceptible to weather patterns (lack of wind and sun, rise in cold weather) and insufficient sources of back-up energy. These conditions were then exacerbated by the war in Ukraine, which made it more difficult for Europe to access Russian natural gas, and which pushed energy prices, in general, through the roof.

Two Norwegian economists, Diderick Lund and Knut Einar Rosendahl (2022), have suggested a novel way by which political authorities could use what we call the Natural Dividend as a price cushion, or buffer, to protect consumers from exorbitant swings in prices. In particular, they point to the utility of using an RRT to secure any extraordinary surplus from energy producers. After all, when retail energy prices escalate, so too does the Natural Dividend. As this Natural Dividend increases, the political authorities can channel some (or all) of this Dividend back to consumers, by way, for example, of a monthly credit. In this way, the average consumer can be compensated for the rise in energy prices (instead of the increase ending up as an unearned windfall for the energy producer).

We do not have the space to elaborate on this proposal, but it is both innovative and attractive. For example, Lund and Rosendahl (2022) describe how the system could be devised in such a way that it would still incentivize customers to reduce their energy consumption as prices rise.

This sort of consumer rebate could also be used in any of the other natural resource markets described in this book, given sufficient political will. For example, such a rebate system could be used to dampen petroleum price fluctuations at the pump, or natural gas prices in a Europe struggling with war. Indeed, in the autumn of 2022, the European Commission seemed tempted to do something along these lines. On 12 September it released a draft proposal to introduce a "solidarity contribution" on the fossil fuel industry, based on "taxable surplus profits", which could be used to help vulnerable households.[1]

---

1. www.euractiv.com/section/energy/news/eu-plans-solidarity-contribution-from-oil-and-gas-firms-during-energy-crisis

ensure that these are legitimate (not inflated or gold-plated). This is not a new or alien task for political authorities; they already maintain income tax and property assessing competences, and the resulting maths (revenue – costs = rent) is not particularly challenging. To calculate the Natural Dividend, political authorities need to compare all costs (including the return on capital) with what is standard (competitive) in similar industries. In markets in which risk plays a large role, this risk premium needs to be included. When excesses are uncovered, they can be marked as rent, and the authorities can then tax this rent at a higher level than the tax on earned income or surplus (i.e. through an RRT). Doing so, as we saw in Chapter 3, will reduce the risks and uncertainties of investing in a sector with an active/volatile spot price. This approach offers a win-win situation for producers, political authorities and the public that own the underlying resources.

In particular, this can be done by making some minor adjustments in phases 2 and 4 of Figure 6.5. The first change is to simply claim the public's ownership of our common resources as part of the enclosure process. Rather than granting full control (*fee simple*), political authorities should clarify that the enclosure grants a form of *usufructuary leasehold* (see Box 4.3 for clarification on these terms). In recognizing the productive potential in natural resources and claiming public ownership over them, political authorities legitimize their claim on the Natural Dividend these resources produce. In the doing, it becomes more difficult to simply gift these resources to individual interests (as is done now).

In claiming public ownership, we are not ignoring or minimizing the value produced by the landlord (in terms of offering a landing site), or the need for the site holder (and the surrounding community) to be compensated for the inconvenience of the production facility that results. After all, if the land is used to produce RE, it is not available for alternative uses. The landowner should expect an annual payment for the access that her site provides – but this payment should not be so large as to shave off the resulting Natural Dividend. Similarly, in recognizing this enclosure, political authorities might require that a certain percentage of energy produced remain with the local community and/or landowner to pay for these inconveniences and services. This would be a more direct claim on the productive capacity of the resource (which is not yet rent), before it has been commodified.

Nor do we wish to minimize the significant effort exerted by the REE to coordinate and bring this productive effort to life. REEs deserve just rewards for their invested time, energy and money. The management regime we are proposing will ensure this. But, once the initial investments are recovered, the wind and sun can produce phenomenal value for the concessionaire with little or no additional value being added.

The next step can be made in phase 4, when political authorities allocate access to the public grid, and decide the terms of that access (remuneration schemes).

To secure the Natural Dividend, political authorities might arrange licence/concession agreements for wind and solar resources in a way that is similar to what we find in the Norwegian regime for managing petroleum (see Chapter 7). In deciding who will be granted access to the most attractive sites, the authorities could create licences in the form of joint ventures (JVs), which pair industry leaders with local producers. This would ensure that the technical competence needed to turn nature into energy is shared with the local community. But such JVs could also be created in a way that allows an NRC to become co-owner in the licence, with a requisite share of returns.

The simplest way to secure the Natural Dividend, however, is by means of a taxation regime that allows the political authorities to identify the Dividend and tax it accordingly, as described in Chapter 3. The political authorities will know the spot price at which the energy is sold; they can gather information about the costs of that production through its regular means of tax collection, and then they can generate a fair estimate of returns on capital and risk. When the overall returns exceed these costs and the fair returns on investment, then the government can tax this excess at a much higher rate, without a detrimental effect on production.

Consider, for example, Europe's extremely high electricity prices in the winter of 2022/23. These prices were being driven upwards by a significantly reduced supply of energy inputs, in large part because of the war in Ukraine (and the resulting embargo on Russian natural gas imports). For those European producers generating electricity using natural gas, the higher prices reflect the difficulty of securing enough natural gas. But for those that can produce energy cheaply (i.e. those that do not rely on Russian natural gas inputs), then the rents from these higher prices can be astronomical (see Box 6.5).

This is neither new nor difficult. The general outlines of the regime we are proposing are the same as those in the LVT regimes described in Chapter 4, and the way in which the Norwegian authorities have secured the massive rent generated by its petroleum sector, as described in the following chapter.

As we saw earlier in this chapter, a growing share of the RE market is now being allocated by tender/auction arrangements. This trend deserves comment, on two grounds. First, it is important to point out that auctions in themselves cannot secure the Natural Dividend. This is because auctions are one-time events, while the Natural Dividend is dynamic (and will change with market conditions, over time). Auctions are used to secure a monopoly form of access to a scarce resource (here the grid); they cannot capture the non-competitive gains that this access provides.

More interesting, perhaps, is that a growing reliance on auctions can generate a larger Natural Dividend and make it easier for the political authorities to collect. This is because auctions tend to concentrate the industry in ways that

BOX 6.5 EUROPEAN ELECTRICITY RENTS: A RECENT EXAMPLE

Norway is not a member of the European Union but it does share much of the European market, and this relationship is governed by the European Economic Area (EEA) agreement. Before 2013 the EEA agreement did not have much impact on Norwegian energy markets, as their respective electricity grids were not integrated. Their subsequent integration offers a natural experiment, in which we can see how the expansion of a market can facilitate the production of greater rents for the most productive producers.

The Norwegian energy market is dominated by hydropower, but with a growing share coming from wind sources. With an abundance of hydroelectric and wind sites distributed across the country, Norway has not needed to develop a highly integrated national grid. In the past this market for electrical power has been mostly limited to local producers and consumers, and the marginal cost of producing power has been very low. In practice, the electricity grid is itself divided into various regions, with limited capacity to transfer excess power from one region to another. Consequently, the spot price for electricity can vary across the country, with the energy prices in southern Norway being different from those in the north and the west.

For 2022 the Norwegian Ministry of Petroleum and Energy (Olje- og energidepartementet: OED) estimated that the average price of power production in the country was about 0.1157kr per kWh (OED 2021). This is the concession price: the price that local authorities are expected to pay when they purchase power, which is set to reflect the real cost of production (i.e. no mark-up). It is the Norwegian government's best estimate of what it costs to produce electrical power. When this Norwegian market is isolated from the larger European market, the price of Norwegian power will reflect these local production costs.

European power draws from several sources, including coal and nuclear, wind and solar, but also natural gas (from Russia). Because Europe has been trying to wean itself off coal, and lacks sufficient hydroelectric reserves, its energy market is very sensitive to current weather conditions (i.e. when the wind blows and the sun shines, power is cheaper), and this market had become increasingly dependent on Russian natural gas to supply the grid. Hence, until recently, the marginal producer of power in Europe used natural gas. When the source of this gas was cut off, European electricity prices increased exponentially.

In 2013 parts of the Norwegian and European electricity markets were joined up. Norway began to lay two long transmission cables (one to Germany, the other to the United Kingdom) in an effort to connect the energy market in southern Norway with the rest of Europe. These cables did not affect the regional electricity markets in the middle and northern parts of Norway, which remained isolated from the broader European market (although each has smaller linkages to Sweden). The energy market in southern Norway became more integrated with the European market, and the local prices came to reflect the (higher) costs of production in Europe (even if the local supplier can still produce power at a much lower cost).

In effect, Norway has three regional electricity markets, with different spot prices in each, but the southern region is integrated with the European market. These unique conditions provide good examples of the source of rent in electricity prices, and how grid–market integration can affect the rents produced.

Let us examine the cost of power, and the size of rents, in these three Norwegian electricity markets: in September 2022 the price in Oslo (southern Norway) was 4.35kr per kWh (the spot price varies during the day, so these are estimates); in Trondheim, mid-Norway, on the same day it was 0.50kr; whereas in northern Norway (Tromsø) it was just 0.25kr (www.hvakosterstrommen.no).

Region	Kroner price	US dollar price
Oslo	4.35kr/kWh	$0.40/kWh
Trondheim	0.50kr/kWh	$0.05/kWh
Tromsø	0.25kr/kWh	$0.02/kWh

It costs producers in southern Norway (e.g. Oslo) 0.12kr per kWh, but they are able to sell at 4.35kr per kWh.[1] The rent produced in mid- and northern Norway is *much* less. In short, the selling price of electricity in the south has nothing to do with the local cost, nor with the acumen of Norwegian producers; it is the result of a poorly managed power market in Europe, inflamed by a war.

Market conditions in Europe are generating a Natural Dividend of 4.13kr (4.25 – 0.1157kr) for each kWh. Norwegian households, on average, consume about 16,000 kWh a year. If there are 1 million households in southern Norway, then the power producers are able to rake in a phenomenal windfall over the course of the year: 66,080,000,000 kroner [(16,000 kWh x 4.13kr) 1,000,000 inhabitants], or $6,149,404,800. This Natural Dividend should be returned to residents of southern Norway or collected by political authorities to be used for the common good. It matters not whether the Dividend is collected by private or public companies; it matters only that this Dividend is returned to its rightful owners. Equally problematic is the fact that cheap electrical power has become the main means for warming Norwegian homes, and has provided a distinct competitive advantage for Norwegian firms that rely heavily on energy inputs. These advantages have been lost in southern Norway by allowing their electricity producers to access European prices for their power.

If southern Norway had not connected to the European power grid, its prices would reflect local production costs. By linking to the European market, electricity producers in Norway are able to generate enormous rents, because they are much more productive than the marginal producer on the continent. An enormous rent, generated largely by the war in Ukraine, is being paid for by their local consumers.

---

1. It should be noted that many of these producers are public authorities (sometimes local, regional, even state), not private actors. In principle, this should make it easier to secure the Natural Dividend, as much of it lies with these public authorities. But retrieving the Natural Dividend is complicated by the EEA agreement mentioned above and, in particular, the European Union's Third and Fourth Energy Packages. We do not want to wade too deep into these waters, as the scope of these energy packages is highly controversial in Norway; the threat of the Third Energy Package to Norwegian sovereignty was even questioned before the Supreme Court of Norway: see SCN (2021).

---

exploit economies of scale to win auction bids. The growing use of auctions (and their ability to attract global bidders) is also evidence that there is money to be made in this sector; it is becoming less and less dependent upon the state supports that were necessary at the start. This concentrated market can increase the productive capacity that inflates the Natural Dividend, but it also limits the number of producers that need to be monitored by the political authorities. In order to minimize the economic and political inequalities this concentration is bound to produce, the political authorities can employ an RRT to tax the Natural Dividend and return it to the community.

As demand for renewable energy increases, and our appetite for large wind parks and solar furnaces decreases, then we can expect the Natural Dividend on clean energy to rise dramatically in the future. Anticipating this, political authorities should be designing management regimes that allow them to capture this Natural Dividend when and where it develops.

Conclusion

Today's RE markets remain remarkably segregated. This segregation limits the scope of potential RE suppliers (and resource types) to those that are able to tap into existing power grids. Within each of these markets, the most productive resource holders are able to generate rents in the same way we have seen with other natural resources. But the scope of the resulting Natural Dividend has been limited by market size and the competition across different resource types (both non-renewable and renewable).

There are at least two reasons why this is likely to change in the near future. First, we can expect electricity markets to expand as states integrate their local and national grids, in search of more reliable access to energy. We have described a recent example of this with the integration of European power grids in Box 6.5. We can also expect the development of new battery technologies that can help store and transfer energy from abundant to scarce markets. Both these trends will create a more global market for RE, with greater potential for political authorities to harvest the resulting Natural Dividend.

Second, RE sources are becoming much more competitive. This potential is clearly noted in a recent World Bank report:

> Over the last decade, the solar power sector has seen installation costs fall dramatically and global installed capacity rise massively. The International Renewable Energy Agency (IRENA) has reported that solar photovoltaic (PV) module prices have fallen 80 per cent in the last decade, while installed capacity has grown from 40 GW to over 600 GW in the same period. These trends are set to continue with new global solar installations of over 140 GW expected in calendar year 2020. (World Bank 2020b: vii)

In recent years we seem to have crossed a threshold: RE technologies are increasingly price-competitive, relative to more dirty and non-renewable forms of energy. Before this happened, wind and solar energy were clearly the marginal producers in the market, their attractiveness buoyed by subsidies. Given these conditions, the Natural Dividend in these markets tended to be captured by the more efficient (albeit dirty) producers in the coal and petroleum sectors. As RE energy becomes more competitive, however, we can expect to see a significant Natural Dividend developing in this sector, and these Dividends will go to those that have secured access to the most productive sites. Our regulatory sights should be set on the allocation of these valuable sites, and the distributional consequences from this allocation.

Renewable energy markets are poised to produce significant Natural Dividends in the future. In recognition of this, political authorities should shift their regulatory focus to managing these resources in a way that can better secure this Natural Dividend. To do this, they can look to examples when political authorities have been successful in managing subsurface petroleum and mineral resources – as these resources have produced the largest Natural Dividends in the past. This is the focus of the chapter that follows.

7

THE EARTH BENEATH: THE MARKET FOR FOSSIL AND MINERAL RESOURCES

The world's largest Natural Dividends are generated in the markets for subsurface fossil and mineral resources. Given our lengthy and insatiable appetite for coal, gas, oil and precious minerals/metals, the Natural Dividends associated with these resources have been phenomenally large, drawing the attention of investors, governments and academics alike.

Consequently, it should not surprise us to find that these resources seem to be the most difficult to manage from a political perspective. Their markets have the capacity to generate unimaginable wealth, but most of the wealth never makes it back to the community. Instead, these Natural Dividends have been pocketed by corrupt political authorities and/or the subcontractors used to secure the resource. It is not without reason that Venezuela's former oil minister, Juan Pablo Pérez Alfonzo, spoke of oil as "the devil's excrement" (Starr 2007), and the UN secretary-general, António Guterres, feels the need to warn us of the extractive industry's "… litany of ills – corruption, exploitation, colonialism and racism; environmental degradation, worsening climate change and biodiversity loss; armed conflict, gender-based violence, population displacement, cultural harm and human rights violations" (Guterres 2021).

Some of these markets are destined to dry up. There is, after all, significant pressure on countries and companies to move away from fossil fuels and into more renewable forms of energy. But many of these new replacement resources are also located underground. For example, recent advances in subsurface technologies promise access to new sources of renewable geothermal energy from conventional hydrothermal and enhanced geothermal systems (US Department of Energy 2017). Existing technologies can already create subsurface reservoirs that offer safe storage capacity for carbon dioxide (CO_2) and opportunities for the environmentally-responsible management and disposal of hazardous materials and other energy waste streams. Deep-drilling experiments have revealed a new terrestrial biosphere that "harbors a significant fraction of the total microbial biomass of the planet" (Puente-Sánchez *et al.* 2018), offering much work (and new markets) for bioprospectors. Further off on the temporal horizon we expect to find physicists, geologists and entrepreneurs working together to tap the potential energy unleashed by the shifting tectonic plates beneath our feet.

In replacing fossil and carbon-based resources with cleaner sources of energy, we will be forced to rely on a new basket of underground resources, all of which will need to be mined in prodigious amounts. The move to "clean" energy will require the mining of millions of tonnes of new raw materials: cobalt, lithium and nickel will be required to build our new batteries (see Box 7.1); the magnets for a new breed of electric generators and motors will require access to massive amounts of neodymium and other rare earth elements; and a huge amount of copper will be needed to wire these sundry components together (and for the component turbine windings).

BOX 7.1 RAW MATERIAL REQUIREMENTS OF A TYPICAL ELECTRIC CAR BATTERY

One important step in the transition away from carbon-based resources is the push to develop electric vehicles that run on stored energy in the form of lithium traction batteries. To give you an idea of the kind (and scope) of the raw materials we will need to mine if we are to fuel this transportation revolution, consider the average make-up of a typical lithium electric car battery weighing 450 kilograms. This is smaller than the battery used in most Teslas (630 kg in Models S and X), but larger than the one found in the BMWi3 (256 kg) (Lima 2022).

Following Smil (2022) – who draws on Berg and Zackrisson (2019) and Azevedo *et al.* (2018) – we can break down this 450 kg battery into several component natural resources, including:

lithium – roughly 11 kg;
cobalt – roughly 14 kg;
nickel – roughly 27 kg;
copper – roughly 40 kg;
graphite – roughly 50 kg; and
steel, aluminium and plastic – roughly 181 kg.

Smil (2022: 101) reckons that we need to process about 40 tonnes of ores in order to supply the raw materials for a single car battery. As these ores tend to lie in low concentrations, securing them will require the extraction and processing of 226 total tonnes of raw materials. Satisfying this new demand will entail a great deal of new mining activity, with enormous environmental, economic and political consequences.

The International Energy Agency's future roadmap for the global energy sector (IEA 2021) predicts a significant increase in the value of the sort of critical minerals used in the new (and necessary) clean energy technologies that we hope will replace our dependence on coal and petroleum products. Figure 7.1 reproduces the IEA findings to show how the agency expects the global value of these critical minerals to replace that of coal over the span of just three decades. Similarly, *The Economist* (2021) has calculated that the price of a basket of five minerals used in electric cars and power grid soared by 139 per cent in 2021. The same article estimates that global mining firms may have to raise the annual production of critical minerals by some 500 per cent.

The potential for new subsurface markets offers both hope and opportunity. The problem is that our existing approach to managing these resources is not politically sustainable, in that too much of the Natural Dividend has been captured by private interests, and the resulting inequality can easily deter future investments and developments. In developing these new markets, it is necessary that we do not repeat the mistakes of the past. We cannot afford another century marred by the "resource curse".

There is little question that these markets produce significant, sometimes astronomical, surpluses. This is one reason why the literature on RRT is rooted in these markets. Even so, most political authorities have proved unable or unwilling to secure the substantial Natural Dividends that these resources can produce. Living in Norway, we have first-hand experience with a management regime that has successfully secured the Natural Dividend from its petroleum resources, and this experience has motivated us to write this book. We are confident that this

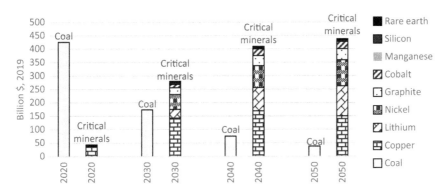

Figure 7.1 Global value of coal and selected critical minerals, 2020–2050

Notes: Total estimated revenue for coal and selected critical minerals. The prices of critical minerals are based on conservative assumptions about cost increases (around a 10 to 20% increase from current levels to 2050). See original source for more details.

Source: IEA (2021: 163).

management regime can be transferred to other states and to other resources, given sufficient political will.

This chapter has three objectives. In the first section we describe how subsurface resources are enclosed, allocated and commodified. This section describes the process by which states allocate rights to access these resources on behalf of the people they represent. The second section then surveys the contemporary markets for these resources to show how their distribution is random (from a political perspective), and capable of generating enormous Natural Dividends. For the most part, these Dividends are now harvested by private interests. These Natural Dividends draw on all three of the component rents – differential, regulatory and locational – and as these have already been introduced it is no longer useful or necessary to distinguish between them. In the third and final section, we demonstrate how it is possible for states to capture this Natural Dividend, on behalf of their citizens, and point to the Norwegian case as an example of just such a management regime.

The market for subsurface resources

There is already a literature committed to securing the Natural Dividend produced by the markets for fossil and mineral resources (usually with explicit reference to taxing the rent and/or securing local content). This section summarizes that literature and is divided into two parts. In the first part we consider how these resources tend to be enclosed and commodified. This description points to two important components of any resource management regime: the legal framework for allocating access to the resource and distributing the associated costs and benefits; and a basket of policies to facilitate that distribution and secure the resulting Natural Dividend. We then turn to see how and where value is created in these markets; this is necessary to establish the source of the Natural Dividend, which is an important objective for any resource management regime.

Management regimes

As with all natural resources, subsurface resources originate in common ownership, as the fruits of the earth, shared by all. Like most of the other natural resources covered in this book, these resources have not been privatized: they remain in the hands of political authorities, ostensibly on behalf of the people they represent. For the vast majority of countries in the world, it is the people (more accurately, their governments) – that own and control the titles to subsurface fossil and mineral resources.[1] Although it is part of a larger political legacy, this legal view came to predominate after the 1962 UN resolution on permanent sovereignty over natural resources, and was subsequently enshrined in the constitutions of many newly independent and mineral-rich countries. This state ownership is widely recognized in the literature, even if it is not always appreciated (Jones Luong & Weinthal 2006: 241–2).

In a recent mapping of mineral ownership regimes, Gary Flomenhoft (2018) compares the national mining laws of 199 countries, finding that a strong majority of these (142, or 71 per cent) allocate mineral titles to the state or "Crown". This tendency contrasts sharply with the accepted international or global practice, wherein common or communal (not state) rights prevail (see Chapter 8), and the baseline assumption of many mainstream economic approaches to resource management, that private ownership is the most common and efficient form of ownership. In Flomenhoft's study (2018: 11), only three countries (Iceland, Latvia and Lebanon) grant mineral titles to landowners, but we know that this practice is also widespread in several US states, where titles to the surface area and mineral rights can be separated, and both can be owned by private interests.[2]

In short, ownership regimes for subsurface natural resources tend to take three forms. The dominant form is state ownership, whereby the nation state allocates access to the resources on its sovereign territory in the name of the people it represents. There is also significant common ownership in those areas of unclaimed sovereign territory (e.g. on Antarctica, beneath the ocean bed of the deep sea, or in the heavens above) where there is explicit reference to common ownership in a number of international treaties. Finally, a very small portion of the global subsurface natural resources finds itself in private hands.

Even if state ownership of these resources is an important point of departure, it is not a solution per se. As Pauline Jones Luong and Erika Weinthal (2006) point out, state ownership is often associated with inefficient management regimes and the economic and political ailments we associate with the "resource curse".[3] We return to this challenge in our conclusion; for now it is enough to recognize

---

1. It is important to distinguish between mineral titles and mineral rights. Ultimate and sovereign ownership of subsoil resources is reserved for those that control the mineral title; mineral rights can be granted by the ultimate owner to private agents (individuals, firms, tribes, provinces) – and in any number of different forms, including inalienable leasehold and alienable freehold, or any combination thereof.
2. In Flomenhoft's study (2018: 22), the United States falls under a "mixed regime", while Australia, Austria, Canada and Greece also provide some scope for landowner rights.
3. It should be noted that private ownership by international corporations is also problematic, in that it can easily create resentment in the local population; see Wegenast and Schneider (2017).

public ownership, so that any (unearned) rent derived from a resource can be returned to its rightful owner.

Like the hypothetical family in the introductory chapter, the state's first decision must be how to develop the resource: it can do so itself (in the form of an NRC); it can hire a private contractor (for example, an international oil or mineral company); or it can pursue some sort of combined public–private venture. If the state decides to go it alone, then many of the subsequent decisions about contract and fiscal regimes are irrelevant (as there are no private companies involved). But, if the state decides to secure private help, or employ some combination of private and public instruments, then it needs to formalize this relationship between government and private solutions. This is done in three steps: through enclosure/allocation, commodification and fiscal restitution.

It is common practice for countries to begin by dividing up their subsurface resources into blocks of territory (on- or offshore), which can vary significantly in size.[4] In doing so, states decide how they will allocate and develop these blocks (and how quickly): they might simply assign them to a lucky developer (friend of the queen, the only interested partner, a national mining/oil company, etc.); auction the blocks off to the highest qualified bidder; or use some other approach. At the end of this process a developer (whether private, public or both) secures a legal right to access the petroleum or minerals (should they exist) on a specified parcel of territory.

It is this first step that provides enclosure, and the sovereign authority allocates it to particular interests. This decision, in effect, allows private interests to set up a "fence" around their parcel, and claim its contents as their own. In doing this, political authorities help to establish the relative value of these blocks and contribute to the resulting Natural Dividend. It is at this early stage that the potential Natural Dividend is established, as the government is acting as a gatekeeper to limit access to its resources. In effect, it is offering monopoly control/access to parcels of territory that might (or might not) contain scarce natural resources in high demand. At this point, neither the government nor the commercial producer knows whether the parcels will generate a Natural Dividend, but producers are willing to pay handsomely for a monopoly right of access.

The government's next step is to decide on the underlying legal framework – i.e. how it will grant rights to explore and develop the nation's resources. Although the scope of variance across these legal frameworks is significant, each is used to determine the distribution of costs and benefits between the host government and the commercial developer. As a general rule, legal frameworks tend to employ one of three contract/licensing arrangements (or a combination thereof): concessions-based licensing regimes, production-sharing contracts and/or service contracts.

---

4. This section draws heavily from Moses and Letnes (2017a: ch. 5).

These frameworks allocate mineral rights in different ways and draw on very different historical and political trajectories. *Concessionary* regimes originated in the United States, where private ownership of subsurface resources was permitted, and provided private companies with ownership of the resource (and its resulting Natural Dividend), once extracted. These frameworks tended to spread with American mining and petroleum companies as they scoured the earth in search of new deposits. *Production-sharing contracts* (PSCs) were a late twentieth-century response to the injustices of concessionary regimes, under which so much of the Natural Dividend was being captured by private companies. In a PSC, private companies and governments negotiate over their requisite share of ownership in the resource produced. For example, in exchange for its help in securing a resource, a government might sign a PSC that secures it 65 per cent of the oil/minerals produced, leaving the private contractor with the remaining 35 per cent. In this way, governments have been able to secure the Natural Dividend associated with *their share* of the oil/minerals secured (and the private company will keep the Natural Dividend associated with its share). Countries that rely on *service contracts* are most like the hypothetical family in the introduction: they maintain full ownership and control (not to mention risk) over the resource but hire a private contractor to do a job for them.

In PSCs and service contracts, the political authorities are able to secure the Natural Dividend by maintaining continued control of the resources (oil/gas/minerals) themselves. By keeping the resources, the authorities are able to keep the resulting Natural Dividend when the oil is sold on the market. In concessionary arrangements, or in the contractors' share of the PSC, private interests are able to secure the resource, and can pocket the Natural Dividend when they bring it to market. Under these conditions, political authorities need to tax the Natural Dividend at a higher rate, to ensure that it is returned to the people who own the underlying resource.

The underlying legal framework is important, because it establishes legal title and allocates access and transfer rights. In deciding how access to the resource will be allocated between public and private actors, the state determines who exactly owns the resource (and the Natural Dividend it may produce) as it moves from nature into commodity form. This decision provides the authorities with a menu of control, risk and reward options from which to choose. Indeed, there is a remarkable degree of overlap among, and nuance within, contract types. In effect, the legal framework allows the state to establish the parameters for commercial development of the sector – it will determine the level of state involvement and many of the main fiscal parameters (how state revenues will be generated, the level of royalties, the allocation of production costs and results) – but the legal framework does not, in itself, secure the Natural Dividend. It secures control of the resource that harbours the Natural

Dividend; the economic value of the Natural Dividend is then secured with the establishment of a fiscal regime that can capture the underlying rents and return them to their rightful owner.

It is this fiscal regime that provides restitution, the third step in this management process; it is used to establish and allocate the relevant costs, profits and rents, as depicted in Figure 3.1. Its main task is to ensure that commercial producers get a fair return on their labour and investment, but do not take the underlying Natural Dividend. How they do this will vary across the different legal frameworks just described, but the Natural Dividend is usually secured by means of local content policies, taxes and participation levels – or any combination thereof.

The source of the Natural Dividend

One essential task of any resource management regime is to discover whether a Natural Dividend is being produced by the resource and develop a means to secure it. This is done by ensuring ownership over the resource, recognizing the existence of rents that are independent of costs and profits and then taxing those rents accordingly, so that it remains with the public. All of this requires a firm understanding of where, and when, the Natural Dividend arises.

To do this, we might consider a typical value chain for these types of resource, as depicted in Figure 7.2. Here we can see that most of the value is secured upstream, in the original process of discovering and producing the resource. This value lies in two components parts: the inherent value from nature; and the state's allocation of access to this value. The first value takes the form of a differential rent; the second can find form in either a regulatory rent, a locational rent or both. This is not to suggest that there is no value added from the exploration, drilling/mining, transport and refining processes. Indeed, the crude product of these efforts is often unsuitable for direct consumption: it needs to be refined to remove impurities and to create the many products we associate with these natural resources. But this value is relatively minor by comparison and does not produce the Natural

	Natural state	Upstream *Exploration and production*		Midstream *Trading and transport*		Downstream *Refining and retail*		Consumption
Value (e.g. oil)	0 →	$65/barrel	→	Little*	→	$ + 15/barrel	→	Spent or recycled

Figure 7.2 Subsurface value chain

Notes: For value sources, see text. *By allocating little additional value at midstream, we are purposefully ignoring the important role played by transfer pricing as a way for private interests to avoid taxation regimes designed to secure the Natural Dividend. See Moses and Letnes (2017a: 94ff.) for more details on how transfer pricing is used in the petroleum sector. *Source*: Authors.

Dividend that interests us here. These types of natural resource are also different from the others considered in this book, in that they are non-renewable; hence, much of their value evaporates when consumed, although some of it may be used in new productive activities and/or be recycled later (e.g. minerals and metals).

In Figure 7.2 we can see how little of the value of the resource is created downstream.[5] This example comes from the oil industry, but its lesson travels easily to other subsurface resources. In particular, we can establish the added value from downstream processing activities by using the "3:2:1 crack spread" (see Box 7.2). Either way, the downstream value added is not particularly interesting from a Natural Dividend perspective.

Because the added value downstream is relatively small, we can set it aside for the time being. The most important part of the Natural Dividend is generated upstream, when something that is provided free by nature can be sold at market

---

BOX 7.2 THE 3:2:1 CRACK SPREAD

The 3:2:1 crack spread captures the difference in the sale price of crude oil and its refined products (e.g. gasoline and fuel oil distillates), and it is used to gauge profit levels in the refinery sector. A typical refinery will use three barrels of crude oil to produce two barrels of gasoline (petrol) and one barrel of distillate fuel (e.g. diesel or heating oil). Like the price of oil, the crack spread varies greatly over time, and was increasing significantly in 2021. With this in mind, we can start with an estimate from prices on 12 March 2021. On that day, WTI crude oil was selling for $64.96/barrel; gasoline (reformulated blendstock for oxygenate blending: RBOB) was selling at $2.12/gallon ($88.9/barrel) and diesel (ultra-low-sulphur diesel: ULSD) was selling at $1.94/gallon ($81.6/barrel).[1] These prices generate a crack spread of $21.5/barrel, whereas the long-term average for the crack-spread tends to be around $11. For this reason, we have suggested that a $15/barrel value increase provides us with a reasonable estimate.

---

1. We should note that the price for gasoline on the West Coast of the United States three months later was $3.30/gallon ($138.60/barrel), which shows a remarkable per-gallon mark-up.

---

5. Note how the price of land is not relevant in this calculation; it is merely a vessel for the resource, and is relatively worthless to the owner, once the resource is extracted. In most cases, the producer does not actually own the land, but uses it for a limited amount of time, and it is (usually) returned to the owner after exploitation.

for $65 a barrel. The key question is: how much does it cost to get this oil out of the ground at any particular production site? To determine this cost, we could return to the example in Table 3.1, which compared the production costs of producing oil in Kuwait and Norway. Alternatively, we might turn to Saudi Arabia, where we find some of the world's most productive oil resources, and where the break-even cost for oil is estimated to be just under $3/barrel (Hecht 2020).[6] In a competitive market, the returns on capital and labour should be the same everywhere; but we know that in some places the oil is more difficult to get than in others. As we have seen from the preceding chapters, differences in productive capacity, regulatory effect and locational advantage combine to generate the Natural Dividend.

Given the oil price in March 2021, oil produced in Saudi Arabia generated a rent equal to about $62 per barrel. This is not small change, when one realizes that Saudi Arabia produced 10,145,000 barrels *a day* in 2019 (BP 2020: 18). The cost of producing oil in other countries will be higher, and, as it approaches $60/barrel, it will become cost-prohibitive. In between these extremes (Saudi Arabia and a break-even producer) lies a great deal of Natural Dividend. The question before us is: who ends up with this Dividend?

State of the rent

We have become incredibly reliant upon fossil fuels. These fuels are not just used to run our planes, trains and automobiles; they also provide the raw materials for a substantial portion of our economic production (e.g. plastics, but also the fertilizers, herbicides and pesticides that help provide food for all the people on our planet).

Our continued reliance on fossil fuels is made abundantly clear in BP's annual *Statistical Review of World Energy*, one of the most important references on global energy. As shown in Figure 7.3, 84 per cent of our world energy consumption is fed by either coal (27.0 per cent), oil (33.1 per cent) or gas (24.2 per cent). Hydro (6.4 per cent), nuclear (4.3 per cent) and other renewable forms of energy (5.0 per cent) are growing quickly but remain remarkably small.

As with the wind and the sun, the geographic dispersion of global reserves of fossil is both concentrated and random (from a political perspective): national

---

6. It should be noted that the concessionaire's operating costs need to include the cost of failed wells, and this is the sort of detail that governments and concessionaries must discuss to establish what constitutes a fair return on investment and what remains as the Natural Dividend. We have avoided this level of detail in the book, but recognize its importance.

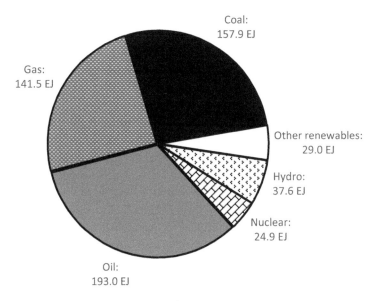

Figure 7.3 Primary energy consumption, by type, 2019

Notes: EJ stands for exajoule, or 10^{18} joules. Renewable power excludes hydro, but includes wind, solar, geothermal, biomass sources of energy and biofuels.
Source: BP (2020: 4).

reserves in the three top countries, for each type of fossil resource, capture about a half of the world market. About 45 per cent of the world's known reserves of oil lie beneath Venezuela, Saudi Arabia and Canada; about 48 per cent of the world's known reserves of natural gas lie beneath the Russian Federation, Iran and Qatar, and about 52 per cent of the world's known reserves of coal lie beneath the United States, the Russian Federation and Australia (BP 2020: 14, 32, 44).

As we saw with the market for RE resources, there is a large geographic gap between the location where these resources are provided by nature and the place where they are eventually consumed. This logistic challenge fuelled a revolution in shipping/transportation technologies, making it easier to transport oil, coal and even gas around the world. In the process, markets for fossil fuels that were once local have become global.

These larger markets allow for greater market concentration and larger rents. The globalization of fossil fuel markets has made it easier for a handful of companies to dominate in each sector. This concentration of capital and expertise has delivered significant efficiency gains – efficiencies that would have been impossible to secure in smaller, unconnected resource markets. (Obviously, this concentration also produces greater inequalities). At the same time, the creation of global market means that the concessionaires with access to the world's most productive resources, or those that are closest to the existing infrastructure, are able to leverage those advantages to secure even greater rents – because they are now competing with concessionaires sitting on much less productive resources. Saudi Arabia is no longer competing with Kuwait in a local market for oil; Saudi Arabia now competes with Norway and others, where the costs of production are significantly higher. The size of the rents grows alongside the size of the market, as global producers are forced out into less productive resource sites, and the difference in production costs (between the least and most productive firms) grows. Although this provides some opportunity for those concessionaries that have gained access to less productive resources, it magnifies the rent available to those with access to the most productive resources in the (now larger) market.

Our reliance on fossil fuels will need to change – and change quickly. In doing so, we can expect significant distributional consequences, as money and interest move out of established and lucrative resource markets and into new and developing ones. These new resources are often characterized as "critical", given their growing economic importance and relative scarcity.[7]

As we transition to these replacement minerals, we face many familiar constraints. Like fossil fuels, the total stock of metals and minerals is finite, and growing scarcer with use. As with oil, gas and coal, the richest, most available reserves have probably already been tapped, and we are moving out into increasingly less productive reserve sites. But metals, at least, are recyclable in principle. Like fossil fuels, but even more so, mineral reserves are randomly spread around the globe in terms of both quantity and quality. There are very high levels of concentration in particular countries, whether it is the Democratic Republic of the Congo's hold on cobalt (53.3 per cent of the world total), Chile's grip on lithium (55.5 per cent) or China's strong holdings of both natural graphite (23 per cent of the world's proved reserves) and rare earth minerals (35.4 per cent) (BP 2020: 63). With the exception of China, note how most of these mineral resources are located far from where they will probably be consumed.

This concentration matters, as it affects our capacity to access the resource, and the (regulatory) rent it will generate, especially as world demand increases for new sources of energy (and their need for storage). Although all of us will need access to lithium in the future, over 55 per cent of the world's known reserves lie in one single country: Chile. How Chile allocates access to this lithium will matter to us, as consumers, but also to the people of Chile, who own the underlying resource.

---

7. See European Commission (2020: 19–22) for a list of minerals that the European Union deems to be critical.

It is not just the size of the resource reserves that is distributed unequally; so too are their quality and accessibility. We have already noted this with respect to the low production costs of Saudi Arabian oil. In some places the natural resource will be of very high quality, easy to access and close to existing infrastructures. In other places the resource is of lesser quality and more difficult to secure. The difference, as we have learned, generates a (differential and/or locational) rent.

The World Bank generates rent estimates for three main types of subsurface resources – oil, natural gas and minerals – and their global aggregates are depicted in Figure 7.4. Although these estimates vary significantly over time, we can clearly see that oil rents are substantially higher than those that are generated by either natural gas or mineral resources. This is because the selling price of oil tends to be between $50 and $100 a barrel, even though it often costs substantially less than this to produce. The difference is rent, but we cannot distinguish its source (i.e. differential, regulatory or locational).

There is much variance between markets. Within each of these markets some resources can secure very high levels of rent as a result of high global demand, high quality, relative abundance, ease of access, etc. Table 7.1 compares the top ten rent-generating countries for each market (oil, natural gas and minerals), to show us where some of the most lucrative resources lie. In the first column in Table 7.1 we find the top ten rent-producing countries for oil in 2019: Libya, the Republic of Congo, Kuwait, Iraq, Angola, and so on. This statistic concentrates our attention on those countries that have the largest and most productive reserves but that are also most dependent upon them (as a share of GDP).[8]

Who, then, benefits from these significant oil rents? To answer this question, we need to look at how oil-rich countries have allocated access to these rents, and whether they have tried (and managed) to retrieve them. Some states may try to secure their Natural Dividend in a more political form by pursuing LCPs, for example. Other states may focus on securing their dividend in more economic forms. As we saw in the previous section, this rent is secured by a legal and fiscal framework that determines the type (and size) of payments that companies must make, in exchange for access to the (potential) resource. One proxy for measuring this scope for rent lies in the (misnamed) statistic for "government take". Although there are several competing measures of

---

8. This World Bank indicator is rather awkward, in that it lists rents/GDP (rather than, say, rents per capita). This makes it difficult to compare some states, as extremely poor states with a moderately sized oil industry will score high on this indicator. This is one reason why Kuwait and Saudi Arabia do not top the oil rent rankings. Below, when we use this indicator to compare Norway with other states, this GDP denominator is particularly problematic. We are aware of these difficulties but use this indicator because it provides a very simple overview, which we leverage in Figure 7.5.

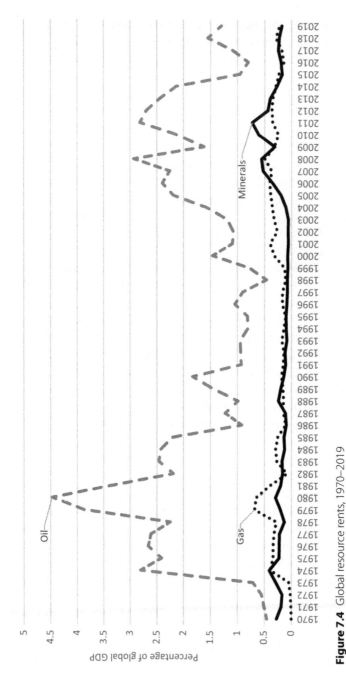

Figure 7.4 Global resource rents, 1970–2019

Notes: The World Bank calculates estimates of natural resource rents as the difference between the price of a commodity and the average cost of producing it. We have already seen this indicator used with Figure 4.4 on forest rents. The World Bank estimates the price of units of specific commodities and subtracts estimates of the average unit costs of extraction or harvesting costs. These unit rents are then multiplied by the physical quantities extracted or harvested (here at the global level) to determine the rents for each commodity as a share of GDP. The minerals included here are tin, gold, lead, zinc, iron, copper, nickel, silver, bauxite and phosphate.

Sources: World Bank (n.d.b, n.d.c, n.d.d).

Table 7.1 Top ten rent-producing states by subsurface resource, as a percentage of GDP, 2019

	Oil		*Natural gas*		*Minerals*	
Ranking	*Country*	*Rent (% GDP)*	*Country*	*Rent (% GDP)*	*Country*	*Rent (% GDP)*
1	Libya	43.9	Timor-Leste	29	Mauritania	11.8
2	Congo, Republic	43.4	Turkmenistan	14.5	Mongolia	7.3
3	Kuwait	42.1	Brunei Darussalam	10.5	Sierra Leone	7.2
4	Iraq	39.6	Uzbekistan	6.9	Congo, Democratic Republic	3
5	Angola	25.1	Equatorial Guinea	6.9	Australia	3
6	Oman	24.9	Papua New Guinea	5.2	Kazakhstan	1.9
7	Saudi Arabia	24.2	Trinidad and Tobago	4.6	Armenia	1.9
8	Equatorial Guinea	22.3	Qatar	3.8	Zambia	1.8
9	Azerbaijan	21.9	Azerbaijan	3.6	Chile	1.6
10	Iran	20.4	Russian Federation	2.8	Laos	1.5

Sources: World Bank (n.d.b, n.d.c, n.d.d).

Notes: For oil rents: Iran's data are from 2018. Syria is not included in this table as it did not report 2019 figures, but its 2007 oil rents were substantial (at 21.3% of GDP). For gas rents: Turkmenistan's data are from 2018. For mineral rents: Eritrea (2011, 24.6%) and New Caledonia (2000, 15.4%) top the mineral rent lists, but as they did not report 2019 data they are not included in the table.

"government take", they are notoriously unreliable, and often misquoted and abused (Johnston 2018: 506).[9]

One (admittedly simple) way to see whether these Natural Dividends are making their way back to the community is to take the top ten oil-rent-producing countries in Table 7.1 and add Norway, which ranks 28th in the World Bank's overall rent ranking (at just 4.8 per cent of GDP). We can then see how these states score on a broad-based indictor of citizen well-being: the Human Development Index (HDI) of the United Nations Development Programme (UNDP).[10] In other

---

9. Johnston (2018) provides a very thorough overview of the challenges with "government take"/ "private take" statistics. See also Johnston (2002). Most of these studies begin from the position of industry, ignore rent and see any attempt at taxation as a "government take" from private interests. Seen in this light, the "government take" is seen as a potential deterrent to investors, and a shaper of global oil prices (e.g. Martén, Whittaker & Martínez de Burio 2015: 1). But if we look at this transaction from the owner's perspective, anything above a normal return on capital and labour is a private taking of rent: it is a "private", not a "government", taking, with no effect on investment behaviour or subsequent prices.

10. The HDI measures social and economic development, along four axes: mean years of schooling; expected years of schooling; life expectancy at birth; and gross national income per capita.

words, we might expect that the states with the highest oil rents are able to afford broad social welfare policies, and we might assume that states are interested in improving the lives of their citizens. Figure 7.5 does this with a simple scatter plot that clearly shows a negative relationship between oil rent and HDI rankings. The regression line imposed on the figure (heading from the top left corner to the bottom right corner) reveals the general relationship; but the story is best told by the three anchor point states. Norway ranked first in the world on the 2019 HDI index, but oil rents made up only 4.8 per cent of that country's GDP. On the other end of the regression line we find the states with the world's highest oil rents: Libya and the Republic of the Congo. But these states find themselves towards the bottom of the UNDP's HDI rankings: at 105 and 149, respectively (out of 189 states; Niger lies at the bottom of the list). In other words, those countries with the highest oil rent rankings are those that rank terribly low on the UNDP's HDI score. Clearly, these states' significant rents are not making their way back to the people who own them.

Of course, there are many factors – in addition to oil rents – that can explain a state's HDI ranking. Most relationships in social science are complicated in this way. But Figure 7.5 provides incentive to dig deeper. We can do this by comparing the underlying resource management regime employed in each of these countries. This is done in Table 7.2. Here we compare the type of legal and fiscal frameworks employed, to see whether there has been a non-ambiguous attempt to recognize and secure the Natural Dividend in these states. These are not run-of-the-mill oil-producing states, of course, apart from Norway. These states have the most lucrative oil reserves in the world, where the costs of getting the oil out of the ground are minimal.

In Table 7.2 we can see that some states still rely on a concession/licensing regime (Kuwait, Norway, Saudi Arabia) to allocate their petroleum rights. Other states have adopted production-sharing contracts (e.g. Angola, Azerbaijan, etc.), while Iran employs service contracts. Although several states employ more than one type of tax, and/or a combination of licence/contract form, this table focuses on the most important form of contract/licence and tax regime.[11] In Table 7.2 we see that no single legal framework predominates,[12] and that the overall level

---

The index is commonly used to follow changes in development levels over time and to compare the development levels of different countries. See UNDP (n.d.a).

11. A more thorough review of each state's legal and fiscal frameworks, listed alphabetically, can be found in EY (2019).

12. This is a common lesson in the literature. For example, Johnston (2008: 39) provides a telling graphic that ranks government take by the type of underlying legal framework. Here it is evident that the choice of a concession regime, or a PSC, is not – in itself – determinant on the level of government (or private) take. Rather, it is the way in which the legal framework and fiscal regime work together that determines a state's capacity to secure the Natural Dividend.

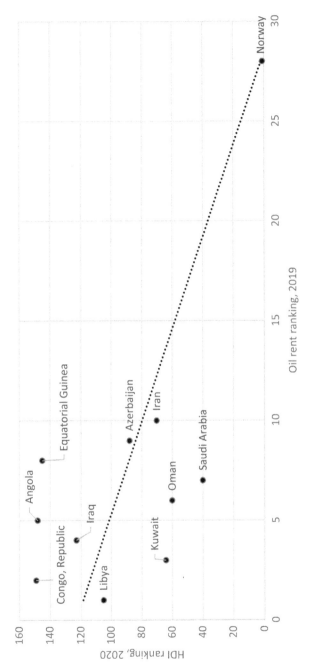

Figure 7.5 Oil rent and HDI: top ten countries plus Norway, 2019–20
Sources: World Bank (n.d.b) and UNDP (n.d.b).

Table 7.2 Resource management frameworks across oil-rich countries

Country	Predominant legal framework	Predominant tax type	Predominant rate
Angola	PSC	Petroleum income tax	50%
Azerbaijan	PSC	Profit tax	20–35%
Congo, Republic	PSC/concession/SC	CIT	30–35+%*
Equatorial Guinea	PSC	CIT	34%
Iran	SC	CIT	25%
Iraq	PSC and SC	CIT	35%
Kuwait	Concession	CIT	15%
Libya	PSC	CIT	65%
Norway	Concession	CIT + RRT	78%
Oman	PSC	CIT	55%
Saudi Arabia	Concession	CIT	50–85%

Notes: Countries listed alphabetically. CIT = corporate income tax. Many countries employ a combination of different contract forms, but this table focuses attention on the most common types of contract, and the tax regime to which they are associated. See EY (2019) for more details on each case. *The Republic of the Congo applies a broad array of contract types. For the concession and service contracts, the CIT is limited to 30%. PSCs are taxed at a minimum of 35%. See EY (2019: 563).

Source: EY (2019).

of taxation is remarkably low. Only two countries recognize the need to have some sort of special tax that is associated with the petroleum sector and that can be directed at securing the Natural Dividend: Angola has a "petroleum income tax" and Norway has an RRT placed on the top of its normal level of corporate income tax. The other states may be using LCPs and/or an NRC to secure the rents, but they do not appear to have a tax regime that recognizes the rent or tries to protect it from private taking.

It should be noted that some of the Natural Dividend might be secured by favourable contracting terms, even if it is not being secured by means of an RRT. Indeed, national efforts to implement LCPs are examples of contract terms aimed to secure part of the Natural Dividend – but in a more political form. As we shall see in the section that follows, Norway employs several different tools to secure the Natural Dividend from its petroleum resources, only one of which is an RRT.

Although it enjoys a much smaller Natural Dividend from oil, the Norwegian authorities have used it to fill one of the world's largest sovereign wealth funds: the Government Pension Fund Global (see below). So, why isn't the world's largest sovereign investment fund located in Libya or the Republic of the Congo – those countries with the highest rents (as a share of GDP) across all three resource types? How can it be that a country such as Norway – whose oil reserves are remarkably costly to bring to market – is able to generate so much more public wealth, with smaller rents? Although this is a complicated question, with many potential variables, a big part of the answer lies in the different management regimes in these different countries.

Securing the Natural Dividend in subsurface resource markets

The Norwegian management regime is an example of what can be done when political authority recognizes its public ownership over common resources, and the Natural Dividend that these resources produce. Capturing the Natural Dividend is eminently achievable. The Norwegian regime has been in place for a long period of time and has secured phenomenal wealth for the Norwegian people, and it has been implemented without deterring investment and subsequent development. To follow the Norwegian example, political authorities need to be able to claim what belongs to their people and to spend the results on their behalf.

It is important to emphasize that there is no particular or magic legal framework or fiscal regime that is necessary for securing the Natural Dividend. States can draw from their own history and experiences to develop their own blend of ownership/licence and fiscal frameworks. We briefly describe the Norwegian management regime, but it should not be followed slavishly by other countries. States with rent-producing resources need only to recognize the Natural Dividend, claim it and then develop and employ fiscal and regulatory instruments designed to capture it for their citizens.

The Norwegian natural resource management regime can be traced back to the country's independence from Sweden at the turn of the last century (1905), and the need for a young country to ensure that the value generated from its natural resources remained in that country.[13] At the time, the most important new energy resource was hydroelectric power, and foreign investors were lining up to buy Norway's most productive waterfalls (see Box 7.3). The question on everybody's lips was: who owned the power inherent to falling water? Was it the private owner of the land where the waterfall was located? Was it the people who sacrificed their farms and livelihoods in the flooding and damming necessary to produce the power? Or did it lie with the political authorities that would regulate the development of this new industry?

This hydroelectric concession regime was established before the First World War. It helped to electrify the Norwegian coastline and provided local industries with cheap power that made them internationally competitive. This concession regime became a cornerstone of Norway's industrial development, and it had

---

13. See Brigham and Moses (2021) and Fuglestad and Almås (2021).

BOX 7.3 MANAGING NORWEGIAN HYDROPOWER

Most of Norway's electricity power comes from hydroelectric installations, many of which were built at the turn of the last century, when Norway was securing its independence from Sweden (in 1905). Norwegian authorities at the time fought to secure sovereign control over the country's abundant natural resource wealth, and much of the resulting political discussion was informed by the work of Henry George (Thue 2003). Policy-makers recognized that differences in productivity were largely determined by accidents of nature (longer waterfalls and bigger dam options would produce more power than shorter falls and smaller dams) – not the capital or ingenuity of the landowner and/or investor. The rents generated by the largest falls would be enormous, whereas the smaller waterfalls might not generate any rents at all.

A set of 1917 laws on industrial concessions (Industrikonsesjonslovene fra 1917) required all hydroelectric production to be kept under public control (today it is roughly 90 per cent), and most of the installations are today owned by municipal, county or national authorities. To compensate the surrounding communities that were negatively affected by these installations, concessions arrangements often required that a portion (e.g. 5–10 per cent) of all electricity produced would be given (free of charge) to the surrounding community. The concessions were also temporary and time-limited (40–60 years), after which facilities were either disassembled or gifted to the requisite political authorities (*hjemfall*).

Finally, it was decided that private interests would be allowed access to valuable hydroelectric sites for a limited time period. These private interests could build huge and expensive power installations, and they would be allowed a healthy return on those investments. But anything that exceeded a normal return – an unearned rent – would be returned to the national and local political authorities (in the form of tax payments and/or free electricity to the surrounding community). At the end of the allotted concession period, when all the returns on investments had been paid, the actual installation and the permission to use it, reverted to the state (*hjemfallsrett,* or escheat), so that access to the waterfall might be granted again, perhaps to a different investor.

In 2018 the Norwegian authorities estimated that the rents associated with hydroelectric production were between 25 and 30 billion kroner (*c.* $3 billion) (Norwegian government 2019c). To secure these rents, the authorities imposed an additional tax burden on larger hydroelectric installations. In addition to paying the 22 per cent corporate income tax, installation owners are required to pay a 37 per cent RRT. In September 2022 the government proposed increasing this RRT to 45 per cent (Finansdepartementet 2022a). Depending on the nature (and location) of the concession, the installation owner may also be required to pay local property taxes and provide the surrounding local community with free or subsidized electricity (for details, see Norwegian government 2019c: 50–1).

proved tried and true by the time Norway discovered a viable petroleum resource in the late 1960s. Given such positive experiences with a mature legal framework that managed private/foreign investment of its natural resources, Norway simply adapted this regime for regulating the offshore petroleum industry. The resulting regulatory framework for managing Norway's petroleum resources is distinct in at least three important ways.

First, and foremost, the regime recognizes, explicitly, that *the resources belong to the people* (both current and future generations) and must be managed on their behalf. In Norway, this democratic anchoring takes the form of the so-called "Ten Oil Commandments", which were used to guide subsequent policy decisions in a more democratic direction (see Box 7.4). Among other things, these "commandments" included limits on the area to be exploited; requirements to develop national competences and economic benefit; and the need to maintain strong political (democratic) control over developments.

> This explicit ownership was still recognized as a central part of the petroleum management regime when the Norwegian Ministry of Oil and Energy discussed the future of the oil industry in Norway in 2011:
>
> Norway's petroleum resources are owned by the Norwegian people and shall benefit the entire community. This has been the main principle for the management of petroleum resources over the past 50 years. The Concession Laws from 1909 concerned the regulation of waterpower but have also been relevant for petroleum activities. The laws ensure *hjemfallsrett* and make it clear that it is the Norwegian people who own the water resources and the resulting resource rent belongs to the people. The same principles have been followed in the management of the petroleum resources. (OED 2011: 5, our translation)

The second distinct feature of the Norwegian petroleum management regime is the unique means by which it allocates licences/concessions. This concession regime, like the one for hydropower, has provided limited concessions, with the right to harvest the resource reverting to the state after a prescribed period (the *hjemfallsrett*, noted earlier). In addition (and unlike elsewhere), the Norwegian government played an active role in assembling the licence partners, or joint ventures, and they used these JV licences not only to develop local (national) competences but also to secure joint ownership in the licences themselves.[14]

Local content policies were a central component of Norway's early management regime. These more "activist" tools were easier to employ in the early 1970s, when Norway was first developing its petroleum sector, but many of

---

14. See Moses and Brigham (2021) and Moses and Letnes (2017a) for further details.

BOX 7.4 NORWAY'S TEN OIL COMMANDMENTS

The Ten Oil Commandments are a declaration of principles underpinning Norwegian oil policy, submitted by the Standing Committee on Industry in a government White Paper from 14 June 1971. These principles clarify how to ensure that the oil activities "benefit the entire nation".

1. National supervision and control of all activity on the Norwegian continental shelf (NCS) must be ensured.
2. The petroleum discoveries must be exploited in a manner designed to ensure maximum independence for Norway in terms of reliance on others for supply of crude oil.
3. New business activity must be developed, based on petroleum.
4. The development of an oil industry must take place with necessary consideration for existing commercial activity, as well as protection of nature and the environment.
5. Flaring of exploitable gas on the NCS is allowed only in limited test periods.
6. Petroleum from the NCS must, as a rule, be landed in Norway, with the exception of special cases in which socio-political considerations warrant a different solution.
7. The state involves itself at all reasonable levels, and contributes to coordinating Norwegian interests within the Norwegian petroleum industry and to developing an integrated Norwegian oil community with both national and international objectives.
8. A state-owned oil company should be established to safeguard the state's commercial interests, and to pursue expedient cooperation with domestic and foreign oil stakeholders.
9. An activity plan must be adopted for the area north of the 62nd parallel that satisfies the unique socio-political factors associated with that part of the country.
10. Norwegian petroleum discoveries could present new avenues for Norway's foreign policy.

(Moses & Letnes 2017a: 74)

---

these tools are still used today by countries that have recently discovered new natural resources. We do not have the space to delve into the many LCP tools that Norway developed, but they can be organized under four different rubrics: local content legislation; the negotiated nature of licence agreements (which required local producers to provide an explicit share of content); the large share of activities that went to Norway's NRC, Statoil; and explicit technology agreements, by which new technologies were to be developed in Norwegian universities and research institutes (Moses & Letnes 2017a: ch. 8). All these tools can be seen as attempts to secure a more political form of the Natural Dividend from petroleum.

By way of its unique concession regime, Norway became a joint owner of oil, in at least two ways. First, it used its licensing regime to prioritize Norwegian firms, ensuring that Statoil (the Norwegian NRC, now Equinor) would receive a significant (usually a majority) share in each licence, with spe-cific requirements that international firms would "show it the ropes". Statoil was protected and nourished, its interests carried,[15] until it could develop its own operational competence. This provided the Norwegian state with oil dir-ectly, but also helped to build up Norwegian local competences in oil produc-tion. This allowed the Norwegian government to secure some of the Natural Dividend in a more political form. Indeed, the nature of the allocation regime allowed Statoil (and the Norwegian state) to secure a larger share of the most productive resources, by means of a so-called sliding scale (see Moses & Letnes 2017a: 157–9). This decision resembles that of the imaginary family in our introduction; but here the government decided it was most useful to learn how to drill for itself, rather than hire a contractor. Norway traded a more efficient short-term solution (letting foreign companies with expertise exploit the resource) for a long-term solution that provided the country with greater autonomy and wealth in the long term. In a nutshell, Norway's Natural Dividend from petroleum took a political as well as an economic form, and the resulting Norwegian oil industry is now competing with other international companies in the global market for petroleum.

Over time, this public ownership was transferred to another (and less-known) Norwegian NRC, Petoro,[16] which represents Norwegian ownership interests in these licences but does not have any operational experience/competence. Instead of actively working the oil fields, Petoro manages the government's own-ership shares in joint licensing ventures, and reaps the gains from this owner-ship. Petoro is an investment body, not an operational oil company. Today, most of Norway's oil wealth comes from this state ownership in joint licences (not

---

15. An interest is "carried" when a partner (e.g. the state, or a state-owned firm) in the exploration or development phase of a contract pays a proportion of the costs and expenses that is dispro-portionately lower than its formal share. Typically, the government's costs are carried through the exploration phase, at which point the government takes up (or "backs in") its contractual obligations (costs) as partner and receives its share of rewards (profit).

16. See www.petoro.no/home.

through its 67 per cent ownership of Equinor): through its direct ownership of oil – and the Natural Dividend this produces.

In addition, Norway employs a substantial RRT on the oil sector. First of all, oil companies must pay an ordinary corporate tax (which stands at 27 per cent, but includes a generous depreciation component to encourage development). In addition, but after a so-called "lift" has been deducted from oil companies' income (as another incentive for investment), companies are saddled with an RRT of 51 per cent (see Moses & Letnes 2017a: 104). In reality, then, petroleum producers in Norway are taxed at 78 per cent (OED 2019). Although this RRT is used to secure the Natural Dividend, oil companies have still managed to secure a solid return on their investments, and their workers secure good wages and working conditions.

These tax and ownership incomes are poured into what may be the most famous component of Norway's management regime: an enormous petroleum investment fund: the Government Pension Fund Global (GPFG).[17] The GPFG is now one of the world's largest sovereign wealth funds, exceeding $1 trillion (Sovereign Wealth Fund Institute n.d.). By way of this fund, the Norwegian people own shares in more than 9,000 companies, invested in 72 different countries around the globe, on behalf of the Norwegian people (Norges Bank Investment Management 2017). Calculated in another way, Norwegians – who constitute less than one-thousandth of the world's population – own roughly 1.3 per cent of the world's listed companies (Moses & Letnes 2017a: 135). This fund has attracted much attention for its size (as one of the world's largest sovereign wealth funds) and its influence (it is governed by an ethics board, which provides specific investment guidelines), but its most important task has been to minimize the threat of "Dutch disease" to the Norwegian economy (Moses 2021b, 2021c).

In effect, the Norwegian government recognizes that its petroleum resources are the national equivalent of the "family silver": they are the country's "natural assets", capable of delivering a Natural Dividend. But Norwegian political authorities also recognize that these assets are non-renewable, so that their consumption occurs at the expense of future generations. In an attempt to compensate for selling the "family silver", Norway reinvests the Natural Dividend from its petroleum in more reproducible forms of capital. In this way, the GPFG hopes to produce returns for future generations, long after the resource has been depleted.

---

17. Although it is called a pension fund, there has never been an explicit political decision as to how the money in the fund should be used in the future; the reference to pensions is simply a convenient way for politicians to signal the need to save for the future.

Conclusion

Over the past century some of the largest Natural Dividends have been uncovered beneath the ground in the energy resource markets that propelled the industrial revolution: coal, oil and gas. The demand for these resources, and the regimes that have managed them (and restricted our access), have created enormous riches (and significant corruption). For most countries, over most of this time, political authorities have allowed private interests to pocket this Natural Dividend, at the expense of its rightful owners.

There is broad recognition of this simple fact. As we saw in Chapter 3, the RRT literature grew out of an acknowledgement that the current management regimes were politically unsustainable and that there was significant scope for finding a middle-of-the-road solution that could benefit producers and owners alike. The development and spread of RRTs constituted one response. The adoption of more favourable PSCs and SCs, as well as the growing number of LCPs and NRCs, can be seen as additional efforts to secure the Natural Dividend, but in a more political form.

The example from Norway shows that it is entirely possible to use a prudential management regime along with RRTs, an NRC and a number of LCPs to secure the Natural Dividend for the public. This was done without alienating investors or undercutting their right to a fair return on investment. By minimizing the risk that is always associated with this sort of resource market, Norwegian governments were able to secure a much larger share of the Natural Dividend, relative to other countries. In return, investors receive a more stable, and less risky, investment environment.

As we move into new, more sustainable mineral markets, we expect to find similarly large potential for Natural Dividends. We hope that political authorities might learn from the Norwegian experience to introduce management regimes that can better secure this Natural Dividend for their citizens.

This lesson may be easiest to apply in the management of resources that the international community holds in common. This is partly because such resources are already recognized as rightfully belonging to the "common heritage of [hu]mankind" (United Nations Convention on the Law of the Sea; see UN 1982: preamble), and partly because private interests have not yet got their hands on them (the regulatory regime is still being developed). It is for this reason that we have saved this last, largely untouched, resource site for our final empirical chapter.

8

A COMMON MARKET? THE MARKET FOR GLOBAL RESOURCES

With this chapter, we shift our parallax. In the preceding chapters we have examined how political authorities have enclosed and allocated access to different types of resources on (or around) their own sovereign territories. Each of these resources has been located on sovereign territory, or in near proximity to that territory – in surrounding coastal waters, immediately above, or below, the sovereign surface. Although the natural resources found in each of these sovereign spaces may produce Natural Dividends, surprisingly few states have been willing or able to secure them for their people.

This chapter considers the challenge of enclosing and allocating access to familiar (and common) resources in the absence of sovereign authority. In short, we begin where the other chapters left off: on managing the resources that remain, after nation states make their sundry claims on the globe. We refer to the global commons, and use that term for the resources that lie beyond sovereign space: outer space, the inner earth, the high seas (and the sea bottom that lies beneath) and Antarctica. These resources resemble the "common goods" (*res communes*) identified by Hugo Grotius in his seminal (1608) *Mare Liberum*, as they belong to everyone and to no one.

Our interest in the global commons is threefold. First and foremost, these common areas offer the next frontier for global resource extraction. Because global demand has outstripped our capacity to provide these resources in sovereign political terrain, we now search for them in the global commons. It is the inadequacy of our current supply in these markets that drives our interest and expansion into the global commons: we go there in search of new sources for familiar, but scarce and valuable, resources. In other words, the markets for these resources are familiar; we are simply extending our reach into new, less charted, political terrain.

This interest is most obvious in space, which has become a competitive playground for the world's richest men, jousting for control over the future market for space tourism. But it is also evident in a number of new enterprises that hope to mine asteroids and planets for rare minerals/metals needed on earth;[1] or with the entrepreneurial dreams to launch high-altitude wind turbines (Levitan 2012) or to secure space-based solar power (*Financial Times* 2021; Frazer-Nash Consultancy 2021). This pull to exploit common resources is equally strong beneath the sea, where we find a quiet, but intense, race to access the valuable minerals that lie on the deep-sea bottom. All these entrepreneurial interests are lining up to access and exploit our common resources, yet we are *almost* entirely devoid of a management regime that can protect our global commons.

"Almost" is the second reason for this chapter. The global commons, in their many disparate forms, remain virgin political territory. The international community has not agreed how to manage these common resources, and many of the ground rules for their future exploitation will be set in the coming decades. Now is the time to discuss how we can, and should, manage these common resources.

The third reason should be the most obvious. The process of enclosing and allocating the global commons has the potential to deliver significant economic and political rewards, and will result in a radical redistribution of wealth. We are concerned that the global community has not committed more energy and thought to the process. We hope to focus attention on these global commons, so that the global community can devise a means to manage them justly, before they are taken from us.

Because we are starting from scratch it should be possible to develop a new, more equitable and just management regime for exploiting these common resource frontiers. In theory, such a regime should be easier to secure because these resources remain in the global commons: they have not yet been enclosed, allocated or commodified. In practice, however, this will still prove difficult. As we have seen in the preceding chapters, it has been difficult enough to secure the Natural Dividend within sovereign states, where democratic pressures can find easier expression. Securing the Natural Dividend from the global commons may prove even more difficult, in an international system where the strongest states have little incentive to create or abide by rules that limit their options. The political challenge does not end there; even if we do agree about how to secure the global Natural Dividend, it is unclear how it should be distributed to the global community.

Because the focus of this chapter is different from earlier chapters, so too is its design. The global resources we consider, and their resulting markets, are already familiar to us. We have seen how these resource markets (e.g. fish, energy, minerals) are established and how the Natural Dividend is produced. This terrain has already been covered in the preceding chapters. Moving forward, our focus

---

1. For a list of companies associated with asteroid mining, see www.wsmcr.org/pages/asteroid-min ing-technology.

BOX 8.1 THE AREA

The United Nations Convention on the Law of the Sea (UNCLOS) defines the outer contours of national jurisdiction with reference to the 12 nm territorial sea; an exclusive economic zone (EEZ) of up to 200 nm; and a continental shelf. This delineation is clearly marked in Figure 5.1. Beyond this national jurisdiction lies "the Area", which is defined as "the seabed and ocean floor and the subsoil thereof, beyond the limits of national jurisdiction" (UN 1982: art. 1(1)).

Although all of the 1982 convention's part XI is committed to "the Area", the convention's preamble makes it clear that the Area, "as well as its resources, are the common heritage of mankind, the exploration and exploitation of which shall be carried out for the benefit of mankind as a whole, irrespective of the geographical location of States." The resources of the Area are administered by the International Seabed Authority, headquartered in Kingston, Jamaica, with the aim of organizing and controlling all the activities in the Area on behalf of the state parties (UN 1982: art. 157(1)).

The Area is enormous, covering roughly 54 per cent of the total area of the world's oceans; a map of the Area can be found at: www.isa.org.jm/media/image/450.

---

is trained on what is unique in the global context: the lack of an established political authority to enclose and allocate access to these familiar resources.

For this reason, we begin by introducing the next resource frontier, and show how it is mostly unregulated. One exception can be found on the deep-sea bottom, beneath the high seas – i.e. "the Area" (see Box 8.1), where a nascent regulatory regime is being negotiated to manage the mineral wealth that lies beyond sovereign territory. As we expect that this new regime will provide the legal groundwork for subsequent management regimes in outer space, the inner earth and maybe even Antarctica, we take a close look at the regulatory regime being developed by the International Seabed Authority (ISA). We close this chapter by considering the many challenges that the global community will face in trying to secure the Natural Dividend that our global commons can produce.

The next resource frontier(s)

It is quite possible that the global commons contain spectacular new natural resources, as yet unfamiliar to us, but with the potential to benefit humankind in a significant way. The script for such discoveries can be found in the 1992 film

Medicine Man, starring Sean Connery and Lorraine Bracco. In the film, a pharmaceutical company sends a couple of biochemists deep into the Amazon's rainforests to isolate a derivative of a new species of flower and use it to create a serum for curing cancer (did we mention it was a Hollywood film?). The pharmaceutical company hopes to patent the serum, save the world and turn a pretty penny.

Medicine Man offers a popularized account of the bioprospecting industry. The UNDP (2016: 1) defines bioprospecting as "the systematic search for biochemical and genetic information in nature in order to develop commercially-valuable products for pharmaceutical, agricultural, cosmetic and other applications".[2] The bioprospecting industry has grown alongside the development of new screening techniques (in the 1980s); the explosive birth of the biotechnology industry; changes in US patent law (which allowed for the patenting of life/micro-organisms); and the export of this legal trend via its inclusion in the WTO's agreement on TRIP: trade-related intellectual property.

Clearly, the global commons contain many new forms of biochemical and genetic information that can be enclosed, marketed and sold on global markets. To ensure that private interests cannot take this common wealth, the global community will need to create management regimes for these resources as well. Bioprospecting offers one very important challenge to managing the global commons in the future, but we now set it aside for the time being.[3]

In this chapter our focus is trained on the recovery of more familiar resources, whose markets have already been described in previous chapters: the fish, petroleum, minerals and renewable energy sources that lie in the global commons. Although these resources vary in significant ways (e.g. some are renewable, others are not), they are all familiar and readily available in established markets with known price and demand levels. We have already seen how a Natural Dividend can be produced by these resources when exploited in sovereign contexts – and the same opportunities exist in the global commons.

Given the phenomenal costs of accessing and securing these resources, they can be commercially viable only when demand for them is insatiable (i.e. their price is very high) and/or when the resource sites are extraordinarily productive (relative to existing sites). In short, the draw to the resources in our global

---

2. Despite significant potential, the global value of bioprospecting contracts is relatively modest, and estimated to be below $100 million a year (UNDP 2016: 2). Even so, the OECD (2009) believes that the industrial application of biotechnology will only grow; by 2030 the organization estimates that biotechnology-based output could account for as much as 35 per cent of the output value of chemicals and other industrial products.

3. We have speculated about how to manage a future bioprospecting industry at the national level in Brigham and Moses (2021). To understand some of the challenges involved, see Brush (1999), Hayden (2003) and Shiva (2016 [1996]).

commons lies in their potential to generate substantial Natural Dividends. It is exactly for this reason that it is essential for us to develop a management regime that can protect our shared interest in the global commons.

The new enclosures

As we turn to exploit the natural resources lying under, over and beyond sovereign territory, we will face a new round of enclosures. Some political authority will eventually decide how to grant access to the resources that lie on the asteroids and planets above, in the inner earth or on the deep-sea ocean bottom. The history of resource exploitation makes it clear that nobody benefits from an unregulated rush on a particular resource. The political challenge lies in the fact that these new enclosures will be granted in places that lack a recognized and established sovereign authority. In these unclaimed political contexts, the political and economic stakes of the enclosure and allocation processes are even higher than we have seen in the sovereign realms. If this is not done correctly, any original allocation of access will lack legitimacy and be subject to reversal. This should worry entrepreneurs and investors.

The stakes are high. In deciding how to enclose and allocate access to our global resources, we will be granting access to some of the greatest Natural Dividends produced by our planet (and beyond). As the US senator Ted Cruz has noted with reference to space exploitation, it is here that the world's first trillionaire will probably be made (quoted in Glester 2018).

Opening up access to this new resource frontier will flood existing resource markets in ways that can generate significant political disruption. Consider just one scenario:

> According to the World Bank, the total gross product of planet Earth was about USD 85 trillion … At the same time, according to John Lewis, professor of astronomy at the University of Arizona, the estimated value of resources that can be mined on a single asteroid (3554), 2.5 km in diameter, is about USD 20 trillion (one quarter of the world gross product in 2018): USD 8 trillion – iron and nickel, USD 6 trillion – cobalt, USD 6 trillion – platinum and other platinum group metals … That is, *the value of one asteroid will far exceed the value of all mineral deposits sold for a year in the world*. It is impossible to foresee and predict the effects of the resources inflow from other planets to Earth, since no analogues have happened in the world history. A long way off is the bankruptcy of Spain, caused by the importation of gold from the New World.   (Zyma 2019: 127–8, emphasis added)

These concerns about flooding the market are also evident in the current negotiations surrounding the governance regime being discussed at the ISA (see below), in which land-based (sovereign) mineral producers are worried that the entry of new, deep-seabed mineral harvests can flood the existing market and undermine the status quo.[4] These concerns are entirely justified, especially with regard to some of the more essential metals. A report for the High Level Panel for a Sustainable Ocean Economy found that the supply of cobalt in the Clarion–Clipperton Zone (just one productive zone in the Area), is estimated to be equivalent to 340–600 per cent of the land-based reserves of cobalt (Haugan *et al.* 2019: 20, tab. 3). It is for this reason that the 1994 implementation agreement of the United Nations Convention on the Law of the Sea (UNCLOS) made clear: "The rates of payments [e.g. royalties] under the system shall be within the range of those prevailing in respect of land-based mining of the same or similar minerals in order *to avoid giving deep seabed miners an artificial competitive advantage* or imposing on them a competitive disadvantage" (UN 1994: annex, sect.8.1b, emphasis added).

In short, the path to enclosing and allocating access to these scarce, valuable and common resources is strewn with political and economic challenges. To ensure that the enclosure and allocation process is seen as legitimate, any regulatory authority will need to assure the global community that access has been granted on their behalf and for the benefit of humankind. After all, any allocation decision will grant particular (private or public) interests access to enormous wealth, with significant distributional consequences.

Who, then, should represent humankind (as the original holder of these common resources) in deciding how to enclose and allocate access to these scarce, valuable and shared resources? The most evident candidate is surely the United Nations, but the reach of UN authority is often constrained by its most powerful member states. Even so, it is here, in the texts of several international treaties, that a future regulatory authority for our global commons will most likely be located.

The absence of regulatory authority

Although there are a number of international agreements and frameworks that govern our global commons, none of them deliver a detailed management regime for how (or even if) we should manage the harvest of our shared resources.

---

4. See also the explicit concerns of the African Group in Remaoun (2019).

The most sophisticated management regime is currently being negotiated at the ISA, which is tasked with managing the resources of the Area for the "benefit of [hu]mankind as a whole" (UN 1982: preamble). Because we believe this regime offers a model for how we might manage the resources in our other global commons, it is the focus of our attention in the next section. This section provides a brief glimpse of the most important treaties currently "governing" the global commons, as they vary significantly. Some of the most important international treaties governing the global commons can be found in Table 8.1.

Table 8.1 Headline international governance treaties

1959	**The Antarctic Treaty** was signed by 12 states, seven of which asserted a territorial claim to some part of Antarctica. There are currently 55 states party to the treaty, 29 of which (including all 12 original signatories) have consultative (voting) status. See www.ats.aq/e/antarctictreaty.html.
1967	**The Outer Space Treaty**. Formally, the Treaty on Principles Governing the Activities of States in the Exploration and Use of Outer Space, including the Moon and Other Celestial Bodies. Today there are 111 countries party to the treaty, including all major spacefaring nations, and another 23 are signatories. See UN (1967) and www.unoosa.org/oosa/en/ourwork/spacelaw/treaties/status/index.html.
1979	**The Moon Agreement**. Formally, the Agreement Governing the Activities of States on the Moon and Other Celestial Bodies. There are currently only 18 state parties to the treaty, and it has not been ratified by any state that engages in self-launched human spaceflight (i.e. the United States, Russia and China). Consequently, the relevance of this agreement in international law is rather limited. See UN (1979) and www.unoosa.org/oosa/en/ourwork/spacelaw/treaties/intromoon-agreement.html.
1982	**United Nations Convention on the Law of the Sea** (UNCLOS), sometimes called the Law of the Sea Convention (LOSC). This convention provides a legal framework for all marine and maritime activities and introduces the International Seabed Authority and the "common heritage of mankind" principle. There are currently 168 parties to the convention, but the United States is not among them.* See www.un.org/Depts/los/convention_agreements/texts/unclos/unclos_e.pdf.
1992	**The Convention on Biological Diversity (CBD)**. One of three conventions agreed to at the 1992 Earth Summit in Rio de Janeiro. This convention aims to conserve the planet's biological diversity and includes the need for "[t]he fair and equitable sharing of the benefits arising out of the utilization of genetic resources" (UN 1992: introd.). Every single UN member state is party to this convention, with only one exception: the United States. See www.cbd.int/convention/text.

Note: *Although the United States ratified the 1958 convention, it is not a party to the 1982 convention. Even so, the United States recognizes that the 1982 convention reflects customary international law, and it tends to comply with its provisions.

Inner earth

It is possible to think of a continuum of regulatory responses to managing our global commons. At one end of the regulatory continuum, we find that much of the global commons lies beyond any international agreement or consensus: some of us see the resources in these common spaces as part of the global commons; others see them as free for the taking. Such is our approach to governing access to the inner earth, where there is currently no agreement about who controls the inner earth, or even where the limits to sovereign (let alone private) authority starts and ends. This is curious, in that the deepest borehole in the world is only 12 km deep (the Kola Superdeep Borehole). Consequently, an agreement limiting sovereign authority to just 100 km (downwards) would provide states with more underground territory than they can possibly utilize in the foreseeable future. Although it would be relatively easy to agree to a common management regime for the inner earth (before it reveals any of its potential value), this has not been a priority.

Antarctica

Antarctica lies at the other end of this imagined regulatory spectrum. The Antarctic region is subject to the Antarctic Treaty (1959) and a number of supporting agreements, known collectively as the Antarctic Treaty System (or ATS). This treaty sets aside Antarctica as a scientific preserve, establishes freedom of scientific investigation and bans military activity on the continent. For our purposes, the most significant aspect of the original treaty is that it makes no reference to the regulation of mineral resources. The same can be said for most of the supporting agreements in the ATS.[5] The one exception is the Protocol on Environmental Protection to the Antarctic Treaty (signed in 1991, and known as the Madrid Protocol), whose article 7 makes it clear that Antarctica is to be protected from commercial exploitation: "Any activity relating to mineral resources, other than scientific research, shall be prohibited" (Secretariat of the Antarctic Treaty 1991: art. 7). In short, and in contrast to our approach to managing the other global commons, the international community

---

5. The 1988 Convention on the Regulation of Antarctic Mineral Resource Activities is part of the ATS, and it would have allowed mining under the control and taxation of an international managing body similar to the ISA. Although the convention was signed by 19 states, it was ratified by none. Consequently, the convention never entered into force, and it has been replaced by the Madrid Protocol, which came into force in 1998.

explicitly recognizes Antarctica to be part of the global commons, and places its resource wealth out of bounds for commercial activity.

The high seas

We find a good deal of variance and legal opacity in between these two place markers on the global regulatory continuum. Take, for example, the way we agree to govern (or not) the global fisheries in the high seas that exist just off the sovereign EEZs introduced in Chapter 5 (see also Armstrong 2022). This area is said to be "governed" by the law of the sea, which is today tethered to the UN Convention on the Law of the Sea – the result, first, of the four treaties that constitute the 1958 convention[6] and, subsequently, the (1982) Convention on the Law of the Sea itself, which came into force in 1994. Not only does the 1982 UNCLOS define and delineate the limits to sovereign territory at sea (as shown in Figure 5.1), it also establishes general obligations for safeguarding the marine environment and protecting the freedom of scientific research on the high seas (as well as introducing an innovative outline for regulating mineral resource exploitation on the underlying seabed, as we shall see below).

The high seas, then, constitute that unclaimed ocean lying just beyond the sovereign EEZs. In effect, fishing in the high seas is a free-for-all. What governance there is comes in the form of a number of self-enforcing voluntary intergovernmental agreements or treaties, known as regional fisheries management organizations (RFMOs), which vary in their scope and objectives. The only global standards for deep-sea fishing are a set of non-binding guidelines issued by the UN's Food and Agriculture Organization, which encourage states to protect vulnerable marine ecosystems (such as deep-water coral)[7] – but these guidelines have been adopted by only a few coastal and flag states (Rogers & Gianni 2010).

In 2018 the United Nations began negotiations on a new treaty that focuses on the conservation and sustainable use of marine biodiversity in the high seas. This new treaty would establish a framework for evaluating and implementing area-based management tools (including the introduction of marine protected areas); establish uniform requirements for conducting environmental impact

---

6. The Convention on the Territorial Sea and Contiguous Zone; the Convention on the Continental Shelf; the Convention on the High Seas; and the Convention of Fishing and Conservation of Living Resources of the High Seas.

7. In particular, the United Nations' Resolution 59/25 from 2004 called on high seas fishing nations and RFMOs to take urgent action to protect vulnerable marine ecosystems from destructive fishing practices, including bottom trawl fishing (UN 2004). UN Resolution 61/105 committed nations that authorize their vessels to engage in bottom fisheries on the high seas to take a series of additional actions (UN 2006).

assessments; determine how the benefits from marine genetic resources should be shared; and build capacity for further management and conservation (Lohan 2020).

What is most interesting about this new treaty text is its embrace of the "benefit-sharing" principle first enunciated in the 1992 Convention on Biological Diversity (CBD: see Box 8.2 and Table 8.1). In particular, the treaty aims to "[p]romote the (fair and equitable) sharing of benefits arising from the (collection of) (access to) (utilization of) marine genetic resources of areas beyond national jurisdiction" (UN 2019e: 5, art. 7(a)). Article 11 elaborates that the benefits arising from marine genetic resources in the high seas shall/may be shared in a fair and equitable manner (and apply to both monetary and non-monetary benefits, per article 11(2)). Although it was broadly expected that the treaty would be ratified in 2020, its passage has been derailed by the Covid-19 pandemic, and its current status is unclear.

Outer space

Compared to the high seas, there are greater restrictions placed on the exploitation of outer space, but these restrictions are under increased scrutiny and pressure (for a pessimistic account, see Deudney 2020).[8] The origins of international space law date back to 1919, when international law recognized each country's sovereignty over the airspace directly above its territory (see Kleiman 2013). Today, however, outer space is mostly governed by two treaties, both of which are described in Table 8.1.[9] The Outer Space Treaty from 1967 holds that outer space is the "province of all mankind" (UN 1967: art. I) and has specific provisions that preclude any country from claiming sovereignty over outer space or any celestial body (UN 1967: art. II). Like the Antarctic Treaty of 1959,

---

8. There is a common misperception that the law of the sea transfers easily to outer space. In doing so, however, we are comparing apples to oranges. This is because the law of the sea has traditionally "governed" the harvest/use of renewable (living) resources. In outer space, resources tend to be in the form of non-renewable minerals and metals. If private interests abscond with some fish from the high seas, they will be replaced by natural reproduction (if not overfished). When private interests abscond with minerals from outer space, the taking is permanent. For this reason, the regime being developed at the ISA is more relevant for outer space (than the free-for-all found in the high seas fishery).

9. In addition to these two treaties, the UN Committee on the Peaceful Uses of Outer Space (COPUOS), along with its legal and scientific and technical subcommittees, is responsible for debating issues of international space law and policy. The UN Office for Outer Space Affairs (UNOOSA) serves as the secretariat of the committee, and it promotes "access to space for all" through a wide range of conferences and capacity-building programmes.

BOX 8.2 BENEFIT SHARING

Before the 1990s cultural knowledge, plants and other genetic/biological resources, regardless of where they were located, were considered part of the "global commons" (Merson 2000) or part of our common heritage (Hayden 2003); these resources could be freely taken out of their natural state, innovated upon and then patented.

In 1992 the UN held the Earth Summit on Environment and Development, at which an international Convention on Biological Diversity was passed and subsequently ratified by most of the countries in the world (though not the United States). The Rio Convention aimed to protect biological and genetic resources by giving sovereign states explicit property rights in them.[1] This convention was followed up by the subsequent Nagoya Protocol on access and benefit sharing (in 2014).

In particular, article 8j of the convention (UN 1992) recognizes the rights of traditional communities to their knowledge and resources, whereas article 16 establishes a novel and explicit requirement of reciprocity: poorer countries can provide access to genetic resources in exchange for some form of compensation, technology transfer or other kind of benefit (later elaborated upon in the Nagoya Protocol).

Under the CBD, bioprospecting is regulated through so-called "access and benefit-sharing agreements". These are bilateral contractual arrangements between biologically rich states or communities (which control access to the resource) and private corporations (which hope to exploit them). The convention provides a clearing-house, the Access and Benefit-Sharing Clearing-House (ABSCH), at which partners can exchange information on access and benefit-sharing agreements, and monitor the utilization of genetic resources along the value chain (see https://absch.cbd.int/en).

---

1. We should point out that the convention grants property rights to states, but it also recognizes that the maintenance of biodiversity often rests in the hands of indigenous communities that have been part of the ecological balance for many thousands of years. The convention (articles 8j and 10c) refers to the need to protect the interests of these indigenous communities as part of any conservation strategy.

---

the focus of the Outer Space Treaty is to create a sort of scientific preserve: it aims to regulate certain activities with an eye towards minimizing conflict, but it is mostly silent on how to deal with commercial activities, such as lunar or asteroid mining.

The same tenor is found in the 1979 Moon Agreement (UN 1979), which turns jurisdiction of all celestial bodies (including the orbits around such bodies) over to the participant countries. In effect, the Moon Agreement would place all space activities under international law and the United Nations Charter. Most interestingly, article 11 of the treaty holds that "the moon and its natural resources are the *common heritage of mankind*" (emphasis added), and article 4 holds: "The exploration and use of the moon shall be the province of all mankind and shall be carried out for the benefit and in the interest of all countries, irrespective of their degree of economic or scientific development. Due regard shall be paid to the interests of present and future generations ..." (UN 1979: arts 11 & 4). Although the Moon Agreement is ambitious, its legal reach is severely limited by its lack of relevant signatories (see Table 8.1).

Individual countries have encroached upon both of these treaties, even when they are a party to them. For example, the US Congress passed the Space Resource Exploration and Utilization Act in 2015, which allows for private ownership claims on outer space resources.[10] Along similar lines, the (then) executive director of the US National Space Council, Scott Pace, said:

> It bears repeating: outer space is not a "global commons", not the "common heritage of mankind," not "*res communis*", nor is it a public good. These concepts are not part of the Outer Space Treaty, and the United States has consistently taken the position that these ideas do not describe the legal status of outer space....To unlock the promise of space, to expand the economic sphere of human activity beyond the Earth, requires that we not constrain ourselves with legal constructs that do not apply to space. (Pace 2017)

The ambition to privatize space resources is not limited to the United States. Luxembourg has followed suit by positioning itself as a major player in the space race, with several other countries (Japan, Russia, China, India) waiting in the wings (Mallick & Rajagopalan 2019). Recently the Hague Space Resources Governance Working Group (HSRGWG) was established "as a forum to discuss and propose solutions for the current lack of a legal framework for the issue of space resources found on asteroids and other celestial bodies" (HSRGWG 2018: 1). In particular, the HSRGWG has identified a number of "building blocks" for a subsequent regulatory framework (HSRGWG 2019). Although such groups provide hope for the nascent space-mining industry, the status of their proposals are still

---

10. It "[d]eclares that any asteroid resources obtained in outer space are the property of the entity that obtained them, which shall be entitled to all property rights to them, consistent with applicable federal law and existing international obligations" (Congress 2015: §51303).

pending. In short, there is much legal ambiguity around who has the authority to provide access to and to regulate outer space mining operations (Kelvey 2014).

Thus, we lack a settled regulatory framework for exploiting the global commons. On the high seas, at the inner earth and in the heavens above we have not yet agreed on how to manage our common resources. In Antarctica we have agreed to let these resources lie (for the time being). Although existing international agreements do not provide much explicit guidance as to how our common resources should be managed and regulated, they do make frequent reference to two common (yet still controversial) claims: the notion that these resources should be governed by what are called access and benefit-sharing agreements (see Box 8.2); and that they are part of the common heritage of mankind, or CHM (see Box 8.3). The latter principle is most firmly connected to the regime being established by the International Seabed Authority.

The nascent regulatory regime at the International Seabed Authority

There is only one place where the international community has agreed upon a regime for exploiting its common natural resources: the deep seabed beneath the high seas, known as "the Area". This nascent regulatory regime has come together because the Area is known to contain valuable natural resources that are already accessible with existing technologies.[11] As our terrestrial reserves of high-grade mineral and metal deposits are being depleted, and as the demand for metals and rare earth elements grows precipitously – especially by new "green" and "high-tech" industries – deep-seabed mining has become more attractive and viable (Hein *et al.* 2013).

Responsibility for governing the Area lies with an international body, the International Seabed Authority, whose legal foundations rest on two international agreements: the 1982 UN Convention on the Law of the Sea and its 1994 implementation agreement (see UN 1982 and 1994 and Table 8.1).[12] Parties to these two agreements established the ISA in order to organize and control the activities in the Area (UN 1982: art. 157). This includes a mandate to secure an equitable sharing of the benefits derived from the Area and a promise to protect the marine environment from any harmful effects that may arise from deep-seabed-related activities.

---

11. Although seabed mineral deposits were first found by the Challenger Expedition (1872–76), when manganese nodules were recovered from the Pacific, Indian and Atlantic Oceans, it was not until the 1960s that it was technologically feasible to reap their economic potential (Glasby 2012).

12. For a good introduction to the history of these agreements, see Nandan, Lodge and Rosenne (2002).

BOX 8.3 COMMON HERITAGE OF MANKIND

The notion of a common heritage of mankind, or CHM, pops up in several inter-national agreements relevant for governing what we have called the global commons (see Franckx 2010, Taylor 2011 and Jaeckel 2020). The roots of the CHM can be traced back to the nineteenth century, when the Latin American jurist Andrés Bello spoke of the global commons (i.e. things that could not be held by one nation without detriment to others) as a sort of "common patrimony" (Nandan, Lodge & Rosenne 2002: 5). But the concept was more fully developed in the 1967 discussions concerning the law of the sea, and is usually associated with Malta's permanent representative to the United Nations from 1964 to 1971, Arvid Pardo. More specifically, the CHM first arises in a *note verbale* of 17 August 1967, put into writing the next day (Permanent Mission of Malta 1967).

Traces of the CHM concept can be found in the 1967 Outer Space Treaty, which says that the exploration and use of outer space "shall be carried out for the benefit and in the interest of all countries … and shall be the province of all mankind" (UN 1967: art. I). But the actual term was not formally introduced until a 1970 UNGA Resolution declared the Area and its resources to be the "common heritage of mankind" (UN 1970: 1), a principle that was later enshrined in the UNCLOS (UN 1982: art. 136). The same wording can be found in the Moon Agreement, which declares that the moon and its natural resources are the CHM (UN 1979: art. 11(1)).

The CHM concept has been extended, if not fully accepted, across three of the global commons: Antarctica; outer space; and the deep seabed. Even so, the concept has been applied unevenly across these three areas. For example, the 1959 Antarctic Treaty does not mention the CHM, but its preamble does note that it is "in the interest of all mankind that Antarctica shall continue forever to be used exclusively for peaceful purposes and shall not become the scene or object of international discord" (UN 1959: preamble). The Moon Agreement declares that the moon and its natural resources are the CHM (UN 1979: art. 11(1)), but it leaves the establishment of an international regime for later (UN 1979: art. 11(5)). Finally, the 1982 UNCLOS provides the clearest and strongest expression of the CHM principle (UN 1982: art. 136), and creates the sort of institutions that can deliver its promise.

Although the 1982 UNCLOS and its subsequent 1994 implementing agreement provide the legal foundation for the Area, the detailed requirements for mining operations, and any eventual sharing of benefits, was left to subsequent negoti-ations. Thus far the ISA has produced regulations covering three different deep-sea resources: the regulations for prospecting and exploring polymetallic nodules, sulphides and cobalt-rich ferromanganese crusts (ISA 2010, 2012, 2013).[13] Although these international agreements and ISA regulations provide a general outline for an eventual regulatory regime, many of the most pressing details – especially with regard to securing the Natural Dividend – have yet to be established.

In many ways, the ISA is torn between its two defining documents. The 1982 convention presents a common-property approach to managing the Area, declaring the Area and its resources to be the "common heritage of mankind". This principle was subsequently enshrined in article 136 of the UNCLOS (UN 1982), as elaborated upon in Box 8.3. The 1994 implementation agreement, on the other hand, waters down the common-property approach, by prioritizing a number of private initiatives and market-based principles. These differences have been exploited by some of the most powerful players in the international community, making it difficult to secure agreement over what, actually, the CHM should mean in practice.

The most contentious part of the 1982 UNCLOS was its provisions (in part XI) for the equitable sharing of benefits derived from the use of the resources in the Area (UN 1982: art. 140). The United States led a rearguard action (which included both the United Kingdom and Germany) aimed at undermining these provisions. Although this resistance was at first futile,[14] the end result was a modified implementation agreement (in 1994), which reduced the ISA to a "permitting organization operating via free market principles" (Zalik 2015: 182). In particular, the 1994 implementation agreement watered down some of the most controversial elements of the part XI regime.[15] Although the United States has still not ratified the 1982 UNCLOS, the 1994 implementation agreement

---

13. For greater elaboration upon how the ISA regulates the Area, from an economic and political perspective, see Moses and Brigham (2021).

14. When the convention was put to a recorded vote, at the request of the United States, it was adopted by 130 states with 17 abstentions, but only four states were actively opposed: Israel, Turkey, the United States and Venezuela (Nandan, Lodge & Rosenne 2002: 53). Unable to sway the global majority, the United States pursued a stopgap strategy. Between 1980 and 1985 six states (the United States, Germany, the United Kingdom, France, Japan and Italy) passed legislation under which they all agreed to recognize one another's claims to seabed mining sites and to enact similar national laws, so as to provide for the regulation of seabed mining activities by their nationals on the high seas. A team of legal experts for the developing countries comprising the Group of 77 (G-77) later argued that these sorts of reciprocating states agreements ran contrary to international law (Brown 2001).

15. For example: a recognition of the interests of so-called "pioneer firms"; a weakening of the ISA's capacity to protect these resources for the benefit of (hu)mankind; requirements for the compulsory transfer of technology and the subsidization of the activities of "the Enterprise"; and new voting procedures that undermined the capacity of the Global South to use its majority position (Oxman 1994).

allows its pioneer firms to profit from ISA contracts, while largely avoiding the requirements of international redistribution and technology transfer mandated by the convention (Zalik 2018: 347).

The international community recognizes the ISA's legitimate stewardship over the Area's mineral resources and has granted the ISA authority to allocate access to these resources in a way that is designed to protect the interests of poorer and less developed member states. This authority rests in three representative bodies, described in the UNCLOS – "an Assembly, a Council and a Secretariat" (UN 1982: art. 158(1)) – and a new organization, known as "the Enterprise", which was originally conceived to be something like an NRC (UN 1982: art. 158(2)).

The ISA is the legitimate political authority for allocating access to the natural resources that lie in the deep-sea commons. As such, it will decide who will gain access to the most productive and/or advantageous sites, assess the ease of accessing those sites (e.g. stronger or laxer environmental regulations) and decide the scope of that access. In other words, the authority has the power to flood the existing market (and hence undermine the existing price) or limit access to the most productive sites (thereby protecting the status quo). In short, the ISA enjoys the authority to make and secure differential, regulatory and locational rents from the global commons. Although its authority is clear, its intent remains ambiguous: we still do not know how the ISA intends to use its political authority, and for whose benefit.

To date the ISA has approved 30 exploration contracts, involving 22 different countries (12 of which are from developing states) and covering more than 1.3 million square kilometres of the seabed (Deep Sea Conservation Coalition 2020). But the ISA has *not yet* allocated any contracts to exploit these resources. To that end, the ISA is in the process of developing a "holistic regulatory framework for the exploitation of the resources in the Area" (ISA n.d.). The original intent was to draft exploitation regulations that could be adopted in 2020, but the Covid-19 pandemic has delayed the ISA's progress, and the process is currently on hold.

In short, the global community stands at the edge of a regulatory precipice (Moses & Brigham 2021). It has the authority and the potential to manage the Area in a way that can capture the Natural Dividend for the global community, but it still lacks the requisite awareness and institutions to secure that Dividend.

Indeed, the legal foundations for securing the Natural Dividend have already been laid. The ISA is mandated to act on behalf of humankind as a whole (UN 1982: arts 140, 157), and the original convention tasks the authority with providing for "the equitable sharing of financial and other economic benefits derived from activities in the Area through any appropriate mechanism, on a non-discriminatory basis ..." (UN 1982: art. 140(2)). The subsequent treaty outline suggests that this benefit would probably take the form of "transfers of technology" (UN 1982: art.

144), but subsequent developments suggest that the ISA is now looking at this benefit in a more financial form (generated by royalties). In a 2020 call for study proposals, we learn that, "The Finance Committee of the International Seabed Authority (ISA) is in the process of developing recommendations on an appropriate mechanism for the equitable sharing of the financial benefits (in the form of royalties) generated by seabed minerals exploitation in the international seabed Area" (ISA 2020: 2). There is no reason to assume that these benefits are only financial; after all, many ISA member states still hope to secure a technology transfer, in one form or another. But it is clear that the global community recognizes that (a) the Area's resources belong to us in common, and (b) the ISA is committed to the idea that these benefits should be shared in an equitable manner.

More to the point, the ISA has created institutions that can regulate access to these shared resources in a way that is consistent with the CHM. It is clear that the ISA will be responsible for enclosing and allocating access to future exploitation rights, and these rights will be granted to concessionaries (both sponsoring states and private enterprises) in exchange for some sort of "annual fixed fee" (UN 1994: sect. 8(1d)). What we lack is a shared understanding of what constitutes the CHM, and how it might be operationalized (see, e.g., Jaeckel 2020 and Collins & French 2020): producers see a common benefit to mankind in bringing scarce and necessary minerals to market; poorer countries hope to develop operational competences and technology transfers that will help them exploit their own sovereign resources; others, such as the ISA's Finance Committee, are focusing on the potential financial gains from a royalty imposed on concessionaires. We believe that the CHM must include the Natural Dividend produced by the global commons.

Most disconcertingly – from our perspective – is the lack of any explicit recognition that the Area might produce some form of resource rent or Natural Dividend. To the contrary, the focus of regulatory discussion has been aimed at ensuring sufficient returns so as to attract investors.[16] Worse, the discussion

---

16. Remarkably, the main contributor to discussions about a potential fiscal regime has been a consulting group with strong ties to the engineering and automotive industry (the Materials Systems Laboratory, or MSL, at the Massachusetts Institute of Technology: MIT). The MSL is quite explicit about its interests and affiliation: "The Materials Systems Laboratory is a research group at MIT that studies the strategic implications of materials and materials processing choices. MSL resides within the MIT School of Engineering. A major portion of our work is carried out in cooperation with the automotive industry, examining structural materials, assembly issues, and electronics and powertrain issues, but we are also notable for our work on projects of interest to the electronics and photonics industries, including electronics recycling, opto-electronic devices. We are also engaged in work with bio-polymers and supply chain studies" (MSL n.d.). The ISA announcement of the MIT report, and links to some of the presentations, are available at ISA (2019). An overview can be found in Kirchain *et al.* (2019), while a critical response to the MIT report, from the African Group, is found in Remaoun (2019).

is dominated by industrial interests, along with those of competing land-based suppliers (and their state sponsors), albeit tempered by a rising chorus of environmental concerns (Sharma 2019; Levin *et al.* 2016; Lodge *et al.* 2014). There is remarkably little academic work that directly addresses the challenges of economic management (but see Van Nijen *et al.* 2019 and Moses & Brigham 2021), even though some of the state parties groups at the ISA have begun to voice concerns (e.g. African Group 2018; Remaoun 2019).

To conclude, the ISA is under immense pressure to create detailed regulations for the exploitation of our common mineral resources in the Area. It has already allocated exploration contracts, and firms hope to leverage these contracts into exploitation rights. The problem is that the ISA has made precious little progress in deciding how to secure the common benefit as owner/custodian of these resources, and/or how to distribute the resulting benefits in a manner that is consistent with a CHM approach (including future generations). The global community enjoys a nascent regulatory regime: baseline mining regulations have been adopted, and a number of exploration licences have been allocated, but we still lack a formal regime for allocating and regulating access to the minerals, and for establishing how the resulting Natural Dividend is to be captured.

Securing the Natural Dividend from the Area

The global community has a political mandate and the requisite institutions for harvesting the Natural Dividend from resources that lie in the Area. The problem is that the ISA still lacks an awareness of its role in producing, and its need to secure, that Dividend. One reason for this regulatory myopia may be uncertainty about the economic benefit that the Area can generate.

Clearly, any Natural Dividend will depend on the profitability of harvesting these minerals, and this profitability will, in turn, be determined by the onerousness of any environmental regulations imposed by the ISA. On the one hand, we can assume that there is much economic potential when so many powerful international corporations are lining up for the right to access these minerals. This demand will only grow as our sovereign-based supply is depleted. On the other hand, the future viability of deep-sea mining activity will depend largely on its environmental impact, and this has not yet been fully assessed (Petersen *et al.* 2016: 185). In sum, it is not yet clear whether seabed mining will yield net benefits or costs (Folkersen, Fleming & Hasan 2019: 2; Jaeckel 2020: 665).

As we learned in the previous section, there is a broad consensus for the need to secure these resources for the benefit of humankind, but we have not agreed what this means in practice. As the details of any future exploitation concessions/agreements are still being discussed, we can only speculate what an eventual global concession regime might look like, and its capacity to secure the Natural Dividend. This speculation can be organized under three rubrics: (a) the details of how access will be allocated (i.e. the concession regime); (b) the nature of the fiscal regime connected to that allocation; and (c) what the global community might do with any resulting Natural Dividend.

On the first point, it is becoming increasingly clear that access to these resources will be granted along lines similar to the mineral and petroleum concession regimes outlined in Chapter 7, but in recognition of the need to ensure that this allocation can protect the interest of poorer and less developed member states. Most of this protection takes the form of a divided or parallel licence regime (a so-called "parallel system"), in which each potential exploitation site is separated into two equally valuable/viable areas, with one of these areas reserved for the broader community. The result of this parallel system will be a patchwork of licences, most (if not all) of which will be exploited by private interests and their sponsoring states. As we have discussed in several of the preceding chapters, the scope of this allocation will determine the relative value of the resource (and the resulting rents), and its allocation will create winners and losers (which will require redress).

This brings us to the second point. Up to now there has been no explicit recognition of the role that the ISA's management regime will have in creating rents, or the need to secure these rents on behalf of their owners. Although the ISA recognizes common ownership of the underlying resources, these resources are simply given away to those companies and joint ventures that are granted access to the Area. The public take, then, is limited to a tax or royalty on the collection process. Although we do not wish to climb into the details surrounding the current discussions over different payment regimes (see Van Nijen *et al.* 2019), current proposals of a 2 per cent royalty are remarkably modest (see African Group 2018).

Securing the Natural Dividend from the Area is complicated by the unique nature of the ISA as the legitimate political authority. It was originally assumed that some of the Natural Divided could be secured in a more political form by way of "the Enterprise", which was modelled as a type of global NRC. "The Enterprise" was to train staff from developing-country member states, who could then transfer this expertise and competence to their home markets/resources. But the role and the scope of "the Enterprise" was radically reduced with the 1994 implementation agreement, and its current role and status are uncertain.

Because the ISA is not a sovereign state but a different type of political authority, it is also unclear how it might secure a more fiscal or monetary form of the Natural Dividend. In particular, the ISA lacks the authority to tax and/or access the sort of revenue/expenditure information that is essential for determining the Natural Dividend (see Clark, Cook Clark & Pintz 2013: 46–54). As a result, the

ISA will be forced to pursue other (non-tax) means to secure the public take (or lean on nation states to help fill the void). To the extent that the ISA is forced to rely on royalties alone, the fiscal regime will be insufficiently progressive, and will need to be awkwardly large if it is not to undermine the competitiveness of land-based producers (see African Group 2018: 7–8; and Clark, Cook Clark & Pintz 2013: 46–7). As each concessionaire is linked to a sponsoring member state, and these member states have the capacity and authority to collect this type of information on behalf of the ISA, this is not an insurmountable problem, but it does introduce another level of uncertainty.

As we have discussed in previous chapters, employing a royalty fee will not suffice to secure the rents being generated by this regulatory effort – unless the royalty is paid out as a share of the harvested resource and/or is substantial in size. But, until the ISA has access to the relevant revenue and expenditures data, it simply cannot know the size of this Dividend (now or in the future). Consequently, the ISA risks giving away our Natural Dividend to private interests (and/or their member-state sponsors). In addition, any fiscal regime that the ISA adopts will be further constrained by the fact that it is not allowed to undermine the land-based minerals sector, by offering (for example) better contract terms (UN 1994: sect. 8, §1(b)).

Finally, even if the ISA were to introduce a fiscal regime that could capture and secure the Natural Dividend, it is entirely unclear how the ISA would use its revenues in a way that is consistent with its mandate. To date, this is not an issue, as the expected revenues from a 2 per cent royalty fee promise to be rather modest. Even so, these modest revenues may suffice for the ISA to recover its administrative costs (UN 1994: annex, sect. 1(14)) and a small deposit in a dedicated economic assistance fund (UN 1994: annex, sect. 7(1a)).

Should there be any money left over, we can expect heated discussions around two dimensions related to how this surplus can be allocated in a way that is consistent with the CHM: time and territory. The first debate will concern how much of the surplus should be invested in global markets (to secure returns for the future) and how much should be distributed immediately, for the benefit of humankind. Obviously, the more that is distributed now, the less will remain to accumulate and grow for future generations. The second debate concerns how to distribute the rewards once they are released. In this discussion, the ISA will need to consider how to distribute any return across political terrain – for example should it focus on states, international organizations or individuals? At the most general level, the ISA might consider three potential allocations:[17]

---

17. These three allocation objectives were first forwarded in a 2021 study proposal to the ISA by the authors and Paul Harnett at REPIM (Research on Economic Policy Implementation and Management).

(1) allocation to *member states* according to a formula that benefits poorer states, as discussed in ISA (2020);
(2) allocation to *global objectives*, such as a "Seabed Sustainability Fund", adaptation or mitigation of climate change, the Sustainable Development Goals (SDGs) or other global objectives that benefit the global community; and/or
(3) direct distribution to the *world's population* as a dividend, as is done in the US state of Alaska, to benefit the world's residents directly.[18]

The ISA is currently investigating these issues (as seen by ISA 2020). In doing so, it seems to assume that the CHM can be secured with a modest royalty fee, and the ISA seems to be unaware of the rents that its own regulatory actions will produce. In ignoring these rents, the resulting fund (and its allocation) is bound to be modest.[19] Should the ISA realize its potential for rent creation, and then try to secure the resulting Natural Dividend for the global community, the size of its fund could be substantial, and grow even more so in the future, as global demand for precious minerals rises (and the sovereign supply continues to dwindle).

Conclusion

We can expect that a growing demand for scarce natural resources will push the demand for exploitation deeper into the global commons, where many of these resources continue to lie, untouched. In most of these global commons we still lack a management regime that can provide legitimate access to these scarce resources and provide for their adequate protection. Clearly, the lack of such a regulatory regime will deter future developments.

The focus of this chapter has been aimed on the Area, and the political authority that is responsible for its management: the ISA. Because it is the first, and most ambitious, attempt at regulating the global commons, the ISA is bound to become a model for subsequent regulatory regimes in space, in Antarctica and at the inner earth.

At first glance there are grounds for hope. The international community recognizes common ownership of these shared resources and acknowledges the

---

18. For a history and overview, see Alaska Permanent Fund Corporation (n.d.) and Smith (2021).

19. For example, let us imagine that the ISA is able to invest $500 million per year into the proposed fund. Let us further assume a 6 per cent return on this investment. This investment would produce only $30 million/year for distribution. If this money was used to fund a basic income for the world's population, the ISA could provide a modest income for just 83,333 of the world's residents. (This calculation begins by setting the basic income at $30/month, or $360/year; 30 million, divided by 360, is 83,333. This number would increase by 83,333 each year, so after ten years the ISA could provide 833,330 people with a basic income.) We would like to thank Paul Harnett for prompting us to consider this little thought experiment.

need to distribute the benefits generated by those shared resources in an equitable fashion. The global community has created institutions similar to those that sovereign states have used to manage their resources, and it is entirely possible to use these institutions to secure the Natural Dividend – just as we have seen the Norwegian state use similar institutions to secure a Natural Dividend from its own resource wealth.

But these hopes are still not realized, and they will not be realized in the absence of greater public awareness and political pressure. So far the global community has been unwilling or unable to learn from the mistakes that have been made with resource management by sovereign authorities in recent history. In the same way that so many states have failed to recognize their role and responsibility in generating a Natural Dividend for the resources found in and around their sovereign territories, the ISA seems to be unaware of the important role it will play in creating significant rents by deciding how much of our global riches will be exploited (or not), and who will have the right to exploit them. By ignoring its significant influence and power, the ISA risks developing a management regime that will simply gift the Natural Dividend to its concessionaires, who will claim it as profit.

9
CONCLUSION

We began this book with a call to action – a call that is propelled by the urgency of our current climate (and nature) crisis. The responses to this call have been manifold and can vary across different timelines. Some analysts have focused on the long run and the need for more radical, systemic changes, such as a complete ban on exploiting non-renewable sources of energy; the rise of degrowth, or "half-earth" alternatives; even the end of capitalism itself (see, e.g., Kallis *et al.* 2018; Wilson 2018; Sweeney 2020). These sorts of big-ticket questions are exciting to contemplate, but difficult to bring about.

We have set our sights a notch lower and focused on a more immediate (short-term) timeline. Although the contours of these brave new worlds remain undefined and debated, we can and should begin the journey in their direction. We can do this by taking several smaller steps along the path to real change. The best way to do this, we think, is to reconsider our current approaches to managing shared natural resources. This is because it is possible to secure consensus about the desirability of these steps, even if we disagree about the final end state.

This need for a new management approach is propelled by two realizations. First, it is increasingly evident that we need to secure more sustainable sources of food and energy, and doing so will force us to explore and exploit several new resource frontiers. In all likelihood, the future will find us mining the deep-sea ocean bottom, harvesting solar power from outer space and tapping the inner earth. This future may be frightening for many, but it can also offer promise; after all, most of our natural resources remain unexplored and untapped: we have only scratched the surface, literally, of our natural bounty. We find promise in the possibility of opening these new resource frontiers. Doing so offers us an opportunity to rethink our approach to natural resource management, because it introduces a new round of enclosures, in which common wealth will be enclosed, allocated and commodified.

This brings us to the second realization: the most dominant approaches to NRM today have focused mainly on the need to secure economic efficiency.

In this regard they have been remarkably successful. Although NRM approaches vary significantly over time and across political territory, each approach aims to enclose, allocate and commodify natural resources with an eye on ensuring their efficient exploitation/harvest. For this reason, most NRM approaches are driven by a concern that nature, in the raw, will fall prey to the tragedy of the commons. The conventional solution to this shared challenge has been to pursue nature's efficient exploitation by limiting and privatizing access to those commons.

More recently we have begun to recognize and mitigate the environmental costs associated with exploiting our natural resources. In response to growing public pressure, many political authorities have designed their NRM regimes to minimize their environmental and climatic impacts. In granting access to our natural resources, political authorities often insist that concessionaries comply with a number of sophisticated and detailed environmental regulations and impact assessments. Here, too, there is significant variation across time and political space – and we hasten to add that much more can be done on this front – but we think it is fair to say that there is widespread recognition of the need to manage our natural resources in ways that can encourage their safe exploitation.

It is important to recognize that, in both these regards (efficiency and environmental protection), mainstream approaches to NRM have been broadly successful: the world community is able to muster significant pools of capital, technology and competence to bring scarce, often inaccessible, resources to market; and do so in ways that limit the potential for environmental damage. We stand in amazement at how many important human resources have been mobilized in the effort to exploit nature.

As we were discussing this chapter draft, a marvellous ship – *Deep Energy* – passed by where we were sitting. Registered in the Bahamas, and on its way to Orkanger (in mid-Norway), *Deep Energy* is one of the largest pipe-laying vessels ever built, stretching nearly 200 metres in length and able to accommodate 140 people. This ship was designed to connect markets once separated by oceans: it sets pipe (for the transit of natural gas or petroleum) on the seafloor bottom in remarkably deep waters (up to 3,000 metres), and can scoot to the job site at an impressive 20 knots. From the shoreline the ship looks like a carnival afloat, its topsides filled with carousels, chutes and ladders. It is loaded to the gunwales with imposing equipment, including a 150-tonne crane, twin 2,800-tonne cable reels and a helipad for refreshing the crew (Knud E. Hansen n.d.). From our distant vantage point, we can only imagine what it might cost to build and employ such a remarkable ship. What is even more incredible is that this ship is just one of a fleet of similarly impressive ships owned by TechnipFMC (see TechnipFMC n.d.). The capital, technology and logistics tied up in this endeavour, and countless similar endeavours, boggle the mind.

We think it is fair to say that mainstream approaches to NRM are very good at incentivizing the private exploitation of our common resources, and largely proficient in protecting the surrounding environments. These regimes are successful in these areas because they prioritize them in their approaches to NRM. By contrast, mainstream NRM approaches have mostly ignored or minimized the distributional consequences they produce. We are concerned that these distributional consequences could hamper further progress. As *The Economist* magazine recently editorialized in its leader, but with reference to Russian concessionaires, "Natural-resource earnings have entrenched a rent-seeking elite that has created an offshore archipelago of yachts, nightclubs and Caribbean front companies, [and] stifled representative politics" (*The Economist* 2022).

Whatever their nationality, this entrenchment of rent-seeking elites needs to stop. We do not need to keep throwing money at global entrepreneurs to safely exploit our shared natural resources. This book has aimed to show that it is possible to design NRM regimes that are economically, environmentally *and* politically sustainable. We have the tools, the experience and the know-how. All we lack is the political will.

These three objectives are tied together. When political authorities succeed in enclosing and limiting access to our natural resources, and when they succeed in limiting the environmental impacts of that access, these successes will result in increased (market) values for the underlying resources. By regulating access to our natural resources, political authorities actually make them more valuable. The question we pose is a simple one: to whom does this additional value rightfully belong?

Securing the Natural Dividend

Mainstream management regimes ignore this additional value, allowing it to flow to the concessionaire who has been granted legal access to the resource. Such a narrow-minded view is most evident in the oldest and most established natural resource market: the market for land. By enclosing some (but not all) land, and allocating initial access to a select few, political authorities hoped to minimize conflicts over land and increase its efficient utilization. In doing so, however, political authorities created significant inequalities in both wealth and power. This is because those who have been granted access to the land have also gained access to the value produced by the land.

This pattern is largely replicated in every natural resource market discussed in this book. Regardless of the underlying ownership regime (public, private, communal), political authorities tend to allocate access to a common resource without securing the sort of institutional arrangements that are necessary to capture the Natural Dividend these resources can produce. Mainstream approaches to NRM have focused myopically on how to allocate access in the most efficient manner (e.g. through auction arrangements), and they have become accustomed to granting concessionary contracts that allow private interests to walk off with the Natural Dividend (if, and when, it arises).

In criticizing political authorities for not securing the Natural Dividend, we hasten to note that this task is a challenging one. The Natural Dividend will vary significantly across resources, resources qualities and market conditions. Today the largest Natural Dividends can be reaped in the petroleum and mining sectors; tomorrow they could very well be found in the power markets fed by wind and solar energy. The Natural Dividend can also vary over time: some resources will require support and subsidies during their infant steps to commodification, but these resource sites can become extremely lucrative in the years that follow. This was the case with the Norwegian oil regime (wherein Norwegian concessions were first very generous, but later hauled in, to secure the Natural Dividend), and is now evident in that country's oligopolistic aquaculture sector (for which the initial regime was also generous, but authorities were at first unable to secure the Natural Dividend once it developed). Recognizing this, political authorities need to introduce management regimes that are flexible enough to respond to changing conditions and introduce them before powerful economic interests manage to capture political authority.

This pattern of allowing private interests to pocket the Natural Dividend is dominant, but not universal. We have endeavoured to show several examples – across countries, time and resource types – in which political authorities have recognized the utility of securing the Natural Dividend, when it arises. Political authorities have done this by requiring local content, securing greater owner-ship shares in the commodified resource and/or by taxing the rents generated by natural resources and our regulation of them. By introducing the established lit-erature on LVTs and RRTs – and by pointing to the support this literature enjoys among economists and analysts – we hope to show that there are many viable and successful management alternatives available. By showing how Norway has managed to build one of the world's largest sovereign wealth funds, by taxing its Natural Dividend from petroleum, we have demonstrated that such policies are not "pie in the sky".

Lessons learned

In comparing the different ways that a wide variety of natural resources are managed, we have seen how each of these resources is capable of producing a Natural Dividend. This Natural Dividend will vary over time, and may even be negative – but its potential remains constant. Under most, but not all, management regimes, this Natural Dividend goes unrecognized: it is swiftly and quietly subsumed as profit by those who have been granted access to the resource. When the Natural Dividend proves to be significant, as, for example, in mineral and petroleum markets, political authorities have come to recognize that it is indeed possible to secure. As we have seen in the Norwegian case, this can be done without undermining the incentives for private investment and initiative, and in a way that benefits both the local community and private interests (who have been hired to exploit these resources on behalf of the larger community). We hope we have shown how this lesson can travel to other resource markets as well – existing markets (e.g. in land and aquaculture), as well as in developing markets (e.g. renewable energy) and in future markets (e.g. deep-sea bottom and asteroid mining).

In particular, we hope you will walk away from reading this book with four distinct lessons. The first of these is the need to focus on both justice and efficiency when managing our natural resources. Our mainstream approaches to NRM are unjust: they facilitate a private taking of common wealth, and this draining of public wealth cannot continue indefinitely. The second lesson is a derivative of the first: to protect our common wealth, we need to recognize the way that value is created in natural resource markets. This means we need to change our perceptions about the original source of value, in order to ensure that any value created is justly rewarded. The third lesson is perhaps the most difficult: we need to recognize the important role played by political authority in creating and securing significant value, and hold that political authority accountable. The last lesson concerns the importance of realizing that there can be no single – "one size fits all" – approach to securing the Natural Dividend. Different communities will use different approaches, and these are bound to vary with the nature of the resource, and the political context in which it lies.

An efficient, safe *and* just allocation

We face a new round of enclosures. Growing pressure from demographic, environmental and climate change factors will force us to explore and exploit a number of new natural resource frontiers in the coming decades. Most of these resources remain in some form of common wealth (they have not yet been enclosed), and accessing them will require some form of enclosure and allocation. Some of these concessions will occur within sovereign territory, where political authorities still have great latitude to decide how to allocate access (on behalf of the people they represent). New types of resource wealth will be found and exploited in states that have little or no previous experience managing such resources. In deciding how to allocate access to their scarce resources, these states will want to manage their resources in an efficient, safe and just manner.

Some of these future enclosures will occur in very new and different global political contexts, however, in which questions of sovereignty remain unresolved. As we begin to exploit the potential of these common resources, a community of nations will have to decide who is allowed access to these resources, and how much of the resulting value will be given away. This will not be easy, as new resource sites take time to develop; they often start off slowly, with a need for subsidies and support, but become more productive over time. Like political authorities in sovereign states, the international community will want to manage our shared natural resources in a way that can ensure their efficient exploitation and protect the surrounding environment, but also ensure a fair distribution of rewards. This means introducing an NRM regime that is flexible enough to capture the Natural Dividend, when and if it arises.

It should be obvious that our approach to managing natural resources is different from most contemporary approaches, in that we emphasize justice – in addition to the need for efficiency and environmental protection – as a necessary and worthy policy objective. We have assumed that it is not problematic or difficult to agree on a fair distribution, but it might be worthwhile to describe what we mean, exactly, by a fair distribution.

A fair distribution of rewards is one in which each input owner receives a share of the returns that is equal to what that owner contributes to the added value. As an example, consider a joint venture between three independent firms: A, B and C. Firm A is the majority owner in the JV, providing 51 per cent of the investment capital; firm B originally contributes 24 per cent; and firm C contributes the remaining 25 per cent. Let us then assume that the JV increased in value by $100,000 over the course of the following year. In this hypothetical scenario, a fair distribution of rewards would provide firm A with a $51,000 reward; firm B would get $24,000; and firm C would receive $25,000. This is not rocket science; it is the nexus of simple mathematics and basic fairness. It would be unfair for firm C to secure more than $25,000 of that year's return, as it did not contribute more than 25 per cent to the added value produced.

The challenge for us lies in determining where value is created when nature is commodified: what percentage of that value is created by nature itself, what percentage is created by monopoly/restricted access to that nature and its relationship to public infrastructure, and what percentage is created by the capital and labour invested in the process? This equation is slightly more complex than the simple JV example above, in that we do not have a good measure of the initial value created by nature and political authority (including access to public investments). But, once we recognize that this value exists, its amount can be determined by a simple process of elimination. This is because we *do* have good measures for a fair-market return on labour and capital; we simply look to nearby examples in the market and take this as our point of departure. After ensuring that labour and capital receive their fair return, what remains – the residual – is the Natural Dividend. This is the community's fair share for its role in creating the value attached to commodified nature.

Now that we know what a fair distribution looks like, we wish to point out three explicit reasons for reintroducing justice as a standard for evaluating our approach to managing natural resources.

The first reason should already be familiar. A focus on justice is not new – such a focus can be traced all the way back to John Locke (1960 [1688]) – but it is one that is too often forgotten. After centuries of trading ownership in land (and the products derived from the land), much of the world now finds it easy and natural to think of land in the same way we think of any other commodity. For many readers, today's allocation of land is seen to be a just result of voluntary exchanges in a free market. We have forgotten the common origins of land, and we have accepted political authority's legitimate role in allocating (and limiting) access to that land. Much of this allocation occurred at a time when there were fewer constraints on political authority, and when land was often used as a form of political capital or gift. In doing so, we have legitimized the unjust allocations of the past, and accepted the remarkable inequalities that result – when single individuals can have formal ownership rights over such a large part of our globe, as evidenced in Table 4.4.

As we are forced to enclose and manage new resource frontiers, Locke's perspective on land management will become increasingly relevant. In his time, land could still be seen as abundant, but its increased scarcity (relative to a growing population) necessitated its eventual enclosure. For Locke, enclosure was necessary in order not just to secure a more efficient exploitation *but also* to minimize potential conflicts over resource claims. After all, if the allocation is contested, or seen to be unjust, then the result can be devastating. These forgotten truths will rise to the surface again as we begin a new round of enclosures. In deciding how to conduct our future enclosures, and allocate their results, we would be wise to remember Locke's caveats and provisos: an unjust allocation may be efficient (or not), but it will not be permanent if it is seen as unjust.

This brings us to the second reason: the world is already crippled by massive inequality, and there is a growing recognition that these political and economic inequalities are not sustainable.[1] In this political context, it will be increasingly difficult for political authorities to continue allowing private interests the opportunity to enrich themselves at the expense of the public good. In short, the Lauderdale paradox (see Box 2.1) stares us straight in the face.

---

1. This literature is massive, but some important headliners include Milanovic (2005); Stiglitz (2012); Piketty (2013) and Bourguignon (2015).

Some of today's greatest political and economic inequalities can be traced back to original enclosures, and this unjust pattern has repeated itself continually throughout modern history: we saw it in the allocation of Crown lands in the colonies; we saw it in the allocation of state lands in the post-Soviet economy; we see it in the enormous private wealth of petro-state leaders (witness the wealth and power of the dos Santos family in Angola[2]), and in the prediction (from Chapter 8) that the world's first trillionaire will probably be made from exploiting our scarce resources in space. A heightened awareness of the inequalities generated by the way we allocate access to scarce resources should force political authorities to reconsider their NRM regimes and place a greater focus on the need for a just allocation.

Finally, a new focus on justice is needed to secure popular support for political decisions that may be necessary but will have serious and negative repercussions for local communities. Consider the decision to dam a waterfall for the purposes of creating hydroelectric power. The larger needs of the community may lie in building a dam that can supply cheap and clean energy, but building such a dam will have a tremendously negative effect on the local community: it will raise the surrounding water level and flood the nearby farms and forests. In short, many of the costs of a dam are paid by the families that once farmed the fertile surrounding riverbanks, now under water. The same sort of costs will fuel NIMBY (not in my back yard) resistance to wind farms, solar arrays, salmon farms, etc. To secure the support of local communities, political authorities can shave off a share of the Natural Dividend and use it to compensate those communities for their losses.

Seen in this light, the Natural Dividend can be used to help secure local political support for costly and controversial resource transformations. It is much easier to secure community support, and maintain it over time, if the rewards from harnessing nature are redistributed to the affected local communities, rather than gifted to some distant investor/entrepreneur.

We hope readers can see the importance of securing a just, as well as an efficient and clean, approach to managing natural resources. By focusing myopically on the need to secure a more efficient allocation of resources we risk undermining the broad political support we will need to exploit our (increasingly scarce) natural resources in the future. To encourage the exploitation of these new resources, political authorities should ensure that a fair share of the value created by their actions is redirected back to those who suffer most from its extraction: the surrounding community. Allocating private access to common resources may be necessary to secure their efficient harvest, but the inequality that results from that allocation can and should be minimized.

---

2. See, for example, Fitzgibbon (2021).

Changing perceptions

The second lesson is closely related to the first. To hinder the private appropri-ation of our Natural Dividend, we need to change public perceptions of how value is created in natural resource markets. This will take some doing, as current perceptions work to the benefit of strong and influential interests, who would prefer they stay unchanged.

In our mainstream approaches to NRM, nature is understood to be worthless (from a market perspective). In its raw state, nature is available to everybody: it has not been enclosed, and it cannot be commodified. Think of the wind, or the sun or the deep sea beyond sovereign territory. Political authorities hope to create some market value by gifting our natural resources to producer-entrepreneurs, who turn these resources into jobs and tax revenues. In this calculation, a concessionaire is granted her main factor of production (nature), she mixes capital and labour to it, and the result is seen as profit (after the sundry input costs are covered). From this perspective – the one that dominates today – profit is seen as a residual, and we assume that this residual belongs to the entrepreneur who saddled the risk and marshalled the necessary capital and competence to commodify nature and bring it to market. From the per-spective of mainstream NRM approaches, any new value created belongs to the concessionaire.

The problem with this perspective is that economists have long recognized that returns on natural resource investments can deliver an *unearned* windfall. This is one of the features that makes these investments so attractive, but the existence of a windfall reveals the non-competitive nature of natural resource markets. If resource markets were competitive markets, many capitalists would move money out of their current investments and put them in natural resource markets to secure the sort of windfalls that resource markets regularly produce. Should this happen (in accordance with the laws of modern economics), the returns on resource investments would fall and equalize at a market-clearing rate. This is the logic of a competitive market.

But this logic breaks down when applied to resource markets. The level of reward in this market does not correspond to the level of risk taken, or cap-ital invested; it is attributable to a number of diverse rents. As with wages in a competitive market, there is no good reason to expect returns on capital to be extraordinarily large in this market (relative to others). These returns are huge because the market for natural resources is anything but competitive: access to these resources is severely restricted by the scarcity of the underlying resource, and the allocation systems employed by political authorities.

Once we recognize that a substantial part of the value produced by nature is a result of nature's productive capacity, and the power of political authorities to regulate and limit access to these resources, then it becomes imperative for political authority to protect this common wealth from private taking.

In the end, we need to recognize the value produced by nature, and the way that we regulate and facilitate access to that nature. We need to recognize the source and existence of differential, regulatory and locational rents – what we call the Natural Dividend – and ensure that these sources of value are granted their just returns. These rents have nothing to do with private initiative, and yet we allow private interests to pocket them in the form of an unearned windfall, disguised as profit.

By securing these rents we can create better regulatory outcomes, in which both political authorities and private investors are better off. Because investors are unwilling to walk away from the world's most productive natural resources, all they require is a return that is sufficiently large to justify their investments (i.e. recover all their costs and earn a fair return). As we saw in Chapter 3, we can do this by minimizing the risks associated with unjust concessionary arrangements (when massive investments are sunk over a long period of time, under questionable – often secret – licensing/concessionary agreements) and developing a fiscal regime that taxes the Natural Dividend at a much higher rate than the normal corporate tax level. Such a management regime is Pareto-optimal – in that political authorities, investors and the general public all find themselves better off – but it requires a substantial shift in our perceptions. We hope that our book can nudge readers in that direction.

Making political authority accountable

Our management of natural resources produces a Natural Dividend that is created by nature and the way our political authorities regulate and facilitate access to that nature. In pointing this out, we shine a very strong spotlight on the role and responsibility of political authority in managing natural resources on behalf of their constituents (to whom these resources ultimately belong). By recognizing the enormous power of political authority in creating this value, we have not meant to suggest that political authority can or should be trusted. We are not naïve about the potential for corruption or abuse. As we made clear from the outset, and as illustrated in Figure 3.3, political authority can also pocket the Natural Dividend unjustly, and use it to enrich its individual members, rather than the community it is meant to represent. Political authority, like private enterprise, is easily corrupted when tempted by significant wealth and power.

In recognizing the Natural Dividend, and the role that political authority plays in creating it, we can more clearly see why resource-rich states are prone to what has been called the resource curse, or the paradox of plenty (see Box 9.1). Any country that discovers significant resource wealth can find its broader economy handicapped (e.g. by Dutch disease), and its political institutions and officials are easily corrupted.

The solution to this problem is not to undermine political authority but to make it more accountable. Not all resource-rich states are prone to the paradox of plenty, and we can learn a great deal from those states that have managed their resources in a way that benefits the larger community. Norway's management of its petroleum resources is an example of this, and we have already written a great deal about how this management regime works (and might be exported to other countries).[3] Even in Norway, though, this success has not travelled to other resources, and the successful lessons of its past appears to have been forgotten by a new generation of political authority and their civil servants (Brigham & Moses 2021).

To prevent abuse, it is necessary to ensure that the interests of political authority are aligned with those of the common good. This means that the needs of the economy need to be made subservient to the larger needs of the community: that economic institutions and governments alike need to be subordinate to constitutional law. This is an enormous and difficult task; in many contexts, it may require a rethinking of the nature and the role of the state (see, e.g., Sweeney 2020). But requiring political authorities to serve the interests of their people is the main aspiration of democratic government. This requirement should not be surrendered lightly.

This need to redirect the state is becoming increasingly evident, even beyond the needs of natural resource management. There is a growing recognition that we cannot solve many of the problems that we face by undermining political authority and hollowing out the state. For the sake of democracy, we will need to re-examine the complex relationship between political and economic power. In this regard, we share Colin Crouch's concern: "Today's dominant politico-economic ideology, neoliberalism, has turned this weakening of the nation-state into a virtue. If it is believed that governments are almost by definition incompetent and that large firms are necessarily efficient, then the less power the former have and the more freedom from them that firms gain, the better" (Crouch 2020: 7).

Whatever the inequities of the international distribution of natural resource wealth and the possibility of its abuse by governments, *there is no moral case for handling the entire value of any such resource to the concessionaire or her contractor.* Governments may or may not act as good stewards of their people's Natural Dividend, but this is at least a role they profess to accept. Private companies, workers and the private concessionaires make no such claim. It should not come as a surprise that these actors are driven by self-interest, as they should be.

---

3. See, for example, Moses (2021b, 2021c, 2021d), Moses and Brigham (2021), Moses and Letnes (2017a, 2017b), Moses, Spencer and Pereira (2021) and Moses, Pereira and Spencer (2021).

BOX 9.1 THE PARADOX OF PLENTY

The Paradox of Plenty is the title of an influential book by Terry Lynn Karl (1997), which compares the economic trajectories of several oil states (Venezuela, Iran, Nigeria, Algeria, Indonesia and Norway) in the wake of the 1970s' oil boom. Through this comparison, we learn that many states have difficulty in managing their resource wealth and that some states have managed their resource markets much better than others. In particular, some political authorities are able to manage resource wealth in ways that can protect the environment, reward private investors and use this resource wealth to build a stronger, richer and more democratic state. Our task should be to learn from this variation in policy outcomes, so that policy-makers can implement the most successful lessons from these comparisons.

The term "resource curse" was first coined by Richard Auty (1993), to describe how resource-rich countries seem to be unable to leverage that wealth to boost their domestic economies. Jeffrey Sachs and Andrew Warner (1995) followed with an influential empirical mapping of the curse. Countries rich in natural resources experienced lower economic growth rates (than countries that had few such resources). Over time – as states have learned to manage their resources more effectively – the resource curse has become less prevalent (contrast Ross 1999 with Ross 2012). This is a good example of how policy-makers have learned from the policy failures of their predecessors.

The idea of a "rentier state" was first elaborated by Hussein Mahdavy (1970), and the term is commonly used to refer to states that depend on an external source of income, such as a heavily taxed Natural Dividend. Whereas Mahdavy's empirical focus was on petro-states in the Middle East, his argument can be extended to political authorities in any resource-rich state that no longer needs the economic support of their constituents to remain in power. By filling the state coffers with resource revenues, instead of levying domestic taxes, these political authorities become less accountable to their domestic constituencies.

The term "Dutch disease" was first popularized by *The Economist* (1977), with reference to the decline of Dutch manufacturing in the wake of that country's offshore natural gas discovery in the 1950s. It refers to the damage created by an unexpected inflow of wealth from a natural resource discovery. Unless this inflow is dealt with, it can appreciate the country's real exchange rate and make it more difficult for the non-resource-based economy to compete in international markets.

In general, the paradox of plenty literature focuses on three main types of challenges facing resource-rich countries (Moses & Letnes 2017a: 6–9): the threat of decreased competitiveness (from a real appreciation of the currency and resource pull effects); poor economic performance (e.g. lower real growth rates and higher levels of government spending); and rent seeking (when officials focus their attention on the needs of international resource companies rather than their domestic constituencies). Consequently, political authorities in these countries tend to be more susceptible to political violence and civil conflict (see World Bank 2011b).

All these threats are real, but each is manageable. Unexpected economic windfalls need to be managed prudently, or they are quickly squandered. The proper response to the paradox of plenty is not "less plenty" or to divert the plenty to private actors (creating greater inequality). The most appropriate response is to manage that plenty better, and make it less paradoxical.

When political authority refuses to claim this responsibility, it falls on private parties, whose interests are explicitly opposed to the public interest. In recognizing this simple fact, our task should be to *improve government*, not starve it, and to make political authority more accountable.

We do not wish to be misunderstood. There is ample justification for the need to protect private investors from the arbitrary actions of host-country governments. Examples of nationalizing or expropriating private property, and/ or returning natural resources to their original state of ownership, provide significant grounds for concern. Following Locke, one of the best ways to secure strong and lasting contracts is to ensure that they are just. This is also the lesson generated by the RRT literature: arbitrary expropriation can be minimized by securing arrangements that are public, transparent and perceived to be just. This can be done by creating management regimes that provide less risky, more predictable, revenue streams for investors.

Olivier De Schutter and Katharina Pistor (2016) provide a very good discussion of the challenges associated with the collective ownership of our natural resources, and the need for both voice and reflexivity when managing them. In their discussion we can clearly see that it is neither naïve nor hopeless to expect governments to represent their constituencies' interests and deal fairly with the foreign and/or private enterprises (which they need to help harvest these resources). After all, this is what government is designed to do: to deal with competing claims that are not easily arranged in a simple or hierarchical manner, and to do so in a just fashion.

It is better to recognize that the task we face is complicated; we should not sweep this challenge under the rug. Following De Schutter and Pistor, political authorities should embrace the important role they play in creating the value of our natural resources when they eventually make their way to market:

> Complexity in governance, we suggest, should not be avoided but embraced. Governing access to resources that are both scarce and essential is complicated normatively, politically, and institutionally. No governance regime is likely to provide a simple solution or to last forever.

> We therefore do not advocate a specific institutional fix or a search for an optimum; what is optimal in one context may be inoperable elsewhere due to different social or environmental conditions. Instead, we emphasize the normative principles that should govern the access to essential resources: Voice and Reflexivity. (De Schutter & Pistor 2016: 38)

No single solution

De Schutter and Pistor's observation leads us directly to our last lesson: it is important to recognize that there is no single institutional fix that is suitable for all countries and/or all resources. Different countries have different needs. The way that Norway manages its gas resources is bound to be different from the way that management should be undertaken in Tanzania, Venezuela or Antarctica.

The biggest divide is probably between countries such as Norway – which was already developed (both politically and economically) when a valuable resource was discovered – and those that are not. When developing a management regime for taxing natural resources in low-income countries, Paul Collier (2010) notes how these countries face distinctive challenges, requiring unique fixes (see also Daniel, Keen & McPherson 2010: 3). Among these are a recognition that the discovery process is usually more important and less developed in these political contexts; that institutions in these countries tend to be less robust – so that we might expect the credibility of government commitments to be impaired; that capital and consumption tend to be scarcer in these countries, requiring a higher rate of return to attract scarce capital; and that governments tend to lack full information about resource potential (vis-à-vis global resource companies). This informational asymmetry is often used by global resource companies to secure contractual arrangements that later reveal themselves to be unjust and/or unacceptable – and thus lead to an obsolescing bargaining mechanism (OBM). A good NRM regime should minimize these kinds of risk and information asymmetries.

Although we have pointed to specific management regimes, in particular countries or organizations, and at different times, this was done to illustrate what is possible. We have not written a policy recipe book, from which political authorities can pick and choose the policy ingredients that best suit their moods or needs. In the end, the needs and expectations of each community, and each resource, and at different points of time, will require unique management solutions. Some communities will want to use their natural resource wealth to build up competences for subsequent development. Like the hypothetical family from our introduction, the political authorities in these countries might recognize that it can be useful to learn how to exploit the resource themselves, as there can be long-term savings and experience gained in doing so. In other places, or at other times, political authorities may decide it is best to employ private entrepreneurs to help bring these resources to market – but in doing so they will not want to lose sight of their own role in creating the (market) value of that resource, once commodified.

Finally, a word about flexibility. In some resource markets, political authorities may find it initially necessary to subsidize the commodification of their natural resources. Over time, however, these very same resources can produce phenomenal Natural Dividends. Hence, the NRM regime needs to be flexible enough to accommodate these changes over time.

The path forward

We have argued for the need to recognize the existence of a Natural Dividend. We have pitched this argument to try and persuade policy-makers, civil servants and academics of the need to rethink our approach to resource management. When the Natural Dividend is acknowledged, we have shown how political authorities can employ policies to secure it for the larger community.

In effect, we offer a modest proposal that shows how resource extraction and capitalism can be made to work for the public interest, in any country on the planet willing to embrace a mixed economy and with a political elite willing to work in the interest of its people. It is entirely possible to implement this proposal in the present (capitalist) economic framework, or it can offer a bridgehead for a more ambitious, post-capitalist, transition.

Even if we have been convincing, the reader may still be left with a feeling of puzzlement. If this is such a just, reasonable and attractive proposal, and if we have evidence of its practical and successful application in a number of different political contexts, why are these policies not employed elsewhere and/or more frequently? If these ideas have been in circulation since the time of Ricardo, Marx and George, why has it taken so long for countries to implement them? And why do we frame this argument in terms of future markets for natural resources, when the threat of environmental destruction and climate change is so pressing?

The answer to all these questions, in a word, is power. Or, more accurately, two words: political power. Even if we can agree about the desirability of a given political objective, it can be quite difficult to bring it about. This is part of the problem associated with securing a "just transition",[4] as strong and vested interests stand

---

4. The concept of a just transition first arose in the 1970s, as US trade unions developed a response to new pollution regulations. The term is now used more broadly, to refer to the need to bridge the apparent gap between destruction (decline) and creation policies in the face of global climate change. See, for example, Newell and Mulvaney (2013), Healy and Barry (2017), Stevis, Morena and Krause (2020) and Normann and Tellmann (2021).

ready to defend the status quo. As we are not political activists, we are uncomfortable proposing a political strategy for securing such a transition – a path forward. Our task has been to describe the desirability and the feasibility of the political outcome. We will leave it to others, more experienced in political action, to consider which strategies are most appropriate for bringing about this just transition.

All the same, our familiarity with the Norwegian case has revealed some interesting patterns, and we think these patterns offer both insights and caveats for those planning the transition to a more just NRM regime. Although Norway might offer an attractive model for its successful management of the Natural Dividend (from petroleum and hydroelectric power), its history also demonstrates the difficulty of securing a similar regime for the aquaculture sector. Likewise, Norway's climate ambitions are clearly hampered by the influence of very established and powerful petroleum interests. We can learn something from this apparent inconsistency.

The first insight concerns *changing ideological climates*. As we hinted in the Introduction, with regard to the issue of privatization, political consensus on these issues tends to swing back and forth over time, like a pendulum. As one of us has described in another context (Moses & Letnes 2017a: ch. 2), the balance of power between states and markets shifts over time, and this changing ideological pendulum provides varying degrees of scope for political action, sometimes greater, sometimes less so. When Norway introduced its management regimes for capturing the Natural Dividend – first in hydroelectric markets in the early 1900s, then in the petroleum sector in the early 1970s – sovereign political authorities enjoyed much greater scope for autonomous action. The 1970s, in particular, were characterized by a new international economic order, in which democratic development was still prioritized over the needs of international corporations and trade.

In the mid-1980s, and for several different reasons, the ideological pendulum began to swing back in favour of markets, away from state power. The rising influence of a neoliberal ideology propelled an expansive network of supranational treaties, regulations, codes and guidelines designed to facilitate free trade and global markets – and to hinder states from erecting barriers to that trade. By the end of the twentieth century the dominant political ideology and the constraints on sovereign authority from a dense web of international obligations made it increasingly difficult for states to pursue the sorts of management policies we have been describing. This changing political and ideological context meant that countries discovering oil in the 1990s or early 2000s found it difficult to pursue many of the policies that Norway used in the early 1970s. Similarly, as the Norwegian aquaculture industry developed and grew during this neoliberal era, it was managed in a way that reflected the dominant political ideology.

As this industry grew, it was simply allowed to abscond with the Natural Dividend once it developed.

During this time the neoliberal ideological influence was pervasive. For example, Norwegian students and civils servants were trained in the field of so-called new public management. This training drew heavily on American and British expertise with management and markets, to the neglect of Norwegian history and experience. As a result, Norway became saddled with a generation of students and civil servants who are largely ignorant of their own management regimes but are well trained in theories that employ stylized markets and equilibria, and that herald the merits of a free market. How else can we explain why Mitsubishi[5] and other international corporations are gifted access to Norway's most productive fjords?

Luckily, this ideological pendulum has already begun to change direction, and it is possible to see a growing recognition of the need for greater state action in the wake of the 2008 financial crisis and the 2020 Covid-19 pandemic, and in Europe's galloping energy prices in the winter of 2022–23. Voters are increasingly concerned about inequality, populism, economic resilience and the need for sovereign control to address these challenges – and the international order is making way for these concerns. Evidence of this shift comes as we were finishing the final draft of this manuscript, when the Norwegian government announced its intent to introduce a new range of RRTs to capture the Natural Dividend from onshore wind, hydro (an increased RRT) and aquaculture (see Box 9.2). Even the European Union has recognized the utility of introducing a new tax regime to secure the phenomenal rents being created by the war in the Ukraine (see Box 6.4). In short, after a long ideological hiatus – when it was more difficult for political authorities to secure sovereign control over natural resources – a new international ideological climate is taking hold. This new ideological climate provides a more nourishing and protective political environment for policymakers hoping to introduce just NRM regimes. After decades of attacks on state power, we now find ourselves in an opportune time for action.

The second insight concerns *vested interests*. It is important to recognize that the introduction of a new, more just, management regime will be seen as a threat to established and powerful interests, and they will resist any change to the status quo. In bringing about a just transition, political activists need to develop a two-pronged strategy for sidelining these powerful interests. The first prong of this strategy should be to recognize that any threats made by these interests tend to be idle. The evidence of this can be clearly found in the Norwegian example, in

---

5. Mitisbushi owns Cermaq, the third largest aquaculture company in the world (see Figure 5.7) and a major player in Norwegian aquaculture markets.

BOX 9.2 SIGN OF THE TIMES: NORWAY'S NEW RRTS

In September 2022 the Norwegian finance minister, Trygve Slagsvold Vedum, referenced Norway's long history of tapping into the spirit of Henry George as he introduced a series of new revenue sources, including three new RRTs: one on hydro; another on wind; and the third on aquaculture.[1]

In particular, the RRT on *hydropower* will increase from 37 to 45 per cent, starting almost immediately, but bypassing smaller hydropower stations (Finansdepartementet 2022a). This change will bring the total marginal tax rate (RRT + normal corporate tax) on Norwegian hydroelectric power closer to what we find in the petroleum sector: it will now be 67 per cent (78 per cent in petroleum). The government estimates that this change will increase government tax revenues by about 11 billion kroner per year ($1.02 billion).

The proposed new RRT on *land-based wind power* will first go out for public consultation, but the government has a parliamentary majority to follow through on its proposal. The proposed RRT for onshore wind energy is 40 per cent, and the new RRT is expected to generate about 2.5 billion kroner in tax revenues (Finansdepartementet 2022b). Because the corporate tax on land-based wind farms is calculated before the RRT, and the resource-rent-related corporate tax is deducted from the basis for the RRT (as it is for petroleum and hydropower), an effective RRT of 40 per cent translates into a formal RRT of about 51.3 per cent. What is most interesting about this proposed tax is the government's promise to split the tax revenues, 50/50, with the municipal sector – so the local communities that are most impacted by wind turbine parks will now receive economic compensation.

In the proposal to introduce an RRT on Norwegian aquaculture in 2023, only the largest producers will be affected (Finansdepartementet 2022c). The proposal has been distributed for public consultation, and the government intends to return to parliament with a concrete bill. Although there has been a massive public relations campaign by the aquaculture industry to resist the proposed changes, the government appears to be holding firm to its commitment. The effective rate of the proposed RRT is set at 40 per cent – a tax that is expected to generate about 3.7 billion kroner a year. As with the land-based wind RRT, the government plans to share these revenues with the affected municipal sectors.

Finally, the government introduced an additional fee on water and power producers for 23 per cent of all the electricity they sell, when the price exceeds 70 øre (0.70kr) per kWh. This "high-price contribution" is expected to increase government revenues by 16 billion kroner per annum (Finansdepartementet 2022d).

Together, these measures are expected to generate 33 billion kroner (roughly $3.1 billion) annually from the private use of Norway's natural resources. By comparison, Norway is expected to have collected only 21.1 billion kroner in car taxes and to have spent 55.1 billion kroner on higher education in 2022 (Ringnes 2021).

---

1. https://tv.regjeringen.no/1.html?mediaId=131480af-76f9-4185-b06b-5e38de2491b4.

which we have seen foreign and domestic interests threatening to flee at every attempt to secure the Natural Dividend.

Such threats are both idle and deceptive. They are idle because the objects of value (natural resources) are bound to sovereign territory, and the most productive resources are remarkably scarce. If investors think they can find more productive fjords for salmon aquaculture, more productive and near-lying reservoirs of natural gas or higher and more conveniently located waterfalls for hydroelectric production elsewhere – let them leave. They cannot leave, because the resources they seek are tied to Norwegian sovereign territory. In this way, land (or nature) is very different from the other factors of production: it is not mobile.

This threat is also deceptive, in that it suggests that these vested interests are being injured or hurt by the introduction of a new management regime. Although these interests can indeed expect smaller returns, it is important to remember that the larger returns (to which they are accustomed) were both unjust and unsustainable. In obtaining a *fair* return, investors are better able to protect themselves from the threat of future expropriation, or an even heavier regulatory burden. More to the point, a properly designed NRM regime promises them a fair return: the Natural Dividend is only captured *after* a fair return has been secured for labour and capital. Investors and producers in Norway have learned that a good management regime will bring steady and healthy rewards, with less risk. We can assure the reader that the oil and hydroelectric industries in Norway are not suffering as a result of the country's management regime. They remain very lucrative and very powerful – perhaps too much so.

Nonetheless, these threats by vested interests are often effective at influencing public opinion. This brings us to the second prong of any strategy for sidelining powerful interests. To prepare for the political pushback we can expect from these powerful interests, it is necessary to secure the support of a broad alliance of interests and social movements. It is easy to imagine several groups and social movements that might be willing to help secure the Natural Dividend: trade unions fighting for energy democracy; climate movements that emphasize the need for the commons; Georgist organizations fighting for the greater use of land value taxes; and so on.

Although these movements must play an active role in helping to secure a just transition, they remain relatively small, marginal and weak (politically). We face a political struggle that pits the general public – whose interests are diffuse and poorly organized – against a powerful, concentrated and influential private interest. This is a collective action dilemma, writ large (Olson 1965). To overcome this dilemma, these smaller movements need to work in unison with the larger community of citizens.

This will not be easy. One of the most evident challenges has to do with securing the support of influential labour movements, whose economic fate may be tied to declining industries. This is where most of the focus of the literature on "just transitions" has been trained, and it is important to take heed. Norway has enjoyed a long tradition of tripartite (labour, capital and government) corporatist bargaining arrangements that secure a consensual style of policy-making. The country's powerful, hierarchical and organized labour movement can have a significant impact on how policy is developed and implemented. This movement needs to be harnessed to secure more democratic control over our natural resources.

At the turn of the millennium it was not uncommon to assume that Norway's form of corporatist policy-making would facilitate a just transition to more climate-sensitive policies (e.g. Scruggs 2003; Jacobs 2011). More recent work has come to question this assumption, with Norway being offered as a typical case of what Matto Mildenburger (2020) sees as the burden of "double representation" – i.e. that fossil fuel interests are represented by both capital and labour, making it difficult to move away from the country's heavy reliance on petroleum (see also Normann & Tellmann 2021 and Sæther 2017). This challenge – of getting organized labour to support the need for a just transition – is equally important for countries that do not employ corporatist policy arrangements.

This brings us to the third, and final, insight: *the importance of timing*. The literature on managing petroleum reserves is littered with references to the OBM. This obsolescing bargaining mechanism recognizes that the relative bargaining power of states and firms changes over the lifetime of an investment, and that political authorities can leverage this mechanism to their advantage. Before any new natural resources are discovered, the state's bargaining position appears to be relatively weak (compared to that of the expert investor/producer), as any potential concessionaire often sits with more information about the likelihood and market value of any resource yet to be found. In other words, states need this private expertise to help them find what is rightfully theirs, and the experts are quite aware of this need.

This relationship changes once the concessionaire begins to sink non-retrievable assets into the country. If a concessionaire spends millions of dollars building a new infrastructure to secure any type of natural resource (e.g. an oil-drilling/-processing platform), it cannot easily pack up these sunk investments in the face of any new regulatory threat or change.[6] The government is free to introduce new regulations, and the concessionaire is forced to accept them, or

---

6. There have been several international attempts in recent years to stop this from happening. These efforts employ so-called investor–state dispute settlement (ISDS) or stabilization clauses in international and bilateral lending and trading agreements. These clauses aim to freeze the regulatory status quo, or to penalize states that try to change their domestic legal and regulatory frameworks.

leave the country (and its sunk investments) for greener regulatory pastures. (Of course, as we have previously noted, if the resource is very productive, then there will not be many comparable alternatives out there, and the threat to leave will prove idle.)

In recognizing this changing balance of power, political authorities are often willing and able to change the original terms of the concession/licence, to their favour, once the value and scope of the country's resource holding becomes more certain. Norway did this, for example, with its second round of allocations for its offshore petroleum blocks (in 1969). Once Norway's policy-makers found that they were sitting on massive offshore petroleum reserves, they quickly changed the initial terms of concession to ensure greater state ownership and higher taxation levels (see Moses & Letnes 2017a: 68ff.). Although the first regulatory regime for petroleum in Norway was very lax (in an effort to attract international oil companies away from the nearby British blocks), the Norwegian government reeled in its licence terms to secure a greater share of the Natural Dividend once its scope had become evident. They could do this in 1969 because there was not yet a domestic petroleum industry in Norway able to resist the change. Norwegian political authorities were able to balance the interests of the country against the interests of (mostly) foreign companies, which desperately wanted something Norway had to offer.

The management regime governing Norway's aquaculture developed in a very different manner. Here, too, the authorities started with a relatively lax regulatory regime, to try and encourage small farmers along the coast to develop a new (alternative) source of revenue. As aquaculture proved to be more lucrative, a domestic aquaculture industry became more concentrated and powerful. While this happened (during the height of neoliberal ideological dominance, as described above) political authorities were unwilling or unable to introduce a regulatory regime that could recognize, monitor and/or capture the resulting Natural Dividend. By the time the enormous scope of the Natural Dividend from salmon aquaculture became evident, it was too late: the aquaculture industry was able to use its powerful political influence to squash any attempt at its capture. Norway's political authorities had waited too long, and an important political opportunity had been squandered. Although it now appears that Norwegians will finally secure this Natural Dividend from salmon aquaculture, we have all learned the very high cost of waiting too long.

We are repeating this slice of Norwegian political history because we think the conditions in Norway are stronger than in most other places for securing a management regime that can recognize and capture the Natural Dividend. By waiting too long, however, the Norwegian authorities were unable to do what they had previously done in managing the nation's waterfalls and petroleum resources. While the Norwegian regulatory authorities waited, the wealth and power of domestic aquaculture interests grew exponentially. In the end, this power was sufficient to postpone the introduction of a management regime that could secure the Natural Dividend from Norwegian aquaculture. At the time of this writing, it remains unclear whether the proposed RRT on aquaculture will be implemented, but we remain hopeful.

This insight from Norwegian practice is especially relevant as the world begins to decide how to access, allocate and commodify new natural resources in the face of significant climate and environmental threats. Some of these new resources will be secured in states that have no previous management experiences or relevant domestic industries. Others will be found in, above, under, or on virgin political territory, such as on the deep-sea ocean bottom, in space or deep below the earth. Wherever they may be located, it is necessary for legitimate political authorities to establish management regimes that recognize our common ownership over these resources, and that are designed in such a way that they can secure the Natural Dividend when and if it arises. But it is just as important to establish these management regimes early, *before* powerful interests can capture the policy process.

It is for this reason we have focused so much on the future. It will be difficult to change the management regimes in contexts already captured by powerful private interests. It is easier to plant them in new political terrain. The longer we wait, the more difficult it will be to secure a just management regime.

In closing

This book has aimed to draw your attention to the creation of an added value found in commodified natural resources – what we call the Natural Dividend – and to argue that this value belongs with its creators: nature and the legitimate political authority that allocates and facilitates access to that nature. When political authority ignores the role that it plays in creating this additional value, and leaves it unclaimed, then the Natural Dividend ends up with those who have been granted access to the underlying resource. This private taking of publicly created value produces significant economic and political inequalities, which aggregate over time. Worse still, these inequalities eventually undermine support for the NRM regime that produces them. Until we can secure NRM regimes that are just, efficient and safe, they will prove to be politically unsustainable.

We began this book by noting how much of nature remains in the commons, and is still beyond the reach of markets. A growing population and its related climate challenges will force us to encroach on this wild terrain, crossing new resource frontiers in the process. In crossing these new frontiers, it behoves us to avoid the most common mistakes of our past management regimes.

The first step in this direction requires that we rethink how value is produced in natural resource markets. This change in perception is probably necessary even without these demographic, climatic and environmental pressures. It is becoming increasingly evident that mainstream approaches to NRM are inherently unjust and produce massive inequalities at the global level. As these inequalities become more difficult to sustain, politically, we should expect increased political pressure to reduce global inequalities. The source of much of this inequality can be traced back to monopoly control over our scarce natural resources.

In the past, we have responded to the need for more natural resources by encouraging the enclosure and privatization of once common resources. We have done this to avoid the tragedy of the commons, and to facilitate a more efficient extraction of those resources. After all, it is commonly held that privatization can encourage a more efficient extraction process, facilitate economies of scale and allow access to capital and markets that may encourage a more efficient exploitation of these resources.

In recognizing these efficiency gains, however, we must not ignore the second important criterion that John Locke posited when deciding how to allocate access to our scarce resources: justice. To ensure a just allocation, we need to recognize the different sources of value creation associated with the enclosure and commodification of our natural resources, and then recognize that different communities will want to harvest that value in different ways.

This gets us to the heart of the matter: we need broad public support when we set off on the next round of enclosures. Privatization may be necessary to encourage efficiencies, larger production, economies of scale, access to markets and capital, etc. If this privatization happens at the expense of the common wealth, however, then the public will probably turn against it.

REFERENCES

Aarset, B. & S.-E. Jakobsen 2009. "Political regulation and radical institutional change: the case of aquaculture in Norway". *Marine Policy* 33: 280–7.

Acheson, J. 2011. "Ostrom for anthropologists". *International Journal of the Commons* 5 (2): 319–39.

AfDB 2016. *Review of Land Tenure Policy, Institutional and Administrative Systems of Botswana*. Abidjan: AfDB. www.afdb.org/fileadmin/uploads/afdb/Documents/Publicati ons/AfDB_BotswanaLandReport_FA.pdf.

African Group 2018. "Request for consideration by the Council for the African Group's pro-posal on the economic model/payment regime and other financial matters in the draft exploitation regulations under review" [submitted to the Secretariat of the International Seabed Authority by the Permanent Mission of Algeria]. 9 July. https://isa.org.jm/files/files/documents/nv.pdf.

Al-Kasim, F. 2006. *Managing Petroleum Resources: The "Norwegian Model" in a Broad Perspective*. Oxford: Oxford Institute for Energy Studies.

Alaska Permanent Fund Corporation n.d. "History of the Alaska Permanent Fund". https://apfc.org/who-we-are/history-of-the-alaska-permanent-fund.

Alchian, A. & H. Demsetz 1973. "The property right paradigm". *Journal of Economic History* 33 (1): 16–27.

Alden Wily, L. 2011. "The tragedy of public lands: the fate of the commons under global com-mercial pressure". Rome: International Land Coalition. www.land-links.org/wp-content/uploads/2016/09/USAID_Land_Tenure_2012_Liberia_Course_Module_2_Commons_Web_Wily.pdf.

Alden Wily, L. 2013. "Enclosure revisited: putting the global land rush in historical perspective". In *Handbook of Land and Water Grabs in Africa: Foreign Direct Investment and Food and Water Security*, T. Allan *et al.* (eds), 11–23. Abingdon: Routledge.

Åm, H. 2021. "A critical policy study on why introducing resource rent taxation in Norwegian salmon aquaculture failed". *Marine Policy* 2: 104692.

Andelson, R. 2000. "Land-value taxation around the world". *American Journal of Economics and Sociology* 59 (5): i–490.

Anderson, J. 1859 [1777]. *An Inquiry into the Corn-Laws; with a view to the New Corn-Bill Proposed for Scotland*. London: Lord Overstone.

Aparicio, N. *et al.* 2012. "Comparison of wind energy support policy and electricity market design in Europe, the United States, and Australia". *IEEE Transactions on Sustainable Energy* 3 (4): 809–18.

Aristotle. 350 BCE. *Politics*, bk 2, trans. B. Jowett. http://classics.mit.edu/Aristotle/politics.2.two.html.

Armstrong, C. 2022. *A Blue New Deal: Why We Need a New Politics for the Ocean*. New Haven, CT: Yale University Press.

Asche, F. & T. Bjørndal 2011. *The Economics of Salmon Aquaculture*, 2nd edn. Chichester: Wiley-Blackwell.

Asche, F., A.-L. Cojocaru & M. Sikveland 2018. "Market shocks in salmon aquaculture: the impact of the Chilean disease crisis". *Journal of Agricultural and Applied Economics* 50 (2): 255–69.

Asche, F. *et al.* 2009. "The salmon disease crisis in Chile". *Marine Resource Economics* 24 (4): 405–11.

Auty, R. 1993. *Sustaining Development in Mineral Economies: The Resource Curse Thesis*. London: Routledge.

Ayers, R. 2017. "Gaps in mainstream economics: energy, growth and sustainability". In *Green Economy Reader. Lectures in Ecological Economics and Sustainability*, S. Shmelev (ed.), 39–54. Berlin: Springer.

Azevedo, M. *et al.* 2018. "Lithium and cobalt: a tale of two commodities". New York: McKinsey. www.mckinsey.com/industries/metals-and-mining/our-insights/lithium-and-cobalt-a-tale-of-two-commodities.

Barbier, E. 2005. *Natural Resources and Economic Development*. Cambridge: Cambridge University Press.

Barnes, P. 2021. *Ours: The Case for Universal Property*. Cambridge: Polity.

Barton, J. & A. Fløysand 2010. "The political ecology of Chilean salmon aquaculture, 1982–2010: a trajectory from economic development to global sustainability". *Global Environmental Change* 20: 739–52.

Baunsgaard, T. 2001. "A primer on mineral taxation", Working Paper 5. Washington, DC: IMF.

Berg, H. & M. Zackrisson 2019. "Perspectives on environmental and cost assessment of lithium metal negative electrodes in electric vehicle traction batteries". *Journal of Power Sources* 415: 83–90.

Berge, A. 2020. "These are the 20 biggest salmon farmers in the world". Salmon Business, 27 July. https://salmonbusiness.com/these-are-the-20-biggest-salmon-farmers-in-the-world.

Birch, K. & D. Tyfield 2013. "Theorizing the bioeconomy: biovalue, biocapital, bioeconomics or ... what?". *Science, Technology and Human Values* 38 (3): 299–327.

Biswas, A., C. Tortajada & P. Rohner (eds) 2018. *Assessing Global Water Megatrends*. Singapore: Springer Nature.

Blaug, M. 1985. *Economic Theory in Retrospect*, 4th edn. Cambridge: Cambridge University Press.

Blaug, M. 2000. "Henry George: rebel with a cause". *European Journal of the History of Economic Thought* 7 (2): 270–88.

BloombergNEF 2022. "Summary: energy transition investment trends 2022". https://assets. bbhub.io/professional/sites/24/Energy-Transition-Investment-Trends-Exec Summary-2022.pdf.

Boadway, R. & N. Bruce 1984. "A general proposition on the design of a neutral business tax". *Journal of Public Economics* 24 (2): 231–39.

Bollier, D. 2014. *Think Like a Commoner: A Short Introduction to the Life of the Commons*. Gabriola Island, BC: New Society.

Bollier, D. & S. Helfrich (eds) 2012. *The Wealth of the Commons: A World beyond Market and State*. Amherst, MA: Levellers Press.

Bookchin, M. 1975 [1962]. *Our Synthetic Environment*, rev. edn [published under the pseudonym Lewis Herber]. New York: Harper & Row.

Bourguignon, F. 2015. *The Globalization of Inequality*. Princeton, NJ: Princeton University Press.

BP 2020. *Statistical Review of World Energy 2020*. London: BP.

Bridge Economics 2020. "Peer review of the economic contribution of salmon aquaculture to Scotland". Hebden Bridge: Bridge Economics. www.sift.scot/wp-content/uploads/2020/04/Peer-Review-Economic-Contribution-of-Salmon-Aquaculture-to-Scotland.pdf.

Brigham, A. 2009. *Just Hungry: Can Land Reform Reduce Hunger in Developing Countries?* Saarbrücken: Verlag Dr Müller.

Brigham, A. & J. Moses 2021. "Den nye oljen". *Norsk statsvitenskapelig tidsskrift* 37 (1): 4–25.

Brown, E. 2001. *Sea-Bed Energy and Minerals: The International Legal Regime*. Amsterdam: Martinus Nijhoff/Brill.

Brush, S. 1999. "Bioprospecting the public domain". *Cultural Anthropology* 14 (4): 535–55.

Burkett, P. 2003. "The value problem in ecological economics: lessons from the physiocrats and Marx". *Organization & Environment* 16 (2): 137–67.

Bustos, B. & Á. Román 2019. "A sea uprooted: islandness and political identity on Chiloé Island, Chile". *Island Studies Journal* 14 (2): 97–114.

Cahill, K. (with R. McMahon) 2010. *Who Owns the World: The Surprising Truth about Every Piece of Land on the Planet*. New York: Grand Central.

Carson, R. 1962. *Silent Spring*. Boston: Houghton Mifflin.

Central Intelligence Agency 2020. *CIA World Factbook 2020–2021*. Langley, VA: CIA. www.cia.gov/the-world-factbook/field/area/country-comparison.

Chan, K. 2009. "The Chinese hukou system at 50". *Eurasian Geography and Economics* 50 (2): 197–221.

Chan, K. 2010. "The household registration system and migrant labor in China: notes on a debate". *Population & Development Review* 36 (2): 357–64.

Chandler, T. 1982. *The Tax We Need*. Berkeley, CA: Gutenberg Press.

Charles, A. 2002. "Use rights and responsible fisheries: limiting access and harvesting through rights-based management". In *A Fishery Manager's Guidebook*, K. Cochrane & S. Garcia (eds), 131–57. Chichester: Wiley-Blackwell.

Chen, J. 2021. "Spot price". Investopedia, 31 January. www.investopedia.com/terms/s/spotprice.asp.

Cheng, Y.-S. & K.-S. Chung 2017. "Designing property rights over land in rural China". *Economic Journal* 128: 2676–710.

Christensen, P. 1989. "Historical roots for ecological economics: biophysical versus allocative approaches". *Ecological Economics* 1 (1): 17–36.

Cicero, Marcus Tullius 1887 [44]. *On Moral Duties* [*De officiis*]. From *Ethical Writing of Cicero: De officiis; De senectute; De amicitia; and Scipio's Dream*, trans. A. Peabody. http://files.libertyfund.org/files/542/Cicero_0041-01_EBk_v6.0.pdf.

Clark, A., J. Cook Clark & S. Pintz 2013. "Towards the development of a regulatory framework for polymetallic nodule exploitation in the Area", Technical Study 11. Kingston: ISA.

Clark, C. 1967. "Von Thunen's isolated state". *Oxford Economic Papers*, new series 19 (3): 370–7.

Collier, P. 2010. "Principles of resource taxation for low-income countries". In *The Taxation of Petroleum and Minerals: Principles, Problems and Practice*, P. Daniel, M. Keen & C. McPherson (eds), 75–86. London: Routledge.

Collins, R. & D. French 2020. "A guardian of universal interest or increasingly out of its depth? The International Seabed Authority turns 25". *International Organizations Law Review* 17 (3): 633–63.

Congress 2015. "HR 1508: Space Resource Exploration and Utilization Act of 2015". www.congress.gov/bill/114th-congress/house-bill/1508.

Congressional Research Service 2020. "Federal land ownership: overview and data", Report R42346. Washington, DC: Congressional Research Service. https://fas.org/sgp/crs/misc/R42346.pdf.

Connolly, C. & A. Wall 2016. "Value capture: a valid means of funding PPPs". *Financial Accountability & Management* 32 (2): 157–78.

Cooper, M. & C. Waldby 2014. *Clinical Labor: Tissue Donors and Research Subjects in the Global Bioeconomy*. Durham, NC: Duke University Press.

Cord, S. 1979. *Catalyst! How a Reform of the Property Tax Can Revitalize Our Cities and Counter Inflation and Recession*. Indiana, PA: Henry George Foundation of America.

Corlett, A. *et al.* 2018. *Replacing Business Rates: Taxing Land, not Investment: Introducing the Commercial Landowner Levy*. London: Liberal Democrats. https://d3n8a8pro7vhmx.cloudfront.net/libdems/pages/43501/attachments/original/1535544506/1039_Business_Ratesfinal.pdf.

Creutzig, F. 2017. "Govern land as a global commons". *Nature* 456 (May): 28–9.

Crouch, C. 2020. *Post-Democracy: After the Crisis*. Cambridge: Polity.

Crown Estate Scotland 2021. "Aquaculture". www.crownestatescotland.com/scotlands–prope rty/marine/aquaculture.

Daniel, P., M. Keen & C. McPherson 2010. "Introduction". In *The Taxation of Petroleum and Minerals: Principles, Problems and Practice*, P. Daniel, M. Keen & C. McPherson (eds), 1–10. London: Routledge.

Demsetz, H. 1967. "Toward a theory of property rights". *American Economic Review* 57 (2): 347–59.

Demsetz, H. 2002. "Toward a theory of property rights II: the competition between private and collective ownership". *Journal of Legal Studies* 31 (4): 653–72.

De Schutter, O. & K. Pistor 2016. "Introduction: toward voice and reflexivity". In *Governing Access to Essential Resources*, K. Pistor & O. De Schutter (eds), 1–48. New York: Columbia University Press.

De Soto, H. 2020. *The Mystery of Capital: Why Capitalism Triumphs in the West and Fails Everywhere Else*. New York: Basic Books.

Deep Sea Conservation Coalition 2020. "Exploration contracts granted by the ISA, March 2020". Amsterdam: Deep Sea Conservation Coalition. www.savethehighseas.org/wp-content/ uploads/2020/03/Table_Exploration-contracts-granted-by-the-ISA_Mar2020.pdf.

Deudney, D. 2020. *Dark Skies: Space Expansionism, Planetary Geopolitics, and the Ends of Humanity*. New York: Oxford University Press.

Doepel, D. & K. Urama 2021. "The stuff of the stars". In *Sovereign Wealth Funds, Local Content and CSR: Developments in the Extractives Sector*, E. Pereira, R. Spencer & J. Moses (eds), v–vi. Berlin: Springer.

Economist, The 1977. "The Dutch disease". 26 November.

Economist, The 2003. "Priceless". 19 July.

Economist, The 2021. "How green bottlenecks threaten the clean energy businesses". 12 June.

Economist, The 2022. "Power play". 26 March.

Enzensberger, N., M. Wietschel & O. Rentz 2002. "Policy instruments fostering wind energy projects: a multi-perspective evaluation approach". *Energy Policy* 30 (9): 793–801.

European Commission 2020. "Critical raw materials resilience: charting a path towards greater security and sustainability", COM (2020) 474 final. Brussels: European Commission.

Eurostat n.d. "Electricity prices for household consumers". https://ec.europa.eu/eurostat/web/ products-datasets/-/nrg_pc_204.

EY 2019. *Global Oil and Gas Tax Guide 2019*. London: EY.

FAO 2001. "Governance principles for concessions and contracts in public forests", Forestry Paper 139. Rome: FAO.

FAO 2005. "Forest area statistics, by country". www.fao.org/forestry/country/32185/en/lbr.

FAO 2020a. "Global forest resource assessment 2020: key findings". www.fao.org/forest-resour ces-assessment/2020/en/?utm_source=twitter&utm_medium=social+media&utm_ campaign=fao.

FAO 2020b. "Global forest resource assessment: data export". https://fra–data.fao.org/SA/ fra2020/home.

FAO 2020c. *The State of the World's Forests 2020: Forests, Biodiversity and People*. Rome: FAO.

FAO 2020d. *The State of World Fisheries and Aquaculture 2020: Sustainability in Action*. Rome: FAO.

FAO 2021a. "Norway: national aquaculture legislation overview". www.fao.org/fishery/ legalframework/nalo_norway/en.

FAO 2021b. "Chile: national aquaculture legislation overview". www.fao.org/fishery/ legalframework/nalo_chile/en.

FAO 2021c. "United Kingdom: national aquaculture legislation overview". www.fao.org/ fishery/legalframework/nalo_uk/en.

FAO n.d. "FishStatJ: software for fishery and aquaculture statistical time series". www.fao.org/fishery/en/statistics/software/fishstatj.

Farber, S., R. Costanza & M. Wilson 2002. "Economic and ecological concepts for valuing ecosystem services". *Ecological Economics* 41 (3): 375–92.

Farley, J. *et al.* 2015. "The Vermont Common Assets Trust: an institution for sustainable, just and efficient resource allocation". *Ecological Economics* 109: 71–9.

Feedback & Changing Markets 2020. "The hidden costs of farmed salmon: exploring why Sainsbury's farmed salmon supplier Mowi doesn't live up to its sustainable image and what Sainsbury's needs to do about it". London: Feedback & the Changing Markets Foundation.

Financial Times, The 2021. "How space-based solar power can save the planet". 23 November. YouTube video: https://youtu.be/oBlOb2z26Do.

Finansdepartementet 2022a. "Increased resource rent tax on hydropower". Press release, 28 September. www.regjeringen.no/en/aktuelt/increased-resource-rent-tax-on-hydropower/id2929115.

Finansdepartementet 2022b. "Resource rent tax on onshore wind energy". Press release, 28 September. www.regjeringen.no/en/aktuelt/resource–rent–tax–on–onshore–wind–energy/id2929117.

Finansdepartementet 2022c. "Resource rent tax on aquaculture". Press release, 28 September. www.regjeringen.no/en/aktuelt/resource–rent–tax–on–aquaculture/id2929113.

Finansdepartementet 2022d. "High-price contribution on wind and hydropower energy". Press release, 28 September. www.regjeringen.no/en/aktuelt/high–price–contribution–on–wind–and–hydropower/id2929111.

Fitzgibbon, W. 2021. "US sanctions Angolan billionaire Isabel dos Santos for corruption". International Consortium of Investigative Journalists, 9 December. www.icij.org/investigations/luanda-leaks/us-sanctions-angolan-billionaire-isabel-dos-santos-for-corruption.

Flaaten, O. & T. Pham 2019. "Resource rent in aquaculture". In *Contributions in Natural Resource Economics*, J. Olaussen (ed.), 103–36. Bergen: Fagbokforlaget.

Flomenhoft, G. 2018. "Historical and empirical basis for communal title in minerals at the national level: does ownership matter for human development?". *Sustainability* 10 (6): 1958.

Foldvary, F. 2004. "Public revenue from land rent". In *Handbook of Public Finance*, J. Backhaus & R. Wagner (eds), 165–94. Amsterdam: Kluwer.

Folkersen, M., C. Fleming & S. Hasan 2019. "Depths of uncertainty for deep-sea policy and legislation". *Global Environmental Change* 54: 1–5.

Food and Land Use Coalition 2019. *Growing Better: Ten Critical Transitions to Transform Food and Land Use*. Washington, DC: Food and Land Use Coalition.

Førsund, F. & L. Hjalmarsson 1974. "On the measurement of productive efficiency". *Swedish Journal of Economics* 76 (2): 141–54.

Franckx, E. 2010. "The International Seabed Authority and the common heritage of mankind: the need for states to establish the outer limits of their continental shelf". *International Journal of Marine and Coastal Law* 25 (4): 543–67.

Francis, Pope 2015. *Laudato Si': On Care for Our Common Home*. Encyclical letter of the Holy Father Francis. Vatican: Vatican Press.

Frazer-Nash Consultancy 2021. "Space based solar power: de-risking the pathway to net zero", FNC 004456–52265R Issue 1B. Dorking: Frazer-Nash Consultancy. https://assets.publishing.service.gov.uk/government/uploads/system/uploads/attachment_data/file/1020631/space-based-solar-power-derisking-pathway-to-net-zero.pdf.

Fuglestad, E. & R. Almås 2021. "Tilbake til grunnrentelandet". *Nytt Norsk Tidsskrift* 38 (3): 208–18.

Gaffney, M. 1970. "Adequacy of land as a tax base". In *The Assessment of Land Value*, D. Holland (ed.), 157–212. Madison, WI: University of Wisconsin Press.

Gaffney, M. 1994. "Land as a distinctive factor of production". In *Land and Taxation*, N. Tideman (ed.), 39–102. London: Shepheard-Walwyn.

Garnaut, R. & A. Clunies Ross 1975. "Uncertainty, risk aversion and the taxing of natural resource projects". *Economic Journal* 85: 272–87.

Garnaut, R. & A. Clunies Ross 1983. *Taxation of Mineral Rents.* Oxford: Clarendon Press.

George, H. 1992 [1879]. *Progress and Poverty.* New York: Robert Schalkenbach Foundation.

George, H. 2006 [1892]. *A Perplexed Philosopher*, digitized Per Møller Andersen. www.grundskyld.dk.

George, H. 2019 [1891]. "The condition of labor: an open letter to Pope Leo XIII". https://schalkenbach.org/wp-content/uploads/2019/08/The_Condition_of_Labor.pdf.

Giles, R. 2017. "The theory of charges for nature: how Georgism became geoism". Redfern, NSW: Association for Good Government.

Gilliland, M. 1975. "Energy analysis and public policy". *Science* 189 (September): 1051–6.

Glasby, G. 2012. "Treasures of the abyss". Geological Society, May. www.geolsoc.org.uk/Geoscientist/Archive/May-2013/Treasures-from-the-abyss.

Glester, A. 2018. "The asteroid trillionaires". *Physics World*, 11 June.

Gordon, H. 1954. "The economic theory of a common-property resource: the fishery". *Journal of Political Economy* 62 (2): 124–42.

Goss, C. 1986. "Petroleum and mining taxation: handbook on a method for equitable sharing of profits and risk", Joint Energy Programme Paper 19. London: Policy Studies Institute & Royal Institute for International Affairs.

Gray, J. 2002. "Forest concession policies and revenue systems: country experience and policy changes for sustainable tropical forestry", Technical Paper 522. Washington, DC: World Bank.

Gray, J. 2003. "Forest tenures and concession experience in Canada and selected other countries". In *Institutional Changes in Forest Management in Countries with Transition Economies: Problems and Solutions: Workshop Proceedings*, 37–50. Washington, DC: PROFOR.

Greaker, M. & L. Lindholt 2019. "Grunnrenten i norsk akvakultur og kraftproduksjon fra 1984 til 2018", Report 2019/34. Oslo: Statistisk sentralbyrå.

Grotius, H. 1916 [1608]. *The Freedom of the Seas [Mare Liberum]*, trans. R. van Deman Magoffin. New York: Oxford University Press.

Grotius, H. 2016 [1625]. *On the Law of War and Peace [De jure belli ac pacis]*, trans. A. Campbell. Altenmünster: Jazzybee Verlag.

Guterres, A. 2021. "Secretary-general's remarks to the global roundtable on transforming extractive industries for sustainable development [as delivered]". United Nations, 25 May. www.un.org/sg/en/content/sg/statement/2021-05-25/secretary-generals-remarks-the-global-roundtable-transforming-extractive-industries-for-sustainable-development-delivered.

Gylberte, H. 1578. "Letters Patent to Sir Humfrey Gylberte, 11 June 1578". Yale Law School. http://avalon.law.yale.edu/16th_century/humfrey.asp.

Haggett, C. 2008. "Over the sea and far away? A consideration of the planning, politics and public perception of offshore wind farms". *Journal of Environmental Policy and Planning* 10 (3): 289–306.

Hall, D. 2016. "Land's essentiality and land governance". In *Governing Access to Essential Resources*, K. Pistor & O. De Schutter (eds), 49–66. New York: Columbia University Press.

Hardin, G. 1968. "The tragedy of the commons". *Science* 162 (December): 1243–8.

Harrington, J. 1992 [1656]. *Commonwealth of Oceana*, ed. J. Pocock. Cambridge: Cambridge University Press.

Harrison, F. 1994. "Prologue: rent-ability". In *Land and Taxation*, N. Tideman (ed.), 7–38. London: Shepheard-Walwyn.

Harrison, F. 2008. *The Silver Bullet: There's Only One Way to Kill Poverty.* London: International Union for Land Value Taxation.

Harvey, D. 1984. *The Limits to Capital.* Oxford: Blackwell.

Haugan, P. *et al.* 2019. "What role for ocean-based renewable energy and deep seabed minerals in a sustainable future?". Washington, DC: World Resources Institute.

Hayden, C. 2003. *When Nature Goes Public: The Making and Unmaking of Bioprospecting in Mexico*. Princeton, NJ: Princeton University Press.

Hayes, N. 2020. *The Book of Trespass: Crossing the Lines that Divide Us*. London: Bloomsbury.

Healy, N. & J. Barry 2017. "Politicizing energy justice and energy system transitions: fossil fuel divestment and a 'just transition'". *Energy Policy* 108 (C): 451–9.

Hecht, A. 2020. "Breakeven crude oil production costs around the world". Yahoo!, 27 April. https://finance.yahoo.com/news/breakeven-crude-oil-production-costs-085329648.html.

Heckscher, E. 1918. *Svenska produktionsproblem*. Stockholm: Bonniers.

Hein, J. *et al.* 2013. "Deep-ocean mineral deposits as a source of critical metals for high- and green-technology applications: comparison with land-based resources". *Ore Geology Reviews* 51: 1–14.

Heine, D., G. Batmanian & E. Hayde 2020. "Executive summary". In *Designing Fiscal Instruments for Sustainable Forests*, 1–38. Washington, DC: International Bank for Reconstruction and Development. www.climateinvestmentfunds.org/sites/cif_enc/files/knowledge-docume nts/designing_fiscal_instruments.pdf.

HenryGeorge.org. n.d.a. "Common property in land". www.HenryGeorge.org/rem1.htm.

HenryGeorge.org. n.d.b. "Public rent collection in practice: the historical record". www. HenryGeorge.org/rem4.htm.

Hersoug, B. 2021. "Why and how to regulate Norwegian salmon production? The history of maximum allowable biomass (MAB)". *Aquaculture* 545: 737144.

Hersoug, B., E. Mikkelsen & K. Karlsen 2019. "'Great expectations': allocating licenses with special requirements in Norwegian salmon farming". *Marine Policy* 100: 152–62.

Hishamunda, N., N. Ridler & E. Martone 2014. "Policy and governance in aquaculture: lessons learned and the way forward", Fisheries and Aquaculture Technical Paper 577. Rome: FAO.

Honoré, A. 1961. "Ownership". In *Oxford Essays in Jurisprudence*, A. Guest (ed.), 107–47. Oxford: Clarendon Press.

HSRGWG 2018. "Information provided by the Netherlands". Vienna: Committee on the Peaceful Uses of Outer Space, Legal Subcommittee. www.unoosa.org/res/oosadoc/data/ documents/2018/aac_105c_22018crp/aac_105c_22018crp_18_0_html/AC105_C2_2018_ CRP18E.pdf.

HSRGWG 2019. "Building blocks for the development of an international framework on space resource activities". The Hague: HSRGWG. www.universiteitleiden.nl/binaries/content/ass ets/rechtsgeleerdheid/instituut-voor-publiekrecht/lucht--en-ruimterecht/space-resources/ bb-thissrwg--cover.pdf.

Hubbert, M. 1956. "Nuclear energy and the fossil fuel". *Drilling and Production Practice* 95: 1–57.

Hughes, C. *et al.* 2020. "Implementing a land value tax: considerations on moving from theory to practice". *Land Use Policy* 94: 104494.

Hume, D. 2006 [1748]. "Of the original contract". In *Hume: Political Essays*, K. Haakonssen (ed.), 186–201. Cambridge: Cambridge University Press.

Hustad, J. 2019. "Grunnrentelandet". *Dag og Tid*, 1 November: 8–9.

Hutto, S. 2017. "This land is our land". Choctaw Nation, 5 July. www.choctawnation.com/news-events/press-media/land-our-land.

IEA 2019. *Renewables 2019: Analysis and Forecast to 2024*. Paris: IEA.

IEA 2020. "Renewable electricity capacity remuneration policy types, 2020–2025". 9 November. www.iea.org/data-and-statistics/charts/renewable-electricity-capacity-remuneration-policy-types-2020-2025.

IEA 2021. *Net Zero by 2050: A Roadmap for the Global Energy Sector*. Paris: IEA.

Industry Standards for Fish 1999. "Norwegian industry standard for fish: quality grading of farmed salmon". Bergen: Industry Standards for Fish. www.yousyokuburi.com/pdf/ Quality_grading_of_farmed_salmon.pdf.

International Council for the Exploration of the Sea. 2021. "Working Group on North Atlantic Salmon (WGNAS)", Scientific Report 3(29). Copenhagen: International Council for the Exploration of the Sea.

IRENA 2020. "Renewable capacity highlights". 31 March. www.irena.org/-/media/Files/IRENA/Agency/Publication/2021/Apr/IRENA_-RE_Capacity_Highlights_2021.pdf?la=en&hash=1E133689564BC40C2392E85026F71A0D7A9C0B91.

IRENA 2021. *Renewable Energy Statistics 2021*. Masdar City: IRENA.

IRENA, IEA & REN21 2018. *Renewable Energy Policies in a Time of Transition*. Masdar City: IRENA, IEA & REN21.

ISA 2010. "Decision of the Assembly of the International Seabed Authority relating to the regulations on prospecting and exploration for polymetallic sulphides in the Area", ISBA/16/A/12/Rev.1. Kingston: ISA.

ISA 2012. "Decision of the Assembly of the International Seabed Authority relating to the regulations on prospecting and exploration for cobalt-rich ferromanganese crusts in the Area", ISBA/18/A/11. Kingston: ISA.

ISA 2013. "Decision of the Council of the International Seabed Authority relating to amendments to the regulations on prospecting and exploration for polymetallic nodules in the Area and related matters", ISBA/19/C/17. Kingston: ISA.

ISA 2019. "MIT comparative study of economic models for polymetallic nodule mining now available online". 29 January. www.isa.org.jm/news/mit-comparative-study-economic-models-polymetallic-nodule-mining-now-available-online.

ISA 2020. "Call for proposals for a study on the scope, purpose and administration of a global fund from the financial payments from deep seabed mining". 9 September. https://isa.org.jm/files/ToR%20-%20Global%20fund%20consultancy_1.pdf.

ISA n.d. "Frequently asked questions (FAQs)". https://isa.org.jm/index.php/frequently-asked-questions-faqs.

Isaac, J. *et al.* 2010. "Review: beyond the tragedy of the commons: a discussion of *Governing the Commons: The Evolution of Institutions for Collective Action*". *Perspectives on Politics* 8 (2): 569–93.

Jacobs, A. 2011. *Governing for the Long Term: Democracy and the Politics of Investment*. Cambridge: Cambridge University Press.

Jaeckel, A. 2020. "Benefiting from the common heritage of mankind: from expectation to reality". *International Journal of Marine and Coastal Law* 35 (4): 660–81.

Johnson, C. 1981. "Taking the take but not the risk". *Materials and Society* 5 (4).

Johnston, D. 2002. "Current developments in production sharing contracts and international concerns: retrospective government take – not a perfect statistic". *Petroleum Accounting and Financial Management Journal* 21 (2): 101–8.

Johnston, D. 2008. "Changing fiscal landscape". *Journal of World Energy Law & Business* 1 (1): 31–54.

Johnston, D. 2018. "Government take". *Journal of World Energy Law & Business* 11 (6): 506–40.

Jones Luong, P. & E. Weinthal 2006. "Rethinking the resource curse: ownership structure, institutional capacity, and domestic constraints". *Annual Review of Political Science* 9: 241–63.

Kallis, G. *et al.* 2018. "Research on degrowth". *Annual Review of Environment and Resources* 43: 291–316.

Karl, T. 1997. *The Paradox of Plenty: Oil Booms and Petro-States*. Berkeley, CA: University of California Press.

Kelvey, J. 2014. "Is it legal to mine asteroids?". Slate, 13 October. https://slate.com/technology/2014/10/asteroid-mining-and-space-law-who-gets-to-profit-from-outer-space-platinum.html.

Kenyon, W. & D. Davies 2018. "Salmon farming in Scotland", SPICe Briefing SB 18-12 rev. Edinburgh: Scottish Parliament. https://sp-bpr-en-prod-cdnep.azureedge.net/published/2018/2/13/Salmon-Farming-in-Scotland/SB%2018-12%20rev.pdf.

Kirchain, R. *et al.* 2019. "Exploring possible financial payment systems for polymetallic nodules". MSL presentation, Kingston, 15 November. www.isa.org.jm/files/files/docume nts/03_kirchain.pdf.

Kleiman, M. 2013. "Space law 101: an introduction to space law". American Bar Association, 27 August. https://web.archive.org/web/20181204054125/https://www.americanbar.org/ groups/young_lawyers/publications/the_101_201_practice_series/space_law_101_an_in troduction_to_space_law.

Knoema 2018. "The cost of producing a barrel of crude oil by country". 4 May. https://knoema. com/rqaebad/cost-of-producing-a-barrel-of-crude-oil-by-country.

Knud E. Hansen n.d. "Technip – pipe lay vessel Deep Energy". www.knudehansen.com/wp-content/uploads/2017/10/Technip-Pipe-Lay-Vessel-Deep-Energy-1.pdf.

Kramer, L. 2015. "Land-based salmon aquaculture: a future with potential". Seafood Source, 14 October. www.seafoodsource.com/news/aquaculture/land-based-salmon-aquaculture-a-future-with-potential.

Krueger, A. 1974. "The political economy of the rent-seeking society". *American Economic Review* 64 (3): 291–303.

Kumar, R. 1991. "Taxation for a cyclical industry". *Resources Policy* 17 (2): 133–48.

Land, B. 2010. "Resource rent taxes: a reappraisal". In *The Taxation of Petroleum and Minerals*, P. Daniel, M. Keen & C. McPherson (eds), 241–62. London: Routledge.

Law, J. 2015. "*Cuius est solum ejus est usque ad coelum et ad inferos*". In *Dictionary of Law*, 8th edn. Oxford: Oxford University Press. www.oxfordreference.com/display/10.1093/acref/ 9780199664924.001.0001/acref-9780199664924-e-4660.

Law, J. & M. Lien 2012. "Slippery: field notes in empirical ontology". *Social Studies of Science* 43 (3): 363–78.

Levin, L. *et al.* 2016. "Defining 'serious harm' to the marine environment in the context of deep-seabed mining". *Marine Policy* 74: 245–59.

Levitan, D. 2012. "High-altitude wind energy: huge potential – and hurdles". Yale School of the Environment, 24 September. https://e360.yale.edu/features/high_altitude_wind_energy_ huge_potential_and_hurdles.

Lien, M. 2015. *Becoming Salmon: Aquaculture and the Domestication of a Fish*. Berkeley, CA: University of California Press.

Lien, M. & J. Law 2011. "'Emergent aliens': on salmon, nature, and their enactment". *Ethnos* 76 (1): 65–87.

Lima, P. 2022. "Comparison of the different EV batteries in 2020". PushEVs, 26 March. https:// pushevs.com/2020/04/04/comparison-of-different-ev-batteries-in-2020.

Linebaugh, P. 2008. *The Magna Carta Manifesto: Liberties and Commons for All*. Berkeley, CA: University of California Press.

Linebaugh, P. 2010. "Enclosures from the bottom up". *Radical History Review* 108: 11–27.

Linklater, A. 2013. *Owning the Earth: The Transforming History of Land Ownership*. London: Bloomsbury.

Locke, J. 1960 [1688]. *Two Treatises of Government*, P. Laslett (ed.). Cambridge: Cambridge University Press.

Lodge, M. *et al.* 2014. "Seabed mining: International Seabed Authority environmental man-agement plan for the Clarion–Clipperton Zone: a partnership approach". *Marine Policy* 49: 66–72.

Lohan, T. 2020. "New high seas treaty could be a gamechanger for the ocean". The Revelator, 7 May. https://therevelator.org/high-seas-treaty.

Lund, D. 2009. "Rent taxation for nonrenewable resources". *Annual Review of Resource Economics* 1: 287–307.

Lund, D. & K. Rosendahl 2022. "Grunnrente til folket". *Klassekampen*, 16 March: 20–1.

McPherson, C. & K. Palmer 1984. "New approaches to profit sharing in developing countries". *Oil and Gas Journal* 82 (2): 119–28.

McGlade, C. & P. Ekins 2015. "The geographical distribution of fossil fuels unused when limiting global warming to 2°C". *Nature* 517 (8 January): 187–90.

Mahdavy, H. 1970. "The patterns and problems of economic development in rentier states: the case of Iran". In *Studies in Economic History of the Middle East from the Rise of Islam to the Present Day*, M. Cook (ed.), 428–67. Oxford: Oxford University Press.

Maitland, J. [the Earl of Lauderdale] 1819 [1804]. *An Inquiry into the Nature and Origin of Public Wealth*, 2nd edn. Edinburgh: Archibald Constable.

Mallick, S. & R. Rajagopalan 2019. "If space is 'the province of mankind', who owns its resources? An examination of the potential of space mining and its legal implications", Occasional Paper 182. New Delhi: Observer Research Foundation.

Malthus, T. 1903 [1815]. *An Inquiry into the Nature and Progress of Rent, and the Principles by which It Is Regulated* [reprint of *Economic Tracts*], J. Hollander (ed.). Baltimore: Johns Hopkins University Press.

Malthus, T. 1993 [1798]. *An Essay on the Principle of Population*, G. Gilbert (ed.). Oxford: Oxford University Press.

Marine Scotland 2014. "Assessment of the benefits to Scotland of aquaculture: Research Summary". Edinburgh: Marine Scotland. www.inclusivebusiness.net/sites/default/files/wp/00450798.pdf.

Marshall, A. 1920 [1890]. *Principles of Economics*, 8th edn. London: Macmillan.

Martén, I., P. Whittaker & Á. Martínez de Burio 2015. "Government take in upstream oil and gas". Boston: Boston Consulting Group. https://web-assets.bcg.com/img-src/BCG-Government-Take-Upstream-Oil-Gas-Dec-2015_tcm85-88922.pdf.

Marx, K. 1967 [1867]. *Capital: A Critique of Political Economy*, 3 vols. New York: International Publishers.

Marx, K. & F. Engels 1985 [1860–64]. *Karl Marx Friedrich Engels: Collected Works*, vol. 41. London: Lawrence & Wishart.

Mathew, S. 2006. "Analysis of wind regimes". In *Wind Energy: Fundamentals, Resource Analysis and Economics*, 45–88. Berlin: Springer.

Mazzucato, M. 2018. *The Value of Everything: Making and Taking in the Global Economy*. New York: Public Affairs.

Meadows, D. *et al.* 1972. *The Limits to Growth*. New York: Universe Books.

Merrill, T. & H. Smith 2001. "What happened to property in law and economics?" *Yale Law Review* 111 (2): 357–98.

Merson, J. 2000. "Bio-prospecting or bio-piracy: intellectual property rights and biodiversity in a colonial and postcolonial context". *Osiris* 15 (1): 282–96.

Milanovic, B. 2005. *Worlds Apart: Measuring International and Global Inequality*. Princeton, NJ: Princeton University Press.

Mildenberger, M. 2020. *Carbon Captured: How Business and Labor Control Climate Politics*. Cambridge, MA: MIT Press.

Mirrlees, J. *et al.* 2011. *Tax by Design: The Final Report of the Mirrlees Review*. London: Institute for Fiscal Studies.

Moe, E. 2017. "Does politics matter? Explaining swings in wind power installations". *AIMS Energy* 5 (3): 341–73.

Moses, J. 2021a. *Workaway: The Human Costs of Europe's Common Labour Market*. Bristol: Bristol University Press.

Moses, J. 2021b. "Norway's sovereign wealth fund". In *Sovereign Wealth Funds, Local Content and CSR*, E. Pereira *et al.* (eds), 249–64. Berlin: Springer.

Moses, J. 2021c. "A sovereign wealth fund: Norway's Government Pension Fund, Global". In *The Political Economy of Natural Resource Funds*, E. Okpanachi & R. Tremblay (eds), 181–206. Berlin: Springer.

Moses, J. 2021d. "Norwegian local content policy". In *Sovereign Wealth Funds, Local Content and CSR*, E. Pereira *et al.* (eds), 423–8. Berlin: Springer.

Moses, J. & A. Brigham 2021. "Whose benefit? A comparative perspective for the ISA". *Marine Policy* 131: 104550.

Moses, J. & B. Letnes 2017a. *Natural Resource Abundance and Wealth: The Norwegian Experience*. New York: Oxford University Press.

Moses, J. & B. Letnes 2017b. "Breaking Brent: Norway's response to the recent oil price shock". *Journal of World Energy Law and Business* 10 (2): 103–16.

Moses, J., E. Pereira & R. Spencer 2021. "Conclusion". In *Sovereign Wealth Funds, Local Content and CSR*, E. Pereira *et al.* (eds), 635–58. Berlin: Springer.

Moses, J., R. Spencer & E. Pereira 2021. "Introduction". In *Sovereign Wealth Funds, Local Content and CSR*, E. Pereira *et al.* (eds), 1–28. Berlin: Springer.

Mowi 2020. *Salmon Farming Industry Handbook 2020*. Bergen: Mowi.

MSL n.d. "Materials Systems Laboratory". http://msl.mit.edu.

Munro, G. 1982. "Fisheries, extended jurisdiction and the economics of common property resources". *Canadian Journal of Economics* 15 (3): 405–25.

Myers, N. 2001. *Perverse Subsidies: How Tax Dollars Can Undermine the Environment and the Economy*. Washington, DC: Island Press.

Nandan, S, M. Lodge & S. Rosenne 2002. "The development of the regime for deep seabed mining". Kingston: ISA. https://isa.org.jm/files/files/documents/regime-ae.pdf.

Nationwide 2014. "London homeowners willing to pay a substantial premium to live near a tube or train station", House Price Index special report. Swindon: Nationwide Building Society.

Nature Conservancy, The 2012. *Protecting China's Biodiversity: A Guide to Land Use, Land Tenure and Land Protection Tools*. Arlington, VA: The Nature Conservancy.

Newell, P. & D. Mulvaney 2013. "The political economy of the 'just transition'". *Geographical Journal* 179 (2): 132–40.

Norges Bank Investment Management 2017. "Holdings". 31 December. www.nbim.no/en/the-fund/holdings/holdings-as-at-31.12.2017/?fullsize=true.

Normann, H. & S. Tellmann 2021. "Trade unions' interpretation of a just transition in a fossil fuel economy". *Environmental Innovation and Societal Transitions* 40: 421–34.

Norwegian government 2019a. "Skattlegging av havbruksvirksomhet", NOU 2019:18a. Oslo: Departementenes sikkerhets- og serviceorganisasjon.

Norwegian government 2019b. "Introduction and summary", NOU 2019:18b [English introduction to NOU 2019:18a]. Oslo: Departementenes sikkerhets- og serviceorganisasjon. www.regjeringen.no/contentassets/207ae51e0f6a44b6b65a2cec192105ed/en-gb/pdfs/nou201920190018000engpdfs.pdf.

Norwegian government 2019c. "Skattlegging av vannkraftverk", NOU 2019:16. Oslo: Departementenes sikkerhets- og serviceorganisasjon.

Nozick, R. 1974. *Anarchy, State, and Utopia*. New York: Basic Books.

Obeng-Odoom, F. 2021. *The Commons in an Age of Uncertainty*. Toronto: University of Toronto Press.

OECD 2009. *The Bioeconomy to 2030: Designing a Policy Agenda*. Paris: OECD.

OECD 2016. *Agricultural Policy Monitoring and Evaluation 2016*. Paris: OECD.

OECD n.d.a. "Agricultural policy: agricultural support". https://doi.org/10.1787/6ea85c58-en.

OECD n.d.b. "OECD data: agricultural support". https://data.oecd.org/agrpolicy/agricultural-support.htm.

OED 2011. *En næring for framtida – om petroleumsvirksomheten*, Meld. St. 28 (2010–2011). Oslo: Olje- og energidepartementet.

OED 2019. "Petroleumsskatt". Norsk Petroleum, 7 October. www.norskpetroleum.no/okonomi/petroleumsskatt.

OED 2021. "Konsesjonskraftprisen for 2022 er fastsatt". 20 December. www.regjeringen.no/no/aktuelt/konsesjonskraftprisen-for-2022-er-fastsatt/id2892973.

Olson, M. 1965. *The Logic of Collective Action*. Cambridge, MA: Harvard University Press.

Osherenko, G. 2006. "New discourses on ocean governance: understanding property rights and the public trust". *Journal of Environmental Law and Litigation* 21 (2): 317–82.

Ostrom, E. 1990. *Governing the Commons: The Evolution of Institutions for Collective Action*. Cambridge: Cambridge University Press.

Ostrom, E. 2003. "How types of goods and property rights jointly affect collective action". *Journal of Theoretical Politics* 15 (3): 239–70.

Ostrom, E. 2009. "Beyond market and states: polycentric governance of complex economic systems". Nobel Prize lecture, 8 December. www.nobelprize.org/prizes/economic-sciences/2009/ostrom/lecture.

Ostrom, E. 2012. "The future of the commons: beyond market failure and government regulation", Occasional Paper 148. London: Institute of Economics Affairs.

Otto, J. *et al.* 2006. *Mining Royalties: A Global Study of Their Impact on Investors, Government and Civil Society*. Washington, DC: World Bank.

Oxman, B. 1994. "The 1994 agreement and the convention". *American Journal of International Law* 88 (4): 687–96.

Pace, S. 2017. "Space development, law, and values". Keynote speech, IISL Galloway Space Law Symposium, Cosmos Club, Washington, DC, 13 December. www.spacepolicyonline.com/wp-content/uploads/2017/12/Scott-Pace-to-Galloway-FINAL.pdf.

Paine, T. 2017 [1797]. *Agrarian Justice*. https://earthsharingdevon.net/wp-content/uploads/2020/09/Agrarian-Justice-5-5-17-Print.pdf.

Panagariya, A. 2005. "Agricultural liberalisation and the least developed countries: six fallacies". *World Economy* 28 (9): 1277–99.

Partelow, S. *et al.* 2022. "Governing aquaculture commons". *Reviews in Aquaculture* 14 (2): 729–50.

Permanent Mission of Malta 1967. "Request for inclusion of a supplementary item in the agenda of the Twenty-Second Session", note verbale A/6695. 18 August. file:///C:/Users/Michael/Downloads/A_6695-EN.pdf.

Petersen, S. *et al.* 2016. "News from the seabed: geological characteristics and resource potential of deep-sea mineral resources". *Marine Policy* 70: 175–87.

Peterson, V. & T. Hsiao 2000. "Kia-chau". In *Land-Value Taxation around the World*, R. Andelson (ed.), 3rd edn, 365–9. Malden, MA: Blackwell.

Piketty, T. 2013. *Capital in the Twenty-First Century*. Cambridge, MA: Harvard University Press.

Pisano, G. 1991. "The governance of innovation: vertical integration and collaborative arrangements in the biotechnology industry". *Research Policy* 20 (3): 237–49.

Pistor, K. & O. De Schutter (eds) 2016. *Governing Access to Essential Resources*. New York: Columbia University Press.

Polanyi, K. 2001 [1944]. *The Great Transformation: The Political and Economic Origins of Our Time*. Boston: Beacon Press.

Porter, G. 1996. "Natural resource subsidies, trade and environment: the cases of forest and fisheries". Geneva: Center for International Environmental Law. www.ciel.org/Publications/NaturalResourceSubsidies.pdf.

Powelson, J. 1988. *The Story of Land: A World History of Land Tenure and Agrarian Reform*. Cambridge, MA: Lincoln Institute of Land Policy.

Puente-Sánchez, F. *et al.* 2018. "Viable cyanobacteria in the deep continental subsurface". *Proceedings of the National Academy of Sciences of the United States of America* 115 (42): 10702–7.

Quality Seafood Delivery 2021. "King salmon prices". https://qualityseafooddelivery.com/salmon/king/prices.

Quesnay, F. 1963a [1767]. "General maxims for the economic government of an agricultural kingdom". In *The Economics of Physiocracy: Essays and Translations*, R. Meek (ed.), 231–62. Cambridge, MA: Harvard University Press.

Quesnay, F. 1963b [1766]. "Dialogue on the work of artisans". In *The Economics of Physiocracy: Essays and Translations*, R. Meek (ed.), 203–30. Cambridge, MA: Harvard University Press.

Quesnay, F. 2004 [1758]. *The Economic Table [Tableau économique]*. Honolulu: University Press of the Pacific.

Remaoun, M. 2019. "Statement on behalf of the African Group: agenda item 11: financial model". 25th session of the Council of the International Seabed Authority, Kingston, 25 February. www.savethehighseas.org/wp-content/uploads/2019/02/Final-African-Group-statement-Financial-Model.pdf.

REN21 2021. *Renewables Global Status Report 2021*. Paris: REN21 Secretariat.

Ricardo, D. 1971 [1817]. *Principles of Political Economy and Taxation*, R. Hartwell (ed.). London: Penguin Books.

Rights and Resources Initiative 2015. *Who Owns the World's Land? A Global Baseline of Formally Recognized Indigenous and Community Land Rights*. Washington, DC: Rights and Resources Initiative. https://rightsandresources.org/wp-content/uploads/GlobalBaseline_web.pdf.

Ringnes, T. 2021. "Dette er statens inntekter og utgifter i 2022". E24, 13 October. https://e24.no/norsk-oekonomi/i/oW9WQ7/dette-er-statens-inntekter-og-utgifter-i-2022?referer=https%3A%2F%2Fwww.aftenposten.no.

Ritchie, H. & M. Roser 2019. "Land use". Our World in Data. https://ourworldindata.org/land-use.

Roark, E. 2012. "Applying Locke's proviso to unappropriated natural resources". *Political Studies* 60 (3): 687–702.

Robert Schalkenbach Foundation n.d. "Progress and poverty (modern edition)". https://schalkenbach.org/progress-and-poverty-modern-edition-pdf.

Røed, H. 2013. *Fiskehistorier: Hvem skal eie havet?* Oslo: Forlaget Manifest.

Rogers, A. & M. Gianni 2010. *The Implementation of UNGA Resolutions 61/105 and 64/72 in the Management of Deep-Sea Fisheries on the High Seas*. London: International Programme on the State of the Ocean.

Ross, M. 1999. "The political economy of the resource curse". *World Politics* 51 (2): 297–322.

Ross, M. 2012. *The Oil Curse. How Petroleum Wealth Shapes the Development of Nations*. Princeton, NJ: Princeton University Press.

Roser, M. 2019. "Future population growth". Our World in Data, November. https://ourworldindata.org/future-population-growth.

Sachs, J. & A. Warner 1995. "Natural resource abundance and economic growth", Working Paper 5398. Cambridge, MA: National Bureau of Economic Research.

Salter, W. 1960. *Productivity and Technical Change*. Cambridge: Cambridge University Press.

Say, J.-B. 2001 [1803]. *A Treatise on Political Economy; Or The Production, Distribution, and Consumption of Wealth*, trans. C. Prinsep. Ontario: Batoche Books.

Schlatter, R. 1951. *Private Property: The History of an Idea*. London: Allen & Unwin.

SCN 2021. "Case no. 20-072085SIV-HRET: appeal against Borgarting Court of Appeals order 18 March 2020". Decided 1 March. www.domstol.no/globalassets/upload/hret/decisions-in-english-translation/hr-2021-417-p.pdf.

Scott, A. 1955. "The fishery: the objectives of sole-ownership". *Journal of Political Economy* 63 (2): 116–24.

Scottish government n.d. "Aquaculture: fish farm consents". www.gov.scot/policies/aquaculture/fish-farm-consents.

Scruggs, L. 2003. *Sustaining Abundance: Environmental Performance in Industrial Democracies*. Cambridge: Cambridge University Press.

Sea Around Us 2016. "EEZ". www.seaaroundus.org/data/#/eez.

Sears, P. 1980 [1935]. *Deserts on the March*, 4th edn. Norman, OK: University of Oklahoma Press.

Secretariat of the Antarctic Treaty 1991. "Protocol on environmental protection to the Antarctic Treaty". Buenos Aires: Secretariat of the Antarctic Treaty. https://documents.ats.aq/recatt/Att006_e.pdf.

Seliger, M. 1969. *The Liberal Politics of John Locke*. New York: Praeger.

Senior, N. 1851. *Political Economy*, 3rd edn. London: Richard Griffin.

Sharma, R. (ed.) 2019. *Environmental Issues of Deep-Sea Mining: Impacts, Consequences and Policy Perspectives.* Berlin: Springer Nature.

Shiva, V. 2016 [1996]. *Biopiracy: The Plunder of Nature and Knowledge.* Berkeley, CA: North Atlantic Books.

Sikor, T., J. He & G. Lestrelin 2017. "Property rights regimes and natural resources: a conceptual analysis revisited". *World Development* 93: 337–49.

Silagi, M. 1984. "Land reform in Kiaochow, China: from 1898 to 1914 the menace of disastrous land speculation was averted by taxation". *American Journal of Economics and Sociology* 43 (2): 166–77.

Skonhoft, A. 2020. "Lønnsomhet og rente i oppdrettsnæringen". *Samfunnsøkonomien* 1: 12–14.

Smil, V. 2022. *How the World Really Works: A Scientist's Guide to Our Past, Present and Future.* London: Viking.

Smith, A. 1976 [1776]. *An Inquiry into the Nature and Causes of the Wealth of Nations.* Chicago, IL: University of Chicago Press.

Smith, P. 2021. "The Alaska Permanent Fund and the Alberta Heritage Savings Trust Fund: divergent paths, divergent outcomes". In *The Political Economy of Natural Resource Funds*, E. Okpanachi & R. Tremblay (eds), 15–36. Berlin: Springer.

Sovereign Wealth Fund Institute n.d. "Top 100 largest sovereign wealth fund rankings by total assets". www.swfinstitute.org/fund-rankings/sovereign-wealth-fund.

Standing, G. 2019. *Plunder of the Commons: A Manifesto for Sharing Public Wealth.* London: Pelican Books.

Starr, A. 2007. "Caracas: living large on oil". *The American Scholar*, 1 March. https://theamericanscholar.org/letter-from-caracas/#.Xg-rgfx7mUk.

Steedman, I. & P. Sweezy (eds) 1982. *The Value Controversy.* London: Verso.

Steele, R. 1711. "Vincit amor patriae". *The Spectator*, 19 October: 677–81. www2.scc.rutgers.edu/spectator/outputdjvu.php?filepath=./specv01/INDEX.djvu&pageno=p0680.djvu.

Steinberg, P. 2001. *The Social Construction of the Ocean.* Cambridge: Cambridge University Press.

Stevis, D., E. Morena & D. Krause 2020. "Introduction: the genealogy and contemporary politics of just transitions". In *Just Transitions: Social Justice in the Shift Towards a Low-Carbon World*, E. Morena, D. Krause & D. Stevis (eds), 1–31. London: Pluto.

Stiglitz, J. 2012. *The Price of Inequality: How Today's Divided Society Endangers our Future.* New York: Norton.

Sunley, E., T. Baunsgaard & D. Simard 2003. "Revenue from the oil and gas sector: issues and country experience". In *Fiscal Policy Formulation and Implementation in Oil-Producing Countries*, J. Davis, R. Ossowski & A. Fedelino (eds), 153–83. Washington, DC: IMF.

Sweeney, S. 2020. "The final conflict? Socialism and climate change". *New Labor Forum* 29 (2): 16–24.

Sæther, A. 2017. *De beste intensjoner: Oljelandet i klimakampen.* Oslo: Cappelen Damm.

Taylor, P. 2011. "Common heritage of mankind principle". In *The Encyclopedia of Sustainability*, vol. 3, *The Law and Politics of Sustainability*, K. Bosselmann, D. Fogel & J. Ruhl (eds), 64–9. Great Barrington, MA. Berkshire Publishing.

TechnipFMC n.d. "Fleet". www.technipfmc.com/en/what-we-do/fleet.

Tecklin, D. 2016. "Sensing the limits of fixed marine property rights in changing coastal ecosystems: salmon aquaculture concessions, crises, and governance challenges in southern Chile". *Journal of International Wildlife Law and Policy* 19 (4): 284–300.

Teece, D. 1986. "Profiting from technological innovation: implications for integration, collaboration, licensing and public policy". *Research Policy* 15 (6): 285–305.

Teece, D. 1998. "Capturing value from knowledge assets: the new economy, markets for know-how, and intangible assets". *California Management Review* 40 (3): 55–79.

Teece, D. 2003. *Essays in Technology Management and Policy.* Singapore: World Scientific Publishing.

TfL 2017. *Land Value Capture: Final Report.* London: TfL. www.london.gov.uk/sites/default/files/land_value_capture_report_transport_for_london.pdf.

Thomas, J. 1975. *The Institutes of Justinian: Text, Translation, and Commentary*. Amsterdam: North Holland.

Thomas, W. Jr (ed.) 1956. *Man's Role in Changing the Face of the Earth*. Chicago, IL: University of Chicago Press.

Thompson, E. 1991 [1963]. *The Making of the English Working Class*. London: Penguin Books.

Thue, L. 2003. *For egen kraft: Kraftkommunene og det norske kraftregimet 1887–2003*. Oslo: Abstrakt.

Tideman, N. *et al*. 1990. "Open letter to Mikhail Gorbachev". https://en.wikisource.org/wiki/Open_letter_to_Mikhail_Gorbachev_(1990).

Treaty of Paris 1783. "International treaties and related records, 1778–1974". General Records of the United States Government, Record Group 11; National Archives.

Tree Plantation 2000. "DOUGLAS FIR, 300 percent return growing Douglas fir trees". Sheridan, WY: Tree Plantation.

Trilling, D. 2017. "Farmed versus wild salmon: research review". The Journalist's Resource, 3 October. https://journalistsresource.org/environment/farmed-versus-wild-salmon-research-explainer.

Tucker, G. 1958. *The Self-Supporting City*. New York: Robert Schalkenbach Foundation.

Tullock, G. 1967. "The welfare costs of tariffs, monopolies and theft". *Western Economic Journal* 5 (3): 224–32.

Tullock, G. 1975. "The transitional gains trap". *Bell Journal of Economics* 6 (2): 671–8.

Tullock, G. 1993. *Rent Seeking*. Cheltenham: Edward Elgar.

Turgot, A. 1898 [1770]. *Reflections on the Formation and Distribution of Riches*. New York: Macmillan.

University of California n.d. "Douglas-fir (Pseudotsuga menziesii)". https://ucanr.edu/sites/forestry/California_forests/http___ucanrorg_sites_forestry_California_forests_Tree_Identification_/Douglas-fir.

UK government 2002. "Land Registration Act 2002". www.legislation.gov.uk/ukpga/2002/9/contents.

UN 1959. "The Antarctic Treaty". 1 December. https://treaties.un.org/doc/Publication/UNTS/Volume%20402/volume-402-I-5778-English.pdf.

UN 1962. "Resolution 1803 (XVII): permanent sovereignty over natural resources". 14 December. https://legal.un.org/avl/ha/ga_1803/ga_1803.html.

UN 1966. "International Covenant on Economic, Social and Cultural Rights". 16 December. www.ohchr.org/en/instruments-mechanisms/instruments/international-covenant-economic-social-and-cultural-rights.

UN 1967. "Treaty on Principles Governing the Activities of States in the Exploration and Use of Outer Space, including the Moon and Other Celestial Bodies". 27 January. www.unoosa.org/oosa/en/ourwork/spacelaw/treaties/outerspacetreaty.html.

UN 1970. "Resolution 2749 (XXV): declaration of principles governing the sea-bed and the ocean floor, and the subsoil thereof, beyond the limits of national jurisdiction". 12 December. http://un-documents.net/a25r2749.htm.

UN 1979. "Agreement Governing the Activities of States on the Moon and Other Celestial Bodies". 5 December. www.unoosa.org/oosa/en/ourwork/spacelaw/treaties/moon-agreement.html.

UN 1982. "United Nations Convention on the Law of the Sea" 10 December. www.un.org/depts/los/convention_agreements/texts/unclos/UNCLOS-TOC.htm.

UN 1992. "Convention on Biological Diversity". 5 June. www.cbd.int/doc/legal/cbd-en.pdf.

UN 1994. "Agreement relating to the implementation of part XI of the United Nations Convention on the Law of the Sea of 10 December 1982". 16 November. www.un.org/depts/los/convention_agreements/texts/agreement_part_xi/agreement_part_xi.htm.

UN 2004. "Resolution 59/25 on sustainable fisheries, including through the 1995 Agreement for the Implementation of the Provisions of the United Nations Convention on the Law of the Sea of 10 December 1982 relating to the Conservation and Management of Straddling

Fish Stocks and Highly Migratory Fish Stocks, and related instruments". 17 November. https://documents-dds-ny.un.org/doc/UNDOC/GEN/N04/477/70/PDF/N0447770.pdf?OpenElement.

UN 2006. "Resolution 61/105 on sustainable fisheries". 8 December. https://documents-dds-ny.un.org/doc/UNDOC/GEN/N06/500/73/PDF/N0650073.pdf?OpenElement.

UN 2010. "Resolution 64/292: the human right to water and sanitation". 28 July. https://documents-dds-ny.un.org/doc/UNDOC/GEN/N09/479/35/PDF/N0947935.pdf?OpenElement.

UN 2019a. *World Population Prospects 2019*. New York: United Nations.

UN 2019b. "Probabilistic population projections based on world population prospects 2019". Median projections. POP/DB/WPP/Rev.2019/PPP/POPTOT. https://population.un.org/wpp/Download/Standard/Population.

UN 2019c. "World population prospects 2019". POP/DB/WPP/Rev.2019/POP/F02. https://population.un.org/wpp/Download/Standard/Population.

UN 2019d. "Probabilistic population projections based on world population prospects 2019". Median projections. POP/DB/WPP/Rev.2019/PPP/POPGROWTHRATE. https://population.un.org/wpp/Download/Standard/Population.

UN 2019e. "Revised draft text of an agreement under the United Nations Convention on the Law of the Sea on the conservation and sustainable use of marine biological diversity of areas beyond national jurisdiction". 27 November. www.un.org/bbnj/sites/www.un.org.bbnj/files/revised_draft_text_a.conf_.232.2020.11_advance_unedited_version_mark-up.pdf.

UNCTAD 2006. "A case study of the salmon industry in Chile". Geneva: UNCTAD. https://unctad.org/system/files/official-document/iteiit200512_en.pdf.

UNDP 2016. "Bioprospecting". New York: UNDP.

UNDP n.d.a. "Human Development Index (HDI)". http://hdr.undp.org/en/content/human-development-index-hdi.

UNDP n.d.b. "Human development insights". https://hdr.undp.org/data-center/country-insights#/ranks.

US Department of Energy 2017. "EERE success story: 'seeing underground' to advance geothermal energy". 17 April. www.energy.gov/eere/success-stories/articles/eere-success-story-seeing-underground-advance-geothermal-energy.

US Fish and Wildlife Service n.d. "Life cycle of Atlantic salmon". www.fws.gov/story/life-cycle-atlantic-salmon#:~:text=Life%20Cycle%20of%20Atlantic%20Salmon%20In%20late%20autumn%2C,up%20through%20the%20gravel%20to%20hunt%20for%20food.

US Supreme Court 1823. *Johnson and Graham's Lessee v William M'Intosh*. www.law.cornell.edu/supremecourt/text/21/543.

USAID 2006. "The role of property rights in natural resource management, good governance and empowerment of the rural poor". Washington, DC: USAID. www.land-links.org/wp-content/uploads/2016/09/USAID_Land_Tenure_Property_Rights_and_NRM_Report.pdf.

USAID 2013. "Definition: land tenure". 10 January. https://rmportal.net/library/content/tools/land-tenure-and-property-rights-tools/copy_of_definition-land-tenure.

USBLM n.d.a. "Livestock grazing on public lands". www.blm.gov/programs/natural-resources/rangelands-and-grazing/livestock-grazing.

USBLM n.d.b. "General oil and gas leasing instructions". www.blm.gov/programs/energy-and-minerals/oil-and-gas/leasing/general-leasing.

Van Hensbergen, B. 2016. "Forest concessions: past present and future?", Forest Policy and Institutions Working Paper 36. Rome: FAO.

Van Hensbergen, H. 2018. "Rethinking forest concessions: improving the allocation of state-owned forests for better economic, social and environmental outcomes", Forestry Working Paper 4. Rome: FAO.

Van Nijen, K. *et al.* 2019. "The development of a payment regime for deep sea mining activities in the Area through stakeholder participation". *International Journal of Marine and Coastal Law* 34 (4): 571–601.

Venables, A. 2016. "Using natural resources for development: why has it proven so difficult?". *Journal of Economic Perspectives* 30 (1): 161–84.

Vikse, O. 1976. "Jord-Skatt-Rettferd: Georgismen i norsk samfunnsdebatt 1885–1909". MA thesis, Department of History, University of Bergen.

Vogt, W. 1948. *Road to Survival*. New York: William Sloane Associates.

Von Pufendorf, S. 1729 [1672]. *Of the Law of Nature and Nations: Eight Books* [*De jure naturae et gentium libri octo*]. London: Walthoe *et al*. https://archive.org/details/oflawofnaturenat00pufe.

Von Thünen, J. 1966 [1826]. *Isolated State* [an English edition of *Der isolirte Staat in Beziehung auf Landwirtschaft und Nationalökonomie*], P. Hall (ed.). Oxford: Pergamon Press.

Ward, C. & M. Aalbers 2016. "'The shitty rent business': what's the point of land rent theory?". *Urban Studies* 53 (9): 1760–83.

Watson, L. *et al.* 2022. "'Offshore' salmon aquaculture and identifying the needs for environmental regulation". *Aquaculture* 546: 737342.

Wegenast, T. & G. Schneider 2017. "Ownership matters: natural resources property rights and social conflict in sub-Saharan Africa". *Political Geography* 61: 110–22.

Weiss, E. 1984. "The planetary trust: conservation and intergenerational equity". *Ecology Law Quarterly* 11 (4): 495–582.

White House 2022. "Fact sheet: securing a Made in America supply chain for critical minerals". 22 February. www.whitehouse.gov/briefing-room/statements-releases/2022/02/22/fact-sheet-securing-a-made-in-america-supply-chain-for-critical-minerals.

Wilson, E. 2018. *Half-Earth: One Planet's Fight for Life*. New York: Norton.

Winthrop, J. 1992 [1629]. "Reasons to be considered for justifying the undertakers of the intended Plantation in New England, and for encouraging such whose hearts God shall move to join with them in it", in *Winthrop Papers, 1929–92*, ed. J. Twichell, vol. 1, 138–45. Boston: Massachusetts Historical Society.

Wood, M. 2014. *Nature's Trust: Environmental Law for a New Ecological Age*. Cambridge: Cambridge University Press.

Woolhouse, R. 2007. *Locke: A Biography*. New York: Cambridge University Press.

World Bank 2011a. *The Changing Wealth of Nations: Measuring Sustainable Development in the New Millennium*. Washington, DC: World Bank.

World Bank 2011b. *World Bank Development Report: Conflict, Security and Development*. Washington, DC: World Bank.

World Bank 2020a. *Tracking SDG 7: The Energy Progress Report 2020*. Washington, DC: World Bank.

World Bank 2020b. *Global Photovoltaic Power Potential by Country*. Washington, DC: World Bank.

World Bank 2021a. "Agricultural land (sq. km)". https://data.worldbank.org/indicator/AG.LND.AGRI.K2.

World Bank n.d.a. "Forest rents (% of GDP)". https://data.worldbank.org/indicator/NY.GDP.FRST.RT.ZS?most_recent_value_desc=true.

World Bank n.d.b. "Oil rents (% of GDP)". https://data.worldbank.org/indicator/NY.GDP.PETR.RT.ZS?most_recent_value_desc=true.

World Bank n.d.c. "Natural gas rents (% of GDP)". https://data.worldbank.org/indicator/NY.GDP.NGAS.RT.ZS?most_recent_value_desc=true.

World Bank n.d.d. "Mineral rents (% of GDP)". https://data.worldbank.org/indicator/NY.GDP.MINR.RT.ZS?most_recent_value_desc=true.

World Bank n.d.e. "Concessions build–operate–transfer (BOT) and design–build–operate (DBO) projects". https://ppp.worldbank.org/public-private-partnership/agreements/concessions-bots-dbos.

World Resources Institute 2019. *Creating a Sustainable Food Future: A Menu of Solutions to Feed Nearly 10 Billion People by 2050*. Washington, DC: World Resources Institute.

WWF 2018. *Living Planet Report 2018: Aiming Higher*. M. Grooten & R. Almond (eds). Gland, Switzerland: WWF.

Yardley, W. 2016. "Who owns the wind?". *Chicago Tribune*, 17 August.

Yergin, D. 2009 [1991]. *The Prize: The Epic Quest for Oil, Money and Power*. New York: Free Press.

Zalik, A. 2015. "Trading on the offshore: territorialization and the ocean grab in the international seabed". In *Beyond Free Trade: Alternative Approaches to Trade, Politics and Power*, K. Ervine & G. Fridel (eds), 173–90. Basingstoke: Palgrave Macmillan.

Zalik, A. 2018. "Mining the seabed, enclosing the Area: ocean grabbing, proprietary knowledge and the geopolitics of the extractive frontier beyond national jurisdiction". *International Social Science Journal* 68 (229/30): 343–59.

Zeller, C. 2008. "From the gene to the globe: extracting rents based on intellectual property monopolies". *Review of International Political Economy* 15 (1): 86–115.

Zyma, A. 2019. "Global administrative law and regulation of extraction of minerals in outer space". *Advanced Space Law* 4: 125–36.

INDEX

abundance *see* scarcity
allocation   5, 11, 12n3, 34–5, 37, 44–5,
     81–2, 101–2, 133, 150–1, 167–8,
     178–9, 195, 214, 216–17
Anderson, J.   55
Antarctica   5, 11, 83, 206–7, 211, 212
Antarctica Treaty   205, 206, 212
appropriation   16, 34–5, 82
aquaculture   110–12; *see also* Norwegian
     aquaculture; salmon
Area, the   109, 201, 204, 205, 211–17
asteroid   8, 17, 27, 200, 203, 210
auction   17, 34, 88, 120, 121, 135, 155–7,
     168, 171, 178

benefit sharing   205, 208, 209, 211, 214
biodiversity   119, 173, 207, 209; *see also*
     Convention on Biodiversity
bioprospecting   173–4, 201–2, 209
Botswana   85

Chile   61, 83, 119, 124, 131, 184, 187
     aquaculture regime,   121–2
China   86, 87, 100, 105, 144, 155–6, 161–4,
     184, 205
Cicero   30
commodification   18, 26, 39–41
     of energy   141, 149–50, 152
     of fish   114–18
     of land   32, 88–9
common
     heritage of mankind (CHM)   10, 32, 201,
         205, 210–11, 212, 213, 218
     pool resources   14
     property *see* property, common
commons   13–15, 16, 18, 21n12, 28–32, 34,
     49, 112n7, 143, 149
     global   83, 199–201, 204–6, 209, 210,
         212, 214
     tragedy of *see* tragedy of the commons

competitive economy   50, 52–3
concentrated solar power (CSP)   139, 143,
     151, 152
concession
     agreement   36, 38, 54, 67, 178–9, 190,
         224, 241
     defined   38
     holder   34, 39n9, 40, 45–6, 56, 75, 182,
         184, 218, 231, 240
concession types
     aquaculture   69, 120–2, 124, 133–4
     Area, the   211–15, 216–17, 224
     energy   147–8, 150, 165, 168
     forests   97–8, 100–1
     hydropower   67, 191–3
     land   84, 87, 89, 96
     petroleum   176–80, 188–90, 224
concessionaire *see* concession holder
Convention on Biodiversity (CBD)   205,
     208, 209
corporatism   240
corruption *see* resource, curse; paradox
     of plenty
crack spread   181
critical minerals   2, 174–5
crop value   33, 46, 97

differential rent *see* rent, differential
Dutch disease *see* paradox of plenty

efficiency   6, 13, 16, 20, 60, 61, 63, 64, 68–9,
     75, 78, 102, 105, 108, 112, 133, 172, 177,
     221–3, 225–8
electric; *see also* energy, market
     car components   174
enclosure   5, 12, 16, 27, 34–5, 39, 82, 83,
     141, 149, 167, 178, 203–4, 225–7, 243
energy; *see also* photovoltaic; wind
     consumption   183
     market   22, 144, 146, 161

263